R50B.15

39L

A Man
Before Others

Rudolf Steiner Remembered

A Man
Before Others

Rudolf Steiner Remembered

A collection of personal
memories from the pages
of *The Golden Blade* and
other sources

Rudolf Steiner Press

Published by Rudolf Steiner Press, P.O. Box 955, Bristol BS99 5QN

ISBN **1 85584 007 3**

Typeset by PPS, Amesbury

CONTENTS

ACKNOWLEDGEMENTS

THE FOLLOWING articles have been reproduced from *The Golden Blade 1958* which in turn were translated from *Wir Erlebten Rudolf Steiner* (1956; Verlag Freies Geistesleben GmbH, Stuttgart; 7th edition 1988).

George Adams, "Rudolf Steiner in England"
Emil Bock, "Religious Renewal", translated by A B
Gottfried Haass-Berkow, "Experiences in the Realm of Dramatic Art", translated by M A
Herbert Hahn, "How the Waldorf School Arose from the Threefold Social Movement", translated by H O
Grete Kirchner-Bockholt, "Widening the Art of Healing", translated by V W
Ernst Lehrs, "The Rising Generation", translated by V E P and C W
Kurt Magerstädt, "One of the Young Doctors", translated by M C
Ehrenfried E Pfeiffer, "New Directions in Agriculture"
Karin Ruths-Hoffman, "At the Waldorf School", translated by D D
Albrecht Strohschein, "The Birth of Curative Education", translated by M C
Guenther Wachsmuth, "The Last Years"
F W Zelymans von Emmichoven, "Rudolf Steiner in Holland", translated by D O
Maria Röschl-Lehrs, "Rudolf Steiner as Personal Teacher", translated by A B
Lory Maier-Smits, "The Beginnings of Eurythmy", translated by V C-B

The following articles have been reproduced from *The Golden Blade 1959*.

Alfred Heidenreich, "The Angry Young Men"
Violet Plincke, "Seeking and Finding"
Gladys Mayer, "The Initiate and the Teacher"
Vera Compton-Burnett, "Prelude to Eurythmy in England"
Juliet Compton-Burnett, "The Last Months"

Helen Fox, "The Origins of Michael Hall School", is reproduced from the *Anthroposophical Quarterly* Vol. 16, No 3 (Autumn 1971)

Martina von Limburger, "From Conversations with Rudolf Steiner" is reproduced from the *Anthroposophical Movement* Vol. XXIX, No. 12 (December 1952)

Eleanor C Merry, "A Day at Tintagel in August 1924", is reproduced from the *Anthroposophical Quarterly* Vol. 1, No. 3 (Autumn 1956)

Louise van Blommestein, "How Rudolf Steiner Taught Us to Paint" is reproduced from the *Anthroposophical Movement* Vol. V, No. 21 (May 1928)

W Loftus Hare, "An Impression of Dr Rudolf Steiner" is reproduced from *The Occult Review* (October 1922)

Freidrich Hiebel, "Rudolf Steiner at the Rostrum" is an extract from his book *Time of Decision with Rudolf Steiner* (1989; Anthroposophic Press, RR4, Box 94A1, Hudson, NY 12534, USA)

Friedrich Rittelmeyer, "A Question of Sleep" is an extract from his book *Rudolf Steiner Enters My Life* (1963; Floris Books, 15 Harrison Gardens, Edinburgh EH11 1SH, UK)

Walter Johannes Stein, "Overcoming Formalities" is an extract from his book *The Death of Merlin: Arthurian Myth and Alchemy* (1989; Floris Books, *idem*)

Ilona Schubert, "The Man with the Coat" is an extract from her book *Reminiscences of Rudolf Steiner and Marie Steiner-von Sivers* (1991; Temple Lodge Press, 51 Queen Caroline Street, London W6 9QL, UK)

Anna Samweber, "Two Incidents" is an extract from her book *Memories of Rudolf Steiner and Marie Steiner-von Sivers* (1991; Rudolf Steiner Press, P.O. Box 955, Bristol BS99 5QN, UK)

PREFACE

IT WAS IN 1958 that the English annual, *The Golden Blade*, published a thematic issue entitled 'Rudolf Steiner – Recollections by Some of his Pupils', a translation of the German title, *Wir Erlebten Rudolf Steiner* ('We Knew Rudolf Steiner') edited by Maria Josepha Krück von Poturzyn and published by Verlag Freies Geistesleben, Stuttgart. (The German book sold so consistently on the Continent that a subsequent volume was researched and published and may appear at some future date in an English translation.) The translation in *The Golden Blade* also proved popular, inspiring further reminiscences from English individuals who had known and worked with Rudolf Steiner and which appeared in later issues of *The Golden Blade*. These have also been included in this volume.

Thirty-five years after its publication, that issue of *The Golden Blade* is difficult to find, even in specialist libraries, and thus it was decided to make its contents available again, supplemented by other recollections, so that personal descriptions of Rudolf Steiner, and the impressions he made on those who encountered him, can be appreciated by new generations of inquirers.

In the Foreword to the original German edition, the editor wrote:

Since 1925, when Rudolf Steiner left the physical plane, a whole new generation has grown up. Many of his first pupils, who were able to work with him and under his eyes in the various fields of anthroposophical activity, are no longer with us. The newcomers have been rightly anxious that a human picture of the great teacher should be called to life from the individual memories and experiences of those who knew him, and we are grateful for all the books which have tried to do this and have been published in the course of years.

The essential aim of the present collection has been to bring together pupils of Dr Steiner from the widest possible range of callings who have not yet recorded their recollections of him, and have played an active part in carrying forward the impulses he gave for the renewal of culture and civilization. Their personal memories are set down here in contributions which follow no fixed pattern and are intended to be no more than sketches; for the comprehensive picture, which the younger generation asks for, is something that no single person ever saw.

The present publishers have gathered material from the above-mentioned issues of *The Golden Blade* and other English-language periodicals such as the *Anthroposophical Movement* and the *Anthroposophical Quarterly*. This book also contains a number of vignettes about Dr Steiner culled from other published works.

Rudolf Steiner –
A Sketch of His Life and Work

John Davy

RUDOLF STEINER WAS BORN in Kraljevec (then in Austria, now part of the former Yugoslavia) in 1861, and died in Dornach, Switzerland in 1925. He thus saw the end of an old era and the birth pangs of a new one. His life echoes the transition intimately. The outer surface of the late nineteenth century gave little hint of the extraordinary events the twentieth century would bring. And a superficial biography of the first part of Steiner's life might not easily foresee the extraordinary activities of his later years. Yet the seeds of the later are to be found in the earlier times.

Outwardly, we see the gifted son of a minor railway official growing up in the small peasant villages of Lower Austria. He attended the village schools, and then the modern school in Wiener Neustadt. His father was a freethinker and saw his son as a railway engineer rather than as a priest (the more usual destination for bright boys from the villages). Steiner took a degree in mathematics, physics and chemistry, and later wrote a philosophical thesis for a doctorate. He supported himself through university and afterwards by tutoring. He was drawn into literary and scholarly work. The famous Goethe scholar, Professor Karl Julius Schröer, who befriended the young man, arranged for him to edit the scientific works of Goethe for a new complete edition. He participated actively in the rich cultural life of Vienna. Then he was invited to Weimar, to the famous Goethe archive, where he remained for seven years, working further on the scientific writings, as well as collaborating in a complete edition of Schopenhauer. The place was a famous centre, visited by the leading lights of Central European culture, and Steiner knew many of the major figures of the artistic and cultural life of his time.

In 1894 he published *The Philosophy of Spiritual Activity*, but was disappointed by its reception (we shall return to the significance of this work). Then, as the end of the century approached, he left the settled world of Weimar to edit an avante-garde literary magazine in Berlin. There he met playwrights and poets who were seeking, often desperately, for alternatives of various kinds. The city was a focus for many radical groups and movements. Steiner was invited to lecture at the Berlin Workers' Training School, sponsored by the trade unions and social democrats. Most of the teaching was Marxist, but he insisted on a free hand. He gave courses on history and natural science, and practical exercises in public speaking. His appeal was such that he was invited to give a festival address to 7000 printers at the Berlin circus stadium on the occasion of the Gutenberg jubilee. But his refusal to toe any party line did not endear him to the political activists, and soon after the turn of the century he was forced to drop this work.

In 1899, Steiner's life began to change quite rapidly. Only later did he give a more personal glimpse of his inner struggles, which matured into a far-reaching decision during the 1890s. On August 28, 1899 he published in his magazine a surprising article about Goethe's mysterious 'fairy tale', *The Green Snake and the Beautiful Lily*. The essay was entitled 'Goethe's Secret Revelation', and pointed definitely, if discreetly, to the 'occult' significance of this story. The article attracted the attention of a Count and Countess Brockdorff, who invited Steiner to speak to one of their weekly gatherings. The Brockdorffs were Theosophists. They gave Steiner the first opportunity to realize the decision he came to during the last years of the century, namely to speak openly and directly out of the inner faculties of spiritual perception he had known since childhood and had been quietly nurturing, developing and disciplining ever since.

Quite soon, Steiner was speaking regularly to groups of Theosophists, which upset and bewildered many of his former friends. There was uproar at a lecture on the medieval scholastics which he delivered to the Giordano Bruno Society. The respectable if often radical scholar, historian, scientist, writer and philosopher was emerging as an 'occultist'. It was truly shocking to many of those around him. Steiner knew he was running risks of isolation. Only in the fringe culture, the Theosophists at first had an ear for what he now wanted to say. Yet he saw around him a culture in decay, and profound crises to come. Much later, he wrote in his autobiography, *The Course of My Life*:

> 'In the spiritual domain, a new light upon the evolution of humanity was seeking to break through into the knowledge gained during the last third of the nineteenth century. But the spiritual sleep caused by the materialistic interpretation of these acquisitions in knowledge prevented any inkling of this, much less any awareness of it. Thus the very time arrived which ought to have developed in a spiritual direction of its own nature, but which belied its nature – the time which began actually to bring about the impossibility of life.'

Steiner's decision to speak directly of his own spiritual research was not prompted by a desire to set up as a spiritual teacher, to feed curiosity or to revive some form of 'ancient wisdom'. It was born out of a perception of the needs of the time. As we approach the end of our century, it is perhaps easier to appreciate what Steiner meant by times which 'begin to bring about the impossibility of life'. This lay behind what he described as 'my heartfelt desire to introduce into life the impulses from the world of the spirit. . .but for this, there was no understanding.'

It took him nearly two decades to create a basis for the renewing impulses in daily life that he sought to initiate. At first he worked mainly through lectures to Theosophists and others, and through articles and books. These works remain an extraordinarily rich resource which is still far too little known in the English-speaking world. Within quite a short period of years, Steiner surveyed with clarity and intimacy the spiritual realities at work in the kingdoms of nature and in the cosmos, the inner nature of the human soul and spirit and their potential for further development, the nature and practice of meditation, the experiences of the soul before birth and after death, the spiritual history and evolution of humanity and the earth, and detailed studies of the workings of reincarnation and karma. The style is sober and direct throughout, and it often calls for an effort to realize the quite remarkable nature of these communications. For they are not derived from earlier sources, nor was Steiner acting as a spokesman for a spiritual guide. They are fruits of careful spiritual observation and perception – or, as Steiner preferred to call it, 'spiritual research' – undertaken in freedom by an individual thoroughly conversant with, and deeply serious about, the integrity of thought and apprehension striven for in natural science.

After seven or eight years, Steiner began to add to his work in 'spiritual science' a growing activity in the arts. It is significant and characteristic that he should see the arts as a crucial bridge for translating spiritual science into social and cultural innovation. (We are now vividly aware of what happens when natural science bypasses the human heart and is translated into technology without grace, beauty or compassion.) Between 1910 and 1913 he wrote four Mystery Plays, which follow the lives of a group of people through successive incarnations, and include scenes in the soul and spiritual worlds as well as on earth. With his wife, Marie von Sievers, an actress, new approaches to speech and drama were initiated. In this period, too, lie the beginnings of eurythmy, an art of movement that makes visible the inner forms and gestures of language and music.

In 1913 the foundation stone was laid for the first Goetheanum at Dornach in Switzerland. This extraordinary building in wood, with its vast interlocking cupolas, gradually took shape during the years of the First World War, when an international group of volunteers collaborated with local builders and craftsmen to shape the unique carved forms and structures Steiner designed. The building stimulated much innovation in the use of form and colour and is now increasingly recognized as a landmark in twentieth century architecture. Yet Steiner was not concerned to build an impressive monument. He regarded architecture as the servant of human life, and designed the Goetheanum to support the developing work of anthroposophy (Steiner's preferred term, which he once said should be understood to mean, quite simply, 'awareness of one's humanity') and particularly the work in drama and eurythmy.

An arsonist caused this building to burn to the ground during the night of December 31, 1922. There survived only the great sculpture of 'The Representative of Humanity' on which Steiner had been working in a neighbourhood workshop with the English sculptress, Edith Maryon. Steiner soon designed another building that was completed after his death and now serves as a centre for the world-wide Anthroposophical Society and its School of Spiritual Science. There is a magnificent stage and auditorium, where the Mystery Plays are given regularly, as well as Goethe's *Faust* in full, other plays and concerts, and frequent performances of eurythmy.

As the First World War neared its end, Steiner began to find ways to work more widely and deeply for a renewal of life and culture in many spheres. Europe was in ruins and could have been ready for quite new impulses. Attempts to realize a 'threefold social order' as a political and social alternative at that time did not succeed, but the conceptual basis Steiner developed exists as a seed that is even more relevant for today.

Steiner's social thinking can be adequately grasped only in the context of his view of history, which he saw, in direct contrast to Marx, as shaped fundamentally by inner changes in human consciousness in which higher spiritual beings are actively participating. Just in this century, quite new experiences are awakening in the human soul. (Since Steiner's time this is a good deal more apparent than it was then.) But we cannot expect to build a healthy social order except on the basis of a true and deep insight not only into the material but also into the soul and spiritual nature and needs of human beings as they are today.

These needs are characterized by a powerful tension between the search for community and the experience of individuality. Community, in the sense of material interdependence, is the basic fact of economic life and of the world economy in which it is embedded today. Yet individuality, in the sense of independence of mind and freedom of speech, is essential to every creative endeavour, to all innovation, and to the realization of the human spirit in the arts and sciences. Without spiritual freedom, our culture will wither and die.

Individuality and community, Steiner urged, can be lifted out of conflict only if they are recognized not as contradictions but as a creative polarity rooted in the essential nature of human beings. Each pole can bear fruit only if it has its appropriate social forms. We need forms that ensure freedom for all expression of spiritual life, and forms that promote brotherhood in economic life. But the health of this polarity depends on a full recognition for a third human need and function, the social relationships between people which concern our feeling for human rights. Here again, Steiner emphasized that we need to develop a distinct realm of social organization to support this sphere, inspired by a concern for equality – not equality of spiritual capacity or material circumstance, but that sense of equality that awakens through recognition of the essential spiritual nature of every human being. In this lies the meaning and source of every person's right also to freedom of spirit and to material sustenance.

These insights were the basis from which Steiner then began to respond to a great variety of requests for new beginnings and practical help in many fields. He was approached by doctors, therapists, farmers, businessmen, academics and scientists, theologians and pastors, and by teachers. From these beginnings have grown the many activities which have survived all the tensions and upheavals of this century, and which continue to spread round the world.

Best known, of course, is the work in education and curative education. The former originated in a request from Emil Molt, director of the Waldorf-Astoria cigarette factory, for a school to which his employees could send their children. There are now Waldorf Schools throughout the world. The homes, schools and village communities for handicapped children and adults are also flourishing.

Biodynamic agriculture originated in a course of lectures at Koberwitz in 1924, held at the request of a group of farmers concerned about the destructive trend of 'scientific' farming. It has made its main impact so far in European countries, but is now attracting rapidly growing interest in many other parts of the world. From Steiner's work with doctors, a medical movement has developed that includes clinics and hospitals and a variety of therapeutic work. From a request by a group of German pastors there developed the Christian Community, a movement for religious renewal. The art of eurythmy, which also serves the educational and therapeutic work, has developed strongly, and there are now a number of eurythmy schools where a full four-year training is given. Other training centres – for teacher training, agriculture, the arts, social work, and general orientation in anthroposophy – have grown up in recent years.

Rudolf Steiner died on March 30, 1925, surrounded by new beginnings. The versatility and creativity he revealed in his later years are phenomenal by any standards. How did he achieve all this?

The last part of the twentieth century is bringing a growing recognition that we live within a deeper reality we can call spiritual, to which at present we have direct access only through altered conditions of consciousness. We are also learning to see that these realities were known in the past, described in other images and languages, and were the source of all great religious and spiritual teachings. They have been obscured and forgotten for a while as our scientific culture devoted itself to the material world revealed by the senses.

Many individuals have glimpses during their lives of spiritual realities. Some recollect a more consistent experience in childhood. A few achieve some form of enduring insight as adults. Rudolf Steiner spoke little of spiritual life in personal terms. But in his autobiography he indicates that from childhood he was fully conscious of a world of invisible reality within the world of everyday. His inner struggle for the first forty years of his life was not to achieve spiritual experience, but to unite this fully with the forms of knowledge and insight of our time, and in particular with the language and discipline of natural science. Historically, this can be seen as the special challenge and contribution of Steiner's life and work. He himself saw the scientific age, even in its most materialistic aspects, as an essential phase in the spiritual education of mankind. Only by forgetting the spiritual world for a time and attending to the material world, he said, could there be kindled new and essential faculties, notably an experience of true individual inner freedom. Steiner indicated that his own capacities to meet, in the most practical way, the life questions and working needs of people from so many walks of life, had their origins in the struggles of his earlier years, when he kept almost complete silence concerning his inner experiences, and gradually learned to grasp and articulate their relationship to the mode of consciousness from which science arises. His book *The Philosophy of Spiritual Activity* embodies a first fruit of these struggles – he himself described it as 'a biographical account of how one human soul made the difficult ascent to freedom'. Studied more intimately, this book contains the basis for a path of knowledge that can lead the soul to discover spiritual experience and reality right into the world of ordinary thought and experience. Along this path, Steiner sought to develop a spiritual science that is a further development of the true spirit of natural science.

This path led him in his thirties to awaken to an inner recognition of the 'turning point of time' in human spiritual history, brought about by the incarnation of the Being we know as the Christ. He saw that the meaning of this event transcends all differentiations of religion, race or nation, and has consequences for all humanity; we are as yet aware only of the beginnings of these. This also led him to know the new presence and working of the Christ, which has begun just in this century, not in the physical world but in the sphere of invisible life-forces of the earth and of mankind.

Steiner was therefore not concerned to bring old teachings in new forms, nor to promulgate doctrines of any kind, but to nurture a path of knowledge in freedom, and of love in action, that can meet the deep and pressing needs of our times. These are the ideals, however imperfectly realized, by which those who find in anthroposophy a continuing inspiration for their lives and work seek to be guided.

Rudolf Steiner in England

George Adams

THE SPIRITUAL LIFE of England and the English-speaking world played an important part in Rudolf Steiner's life-work. This was a natural outcome of his allotted task in relation to the Spirit of the Time. For in the phase of history beginning in the 15th century AD (known as the Fifth post-Atlantean Epoch), the Celtic, Anglo-Saxon and Germanic peoples became the bearers of the forward trend in human evolution, even as the Greek and Latin peoples had been in the preceding epoch. The spiritual gifts of these more Northern peoples are revealed in two more or less complementary directions, finding their characteristic expression hitherto where the English and the German languages are spoken. Precisely inasmuch as he was so deeply rooted in the cultural heritage of the German-speaking people among whom he was born, and in particular of his Austrian homeland, Rudolf Steiner's worldwide mission stood in the midst of this polarity. Thus in the very first of his philosophic works, his introductions to the scientific writings of Goethe, he enters into the conscious and unconscious wrestlings of the great German poet with the world-outlook which through the English scientists and thinkers – Bacon, Newton and Locke before Goethe's time, and Darwin shortly after – has so greatly influenced the modern world.

Yet in an even wider compass, far beyond theoretical and scientific questions, Rudolf Steiner had a deep inner connection with the spiritual sources that underlie the native trend of English life and thought. Among his closest friends during his early years in Vienna were men and women such as Friedrich Eckstein and Marie Lang, who throughout their lives were in close contact with the English-speaking world and drew many of their leading inspirations from it. Indeed, it was in those early years that the foundations were laid for the decisive step he was to take 15 years later, when to the utter amazement of the scholarly and literary circles among whom he lived and moved in Berlin, he suddenly became a leading figure in the Theosophical Society. Nourished though it was to a large extent from oriental sources, the Theosophical Society derived its character from the mental outlook and spiritual aspirations of the American and English people among whom it was founded. In his autobiography Dr Steiner relates how among the English-speaking members of this society, though he himself could not have worked in their style, he found 'a spiritual focus from which one could worthily take one's start if one was deeply and truly concerned for the spread of spiritual knowledge'. And in a lecture where he gives an outline of his early life, he tells how in Vienna in the 1880s he was among the first to acquire and pass on to others the booklet which became one of the classics of the theosophical movement, *Light on the Path*, written down by Mabel Collins.

In Rudolf Steiner's open heart and comprehensive mind, every shade of the spiritual wrestlings of his time was living. His clear thinking and yet heartfelt participation in all contemporary trends came to life again in his personal relation to his pupils, who found their way to him from every conceivable direction in the manifold and often contradictory life of our time. He would encourage every one of us along his chosen path, no matter how great the seeming contradictions in the advice he gave to one individual or another. Each of us, therefore, will have amazingly diverse things to relate from our intercourse with him. This aspect of his being, too – reflected however imperfectly in those who became his pupils – reveals the true picture of mankind in modern time. I mean not only what we have to tell about him, but what we ourselves became, quickened by our encounter with him. The picture of Man for which the present age, through all mistakes and failings, is sincerely striving, is made manifest in the way Rudolf Steiner entered into the inmost ideals and individual destinies of every one of his disciples.

I write these words because the purpose of this book is that those who knew Rudolf Steiner in earthly life should tell of their experiences with him. Many among his English friends who may have known him better than I did, and would have had quite other things to relate, have followed him into the spiritual world. I for my part, to tell especially of my first meeting with him, must relate some of the circumstances which led up to this. Like Rudolf Steiner himself, I was born, though not of Slavonic blood, in the Slavonic East of Europe. I think I owe to this the mobility in language which enabled me as a young man to become his interpreter. The speaking and hearing of several languages side by side is – or at least was at that time – part of the social structure of those countries on the Eastern fringe of Middle Europe; it belongs to the very air one breathes, the etheric atmosphere of the landscape. My father, born in Australia of German and English immigrants, had come back to Europe shortly before my birth, and was among the pioneers – mostly Irish Canadians and Poles in those early years – of the oil industry in the Carpathian foothills where we lived. It was a part of Poland (now incorporated in Soviet Russia as the Western Ukraine) belonging still at that time to the old Hapsburg monarchy; therefore I also felt the touch, though in a far outlying province, of the pervasive and rather fascinating qualities of Rudolf Steiner's Austrian home country. My own mother-tongue was English, and so was my upbringing. I had British citizenship by virtue of my father's birthplace.

At the outbreak of the First World War I was an undergraduate at Cambridge. That was the moment when I first heard of Rudolf Steiner. During an unforgettable holiday at a lonely spot on the Suffolk coast I read right through his *Occult Science: An Outline*. The book impressed me deeply. Unlike some other theosophical works, it made no attempt to come to terms with scientific orthodoxy, but the author did at every point state clearly and in a scientific spirit the ground on which he stood. You knew where you were; you felt the writer understood and shared the scientific outlook. As to its spiritual content – it was the English edition, with that impressive portrait where he is sitting with his hands half-folded looking straight at you and yet far beyond – it made a 'timeless' impression on me. I cannot remember thinking, 'When did the author live, or is he living now?' Despite the modern style and context, he seemed to write from beyond all special times.

In the summer of 1916 I joined the 'Emerson Group' of the Anthroposophical Society in London. The meetings began with the verse, 'From the luminous heights of the Spirit...', specially given by Dr Steiner for this group to its leader, Mrs Cull, when it was founded a year or two before the war. She was a wise Scottish lady, daughter of principal Tulloch of St Andrews. In the mountains of Ceylon, before she met Rudolf Steiner, she made some acquaintance with Buddhist esotericism; she told me of the indescribable spiritual presence which she felt when she heard Rudolf Steiner in his lecture-cycles speaking of the Buddha.

To me, as one of mixed descent (my father's father was German, my other three grandparents English), the war became a personal problem in a special sense. In my subjective feelings, however, my mixed descent played little part or none at all. I was full of belief in the oneness and peaceful progress of mankind – an idealism, no doubt, far too easy, but sincere. It was a time when the traditions of 19th-century liberalism were still living. Lord Morley and others, believing the outbreak of war to have been avoidable, had resigned from the Asquith government. Bodies were formed, such as the Union of Democratic Control, with the resolve that the methods of international intercourse should be so changed as to prevent the future occurrence of such catastrophes over the heads, as we thought, of the common people of either country. I myself naturally gravitated towards pacifist and social-revolutionary movements, and was among those who refused military service. I mention these things because of the part they were to play in my first conversations with Dr Steiner.

At Cambridge I made the acquaintance of the family of Josiah Wedgwood, MP. He, and also Mrs Wedgwood (Ethel Bowen-Wedgwood – they were already separated at that time), received me with great kindness. Commander Wedgwood, as he then was, had been severely wounded in the Gallipoli campaign. He was an active member of the House of Commons, believing the war to be inevitable, yet not withholding sympathy and help from those who thought otherwise. He was the soul of chivalry and had a deep and real belief in freedom. Like one of Rudolf Steiner's closest friends in Berlin in the 1890s, the Scottish-German poet John Henry Mackay, the Wedgwoods – philosophic anarchist rather than socialist in outlook – were followers of Henry George; they had some contact too with the Tolstoyan movement. Towards the end of the war, while I was her guest, Mrs Wedgwood heard of Rudolf Steiner's work through me. She read with deep interest his lectures on the Apocalypse, in which the spiritual-scientific conception of human history and evolution is set forth. Then in the spring of 1919 came his newly written book on the Threefold Social Order. Mrs Wedgwood had always taken an active part in public life. In her girlhood she had known the aged Gladstone, a personal friend of her father's. Her lifelong interest and belief in a renewal of the body politic in the true human spirit of the time was quickened and enhanced by the terrible events of the war, to which her generous nature responded with intense human sympathy and with indignation against any falsehood or injustice. With all the enthusiasm of her choleric temperament, she now entered into the solution which emerged from Dr Steiner's masterly analysis, in which all her experience appeared confirmed and her ideals realised, not with Utopian proposals, but with a practicable and progressive path to their fulfilment.

We wrote to Rudolf Steiner: it was important that this book should quickly be made available to English readers. We offered to translate it. In his reply Dr Steiner put us into touch with the sculptress Edith Maryon, who was helping him with the Goetheanum building and above all with the great wooden sculptured Group – the Christlike figure of the 'Representative of Humanity' between the adversary powers, Lucifer and Ahriman – which was to occupy the central position between the pillars at the eastern end of the completed building. Miss Maryon throughout those years was one of his closest collaborators in other respects too, for the studio in which the work was going on became his study for a great part of the day. Here he received his visitors, and she was acting very largely as his secretary. Now he himself had been anxious for an English edition of the book, and as no one else was at hand, Miss Maryon had undertaken to translate it. She, too, now wrote to us and eventually sent us her draft. In style, however – like many of the attempted translations of Dr Steiner's works in those early days – it was impossible, certainly for a work that was to reach a wider public, and we said so frankly. We were then invited to Dornach to go into the whole question.

Late in September, 1919, we arrived there. Dr Steiner was away in Stuttgart, where the first Waldorf School had just been opened. We were received in the most friendly way by the Dornach members and above all by Miss Maryon herself. She gave us mallet and chisel and let us help with parts of the sculptured group where there was much superfluous wood and our unskilled hands could do no harm. One day we were thus engaged when Rudolf Steiner suddenly appeared at Miss Maryon's side, up the steep steps of the scaffolding. He was very simple, courteous, friendly – and happy. That was my very first impression – his delight in telling of the school and of the children. These are the first words that have stayed in my mind: *Die Kinder toben* – the children are romping wildly. *Wenn ein Kind nicht toblustig ist, wird's nachher kein tuchtiger Mensch.* A child that is never rampageous won't grow up into a capable man or woman. (An approximate translation! The word *toblustig*, I am told, is in no orthodox vocabulary. That too is characteristic.) I thought a little ruefully of my own rather subdued and melancholic childhood.

My impression even in those first few days was, so to speak, of many Rudolf Steiners. There was the simple, friendly gentleman whom we had seen at this first meeting. Then there was Dr Steiner lecturing – deeply impressive and stern, vivid in characterisation then often moving into anecdote, good-natured satire, rollicking fun and humour. And there was Dr Steiner speaking in a more esoteric meeting – more as you see him in that portrait in the old editions of *Occult Science* – the

Initiate from timeless realms. Moreover, there was Dr Steiner as you might see him during a personal interview, when you told him of your life's difficulties and ideals and he answered your questions – the deep, silent look in his eyes, the warm kindness and encouragement at some moments, and at others the absolute quiet, so that it was left entirely to you to come out with what you had to say, with seemingly no help from him, but silent waiting. And then again there was Dr Steiner as I saw him at the large public gatherings in Germany in 1921-22, often with audiences of two or three thousand, partly indifferent or merely curious or even hostile – the way he held them, the firmness and buoyancy of his carriage, the utter lack of compromise or any attempt to influence them. He rather put them through the mill, building up the ground of spiritual science or the stages of higher cognition with closely knit trains of thought, speaking for two hours or more at a stretch and yet holding his audience completely.

Mrs Wedgwood and I saw Dr Steiner several times during those days. We had to tell him why and how we thought Miss Maryon's translation inadequate. She herself was present, busying herself with sundry other things. I remember when Mrs Wedgwood, as tactfully as she could in her forthright, choleric way, had explained how impossible the translation was, I assenting, and Dr Steiner's matter-of-fact and kindly answer: '*Das ist Ihre berzeugung*' – that is your conviction. There was no pointed emphasis in the sentence, no implication for or against – it was a simple statement of the fact: we start from here. Presently he asked for examples, which we began producing. '*Maryon, kommen Sie mal,*' he called out, and he explained to her the disparities we had been pointing out. Impersonal, unselfish and detached, in the end she said that she had only offered to do it because no one else was at hand, she did not really feel competent in this realm and gladly withdrew. Soon afterwards, Mrs Wedgwood's translation (for it was very largely hers – I only gave incidental help) was published in London by Allen and Unwin, entitled *The Threefold State*. The book was well received. Mrs Wedgwood afterwards retranslated it for a new edition, which we renamed *The Threefold Commonwealth*.

Each of us also spoke with Dr Steiner alone. I remember as he sat there in his studio beneath the great figure of the Christ on which he was still working, with manifold sculptures and clay models all around, there on his shelves were the books I had known so well in the war-time years in England, where the questions of the outbreak of the war and of the economic and political background of warfare generally in the modern world were thrashed out – controversial books by ED Morel, CH Norman and others. It was typical of Rudolf Steiner: however deeply he might see into the supersensible background of events, he spared no pains in getting to know the precise details of outer happenings, the prevalent opinions and the thoughts of others. We naturally came to speak of my war-time experiences, and he took seriously the movement with which I had been associated. He valued the fact that there were men and women who in the last resort followed their own individual conscience, and that there was a country in which one was able in this way also to play an active and fruitful part in public life. The system of separate nation-states, each with its citizen or conscript army – a heritage from Napoleonic times – cannot go on for ever. Face to face with the appalling lethal powers which modern technical science has conjured up, Rudolf Steiner saw a time approaching when the Spirit of Mankind will give individuals the courage to take upon themselves far-reaching decisions, in the face of all prevailing powers and conventions.

Of her conversations with him during those days, Mrs Wedgwood told me something which reveals again how he was wont to see a question from many sides, and I will relate it, though at second-hand. It concerns his attitude during the war of 1914–18, about which a few words more may here be said, for it presented a problem to his English friends. He certainly did not see in that war a straightforward issue of right and wrong, brought about by aggressive military designs on the part of the central powers; rather he seems to have been convinced, especially in the initial stages, that Germany and Austria were fighting in self-defence. In the Wilsonian conception that underlay the peace treaties of 1919 – the setting-up of many smaller nation-states – he recognised a profound mistake. Let your political principles, he says in effect (in *The Threefold State* and other writings), guarantee the rights and liberties of man as such – individual man – and the freedom of nationalities will follow; it cannot be achieved the other way about.

He saw the war in a far deeper and wider context; to quote the title of one of his war-time lecture-cycles, it was the inexorable *Karma of Materialism*. He composed meditations addressed to the guardian angels of those who were at the front or had been killed, and to the Souls of the Nations – the archangel-beings 'in the choirs of the spheres of peace'. Of such a kind that they could equally well be used in all the warring countries, these meditations quickly reached us through friends in Switzerland and elsewhere. They were translated – more easily perhaps than some of his other verses – and in the anthroposophical groups one heard them regularly.

During those years Dr Steiner spoke again and again about the Spirit of the Time and the Souls of Nations. Some of his deepest and most loving characterisations of the English, French and Russian peoples were given in his lectures at Berlin and Dornach a few weeks after the war had broken out, and in the years that followed. His own people he kept calling to their true spiritual task, exposing the perilous sources of illusion which were unhappily to prevail not many years after his death.

Mrs Wedgwood, ardent in her wish for truer international relations, had been resisting the one-sided and often extravagant war-propaganda of her own country, and at that moment she was incensed by the harsh provisions of the Versailles Treaty. Rudolf Steiner's answer was to temper her indignation. Yet after all, he said in effect, perhaps it is as well that victory was not on the other side. And he went on, thinking no doubt of Ludendorff and others like him: We have to bear in mind the kind of militarist mentality which gained control in Germany towards the end of the war. These people would not have treated a defeated enemy with magnanimity or made a wise peace-settlement in the true interests of human progress.

I asked Dr Steiner for his spiritual guidance and he gave me a fresh appointment. When I came again a few days later he had written out for me an evening and a morning meditation, based on the opening words of St John's Gospel. He explained in detail how it should be done, and then continued: This is only half of what is necessary. The other half is, you must be aware that the regular doing of your meditation is the one entirely free deed of the day. However much the other things you do spring from your own resolves, the circumstances that lead up to them are determined by your particular destiny in this present life. But nothing is obliging you to do the meditation; that is entirely the outcome of your own free decision.

I think this, too, was typical of Rudolf Steiner. What in the spiritual schools of former times would have been a binding vow, he would translate into a deed of purest freedom. This metamorphosis – this inversion, one might almost say – he practised in ever so many ways, not always equally explicit; and we, his pupils, were often slow to perceive it. We thankfully received the new content of his teaching and poured it too often into old bottles of would-be piety and sheltered 'goodness', not really true to the spirit of the time. Or else we took the new freedom too lightly. One sometimes had the impression that this, more than anything, saddened and made him lonely.

Dr Steiner entered with great kindness into the question of my future life and career. I had ambitions in scientific research and had made a promising beginning. But as an outcome of the war and the upheavals in which it ended, the social needs of mankind were in the foreground, and I was wondering in which way to turn. In answer to my question, Rudolf Steiner said: These issues are more urgent now than purely scientific work. Now at that moment I had been offered a job which would have brought me into close contact with events. During the war I had enjoyed the friendship of the distinguished journalist, Michael Farbman. A warm-hearted and highly intelligent Russian Jew, he had been working at a book in which he vainly tried so to influence Allied policy that his weary country would not be driven, as in fact it was, into the arms of the Bolsheviks. His command of English was not perfect. I loved the Russian language and was deeply interested in all that was going on in Russia. I helped him put his work into good English. Farbman was now about to become Russian correspondent of a leading English daily, with his headquarters in Berlin to begin with, and wanted me to go with him as his secretary. I told Dr Steiner of this. Our conversation naturally turned to the Russian revolutionary leaders. 'Lenin himself,' said Dr Steiner, 'I hold to be an honest man and an intellect of no mean order.' *Lenin selbst halte ich für einen ehrlichen und geistig nicht unbedeutenden Menschen*, were his exact words; I only remember the gist of what follows: What he is doing, however, is ruthlessly to exploit and destroy the old civilisation. This civilisation, it is true, is inexorably dying out; be under no illusions about that. But one should not play fast and loose, destroying it the more quickly (*Raubbau treiben* were the words he used); rather should one be sowing seeds of what is truly fruitful for the future.

Speaking of Berlin, he went on to say: Of course you might go there, but do

not imagine that the future lies there. It was in the later l9th century that it attained
its recent greatness. That was a time of spiritual void – here he took pencil and
paper and sketched an empty hole – a time when the old spirituality was no more
and the new was not yet born. Vienna may now seem utterly broken, suffering far
worse starvation, but its roots are true and it will rise again.

In the late autumn of 1919 I went on from Switzerland to Germany and shortly
afterwards to Poland – to the south-eastern borders of that country, where my
home had been. The towns and villages were laid waste; famine and typhus were
raging. My wife and I joined the War Victims' Relief Mission, organised by English
and American Quakers. In the autumn of 1920 – *The Threefold State* having in the
meantime been published – we decided to return to England, hoping to help build
up a movement for the Threefold Order. There was a public conference at Dornach
– the first opening of the Goetheanum building – so we made the detour, receiving
unforgettable impressions in the great auditorium, with ever-varied lights and
shades from the coloured windows playing on the rough-hewn wood, the unending
life and variety of sculptured forms. This time I did not ask to see Dr Steiner
personally. But a not very respectful friend, wanting to reach me quickly, had sent
a telegram with the rough and ready address: c/o Dr Steiner, Dornach. To my no
small embarrassment there was Dr Steiner making his way to us through the
crowded ranks to the middle of the hall where we sat, just before one of his lectures.
'Why, you are not to be recognised,' he said laughingly as he handed me the
telegram. (I had been growing a beard in the meantime.) This was the first time
Mary Adams met him. He was very good to her and gave her much spiritual help
in the years that followed.

Back in England, we soon found ourselves in collaboration with other
anthroposophists, notably of the younger generation. The only lasting thing that
grew out of our attempts to awaken interest in the Threefold Order was the
educational movement, for among those keen on the social question were the first
teachers in the Rudolf Steiner Schools in this country. (Michael Hall, known to
begin with as 'The New School', was founded after consultations with Dr Steiner
at Ilkley in 1923; it began in South London in January 1925.)

In London the several anthroposophical groups had in the meantime formed a
loose association, out of which three years later the 'Anthroposophical Society in
Great Britain' was to arise. Small as the effort seemed to be, Rudolf Steiner took
it very seriously from the outset, and he himself was present when on the 2nd
September, 1923, the actual foundation of our society took place; on the proposal
of Mr D N Dunlop, he consented to become president for life.

The first anthroposophists in England had come to the movement from manifold
directions. There were well-to-do ladies and gentlemen – mostly conservative in
social outlook – seriously interested in occultism or seeking for the esoteric
background of Christianity. Among them were members of the theosophical and
other occult movements, for whom the 'Rosicrucian Theosophy' taught by Rudolf
Steiner brought the fulfilment of their longings, and also Freemasons, who found

it in the deeper spiritual background of their craft. Then there were others who, like myself, intent on new social forms and international ideals, were more in sympathy with the rising Labour movement. They, too, played a leading part in building up the anthroposophical work in this country.

Rudolf Steiner himself sometimes referred to the very great differences between Britain and all Continental countries as to the forms of social and spiritual life. In Britain, the most diverse, seemingly contradictory currents are apt to cross and mingle; so too, the mental attitudes and moods of soul. National self-assurance will go hand-in-hand with childlike receptivity to foreign influences; pugnacity in public life with the widest tolerance. There is a certain joy – is it a heritage from Shakespeare? – in the play of contrast among men. We too, in those post-war years, were glad to meet across wide gulfs of divergent outlook. The one thing that united us was that trait of spiritual realism on which Rudolf Steiner always reckoned when he came to England. Once he has got beyond the universal barriers of our time – intellectual pride and materialist agnosticism – an Englishman will generally approach the knowledge of the spiritual world in a simple and expectant frame of mind; he is not overwhelmed with theoretic difficulties. There is a spiritual world, he says to himself; the seer, the true sage, will be able to tell us what it is like. Then it is only a question of well-founded confidence.

In fact, Rudolf Steiner gave some of his deepest occult revelations in England. I think, for instance, of the lectures he gave immediately before he left this country for the last time in 1924 concerning the cosmic and historic streams of Christianity; or of his lectures on 1st and 2nd May, 1913, in the room of the Zarathustra Group, led by Mr H J Heywood-Smith and Mrs A Drury-Lavin in South Kensington, about the Archangel Michael and the 'renewal' of the Mystery of Golgotha in the 19th and 20th centuries. At Easter, 1922, we heard him in the same room addressing a more intimate circle. He spoke of spiritual history leading up to the present time and of the dangers now threatening mankind. I can still see his dark penetrating eyes at that moment, looking as if into long avenues of time.

Our leading member was Mr Harry Collison, editor until his death in 1946 of the English editions of Dr Steiner's works. A many-sided man, he was a barrister and also a professional artist – a very competent portrait painter. Well-to-do and of aristocratic leanings, he was entirely conservative, not to say authoritarian, in political and social outlook, and an active Freemason. Collison was an entertaining man with a lively sense of humour; often it seemed as though a mischievous sprite were perched on his shoulder, ready to play unexpected pranks at any moment. Rudolf Steiner liked him for his versatility and *savoir faire*. He was a man of the world, who could express deep earnestness without exaggerated feeling or any hint of fanaticism. I remember seeing them together in the old Shakespeare Memorial Theatre at Stratford, laughing delightedly at the antics of Sir Toby Belch. The following anecdote was told me in later years by Collison himself. During the First World War, much had been said and written against the Prussian aristocratic or Junker class, till it became a phrase on everybody's lips – the oftener repeated, the less clear idea of what was meant. Once on a long motor-drive with Dr Steiner, Mr Collison, who had a good command of German, put the question: 'Dr Steiner, what exactly is a Junker?' Looking straight at him with a twinkle in his eye, Dr Steiner answered: 'You, Mr Collison – you are a Junker.' The old boy, who had a keen dramatic sense, was highly tickled at this unexpected turn.

I come now to the unforgettable last three years, when Dr Steiner visited England on no less than five occasions, generally for several weeks at a time. It was the growing reputation of the Waldorf School which first brought him to us. In common with several others among Rudolf Steiner's earliest English pupils, and incidentally with some of the most influential figures in life and letters about the turn of the century, Miss Maryon had been a member of the esoteric movement known as the 'Golden Dawn'. She had there made friends with Mrs Millicent Mackenzie, afterwards Professor of Education in the University of Cardiff and a leading figure among progressive educationists at that time. Miss Maryon wrote to her friend, drawing her attention to the pioneering work of the Stuttgart school. Mrs Mackenzie thereupon arranged to take a party of English teachers to Dornach. At Christmas and New Year, 1921–22, Dr Steiner gave his well-known 'Lectures to Teachers' at the Goetheanum, primarily for the benefit of the visitors from England. The lectures were held in the famous upper room in the south wing of the Goetheanum – the room where the Christian Community had been initiated a few months before and in which, a year later, the smoke of the fatal conflagration was first detected.

That was the first occasion when it fell to me to interpret Dr Steiner into English. From then until his death I interpreted well over a hundred lectures to English audiences, not including answers to questions, conferences and informal discussions. Dr Steiner would nearly always divide the lecture into three parts, speaking for 20 to 25 minutes at a time. The lecture was thus completed in three stages. While listening to him, I scribbled notes for all I was worth – never in shorthand, which I purposely refrained from learning. My principle was to follow and enjoy the lecture, and above all never to get flurried; sometimes at the most difficult moments I would stop writing and relax. I invented signs. At Cambridge I had known Bertrand Russell, one or two of whose pupils had been among my friends. I had picked up a smattering of symbolic logic, which I now turned to good account, though no doubt using the signs in highly unorthodox ways. For the rest, I jotted down English or German words or *ad hoc* abbreviations, or mere capital letters with a quick mental note. Thus I was able to keep the translation alive; however imperfect, still it was like the lecture being given again by an unembarrassed and enthusiastic pupil. And there sat Rudolf Steiner a little way off at the side, often in the chair I had vacated.

Looking back on it now, it seems to me that I was doing it with childlike, youthful life-forces, of which an abundance had been given me. There was a great trust in it – an unconscious act of faith. In other respects I was rather shy and diffident in Dr Steiner's presence; I was less near to him than others among his pupils, who had more experience and confidence or were farther along the path of knowledge. Sometimes he had unexpected ways of putting me at my ease, as on a peaceful summer afternoon at Oxford in 1922. Walking through the college garden, I met him and a few others coming from the opposite direction, or waiting for someone else to join them. I paused and greeted them. Presently Dr Steiner bent to a nearby flower-bed, picked a large snapdragon and began fitting it on the tip of my nose, looking at me with his friendly smile.

But when interpreting his lectures I was never shy. I went all out, there was adventure in it, and all the time, whether he were speaking or listening, I felt quiet encouragement in his presence. Sometimes in his closing address at the end of a conference or summer school, he would speak warm words of thanks and appreciation. On one occasion as I was saying goodbye to him, he thanked me personally, adding with emphasis: *Es ist ein grosses Opfer* – it is a great sacrifice. Oh no, Dr Steiner, I said, I do it so very gladly. But he insisted, and repeated more than once: *Es ist ein grosses Opfer*.

Both in his lectures and in conversation with English friends, Rudolf Steiner would draw attention now and then to some finesse in words or forms of speech – the manifestation of the nation-souls through the genius of language. He used to say, as Hilaire Belloc does in his delightful little essay on translation, you cannot really translate by the dictionary. *Cheval* is not equivalent to horse, nor *tete* to *Kopf*. During the Teachers' Course at Dornach, for example, speaking of ethical and religious education, he put side by side the English word 'duty' and the German *Pflicht*. *Pflicht*, he said, comes from the verb *pflegen*, meaning to tend, to nurse, to care for. (Etymologically the word is akin to the English *plight*.) The dutiful man is he who does not turn aside from the world's plight, but tends it with all care. Duty, on the other hand, is akin to *Deus*; it is for Man to stand as worthy representative, on Earth, of the Divine. Related as I was by destiny to both peoples, with the task given me to help build a bridge, it was an inspiration to me when he spoke in this way. For this no longer tended (as well-meant forms of internationalism were doing at that time) to blot out distinctions, making a featureless sameness; rather it brought them out and in so doing made manifest the essential good, the Divine genius that lives in every nation.

In this respect I had interesting experiences with Rudolf Steiner. Often I had to look for an adequate rendering on the spur of the moment, and went far afield in doing so; now and then I failed completely. I was often present, too, during his interviews with others. At Ilkley in 1923 one of our friends had asked him for a meditation. Dr Steiner asked him and me to come at an appointed hour; when we came he had the meditation ready written out in English and asked me if the language was right. In most instances, however, I think he gave meditations to his English pupils in German, and indeed many of them, while they could scarcely speak or even understand the language in trivial and profane intercourse, became at home in it as a medium of spiritual science and, above all, of meditation. This experience accords with what Dr Steiner himself foresaw – namely, the possibility of German becoming to some extent a universal language, not for external intercourse, but as a vehicle of spiritual life, as other languages – Sanskrit, Greek and Hebrew, for example – have been from time to time. At one of the conferences held at Dornach late into the night during the time of the 'Threefold' movement, I heard him speak to this effect, though if I understood him rightly the possibility was contingent on historic events which are to this day undecided; moreover, if fulfilled, it would mean rather a sacrifice of life for the German nation than any access of external greatness.

In a matter of language, I once knew Rudolf Steiner to be really angry; seeing me crestfallen, he quickly added: I do not mean you personally. In the accustomed English pronunciation of *Michael* – unlike the names of the other Archangels – we practically swallow the last two syllables. (It is a shock to admit it, but we pronounce the name in effect as though we should say 'raffle' instead of Raphael.) Towards the end of his life, Dr Steiner was often speaking of the present historic time – beginning with the year 1879 AD – as the 'Age of Michael'. So, too, he did in his lectures at Torquay, in interpreting which I naturally pronounced the name as we always do; it did not occur to me to do otherwise. When I visited him at his hotel that evening he was indignant. The ending *-el*, he said, is the name of God; how can you slur it over in that way? Pronounce the vowels by all means in the accustomed English way, but do not slur them. It is a different matter when you give the name to a man or boy. In German, too, we have the Christian name Michel (which, in effect, is pronounced 'Michl'), but when referring to the Divine Being you should articulate the full three syllables, *Mi-cha-el*. Then, being evidently under the impression that I might think this impossible in English, he went on: You put a stop to spiritual progress if you will insist that your mother-tongue can only be spoken according to present-day conventions. Think, for example, of the word *Weltanschauung* (philosophy of life); one would suppose it the most typical of German words. Yet in a standard dictionary before Goethe's time you will not find it. The vital streams of spiritual life are ever forming and re-forming language; you become sterile if you set yourselves against this.

He knew us only too well. Often since then our friends have attempted to pronounce the Divine name, Michael, no less articulately than, for example, Gabriel or Raphael, but time and again we fall back into the old habit. Rudolf Steiner knew how great is the power of habit and convention in English at the present time. But there are better and deeper things of which he was equally well aware. He sensed the significance of the peculiarly English form of oratory: the abrupt phrases, the sudden beginnings and endings, the unexpected intervals of silence, the avoidance of fluent rhetoric. In contrast to French and German, he once described the ideal – as it were, the spiritual Archetype – which underlies the English way of speaking. It is concerned with the ethic of language rather than with the rhetoric or the logic. This finds expression in silence rather than in speech as such. To put it paradoxically, we speak to give occasion for the intervals of silence in which a common experience is evoked of what is deeper than any outward words.

The English Teachers' Course at the Goetheanum led up to further plans, which in the year 1922 brought Dr Steiner to the historic centres of English cultural life – Stratford-on-Avon and Oxford. Among those who came with Professor Mackenzie to the course at Dornach was Miss M Cross, of the Priory School at King's Langley. For its initial impulse the Rudolf Steiner educational movement in this country is very greatly indebted to Miss Cross. She was a member of the 'New Ideals in Education' committee, which arranged annual conferences, and at her suggestion Rudolf Steiner was invited to the conference for 1922, held at Stratford during the Easter vacation and in connection with the Shakespeare Festival. 'Drama and Education' was the subject for this year, and Dr Steiner was invited both as an educationist and as a distinguished authority on Goethe. His two lectures aroused such interest that he was asked to give a third. He was here speaking side by side with foremost representatives of English life and letters, John Masefield and John Drinkwater among them. I remember the latter at a social gathering asking me many questions about Rudolf Steiner.

At Stratford I used to have lunch at the house where Dr Steiner was staying. Present among others were Millicent Mackenzie, Frau Marie Steiner, and two or three leaders of anthroposophical groups in London. Two moments of the conversation stand out in my mind. One morning there had been two lectures – by Professor Cornford of Cambridge and Sir Henry Newbolt – the former scholarly and learned, the latter masterly in style, though I confess this did not appeal to me as did the homely, rough-hewn manner of John Masefield a day or two before or after. Commenting on the two lecturers that morning, Dr Steiner said: A lecture like Professor Cornford's you might have heard in Germany; Sir Henry Newbolt's, never. Then he bethought himself a moment: In Austria, however, you might well have heard it. And he went on to say: This peculiar accomplishment in form and bearing came both to England and to Austria originally through Spanish influences.

On another occasion Dr Steiner, addressing himself to the elderly English anthroposophists who were present, foretold: You will be reincarnated before very long in mid-Europe; that will be at a time 'when Mid-Europe will be going barefoot'. And speaking of the character and task of the German people, he went on to say: 'The Germans are not really nationalistic'. This was met with evident surprise; the war had not long been over. Dr Steiner repeated his statement and proceeded to illustrate it with a story from the opening weeks of the Waldorf School – a time when the war, officially at least, was scarcely ended. The children in Rudolf Steiner schools are taught foreign languages – French and English in this instance – beginning at the earliest age, by playing and singing. Of all the tunes and words they had been learning, said Dr Steiner, the children, running up and down the corridors and in the playground, would keep singing, not any German Lied or folksong, but 'My Heart's in the Highlands'.

How often during the years and decades that followed have I had occasion to think of the deep truth that lay in Dr Steiner's words, despite all appearances to the contrary. The Germans lack the instinctive national coherence which belongs to most European peoples of modern time, which impels their deeds and destinies for good or ill and somehow forms and guards them like a gift of nature. If they are nationalistic they are so on more theoretic or philosophic grounds, having convinced themselves that this is the true idea to follow. This is the very reason why they could carry it to such ridiculous and even criminal extremes. Nature will not protect nor moderate what does not spring from nature. A farseeing man – himself a patriotic member of a people that was at war with Germany – said to me once during the First World War: 'The Germans are idealistic'. I looked at him questioningly. They are sincere indealists, he went on to explain; right or mistaken, they are always looking for ideals – wanting to devote themselves to some ideal.

In the late autumn of 1923 I went over to Holland to see Dr Steiner. I had to bring him some message – with which I myself was at least partly identified – in which he felt a lack of understanding on our part; indeed, I scarcely ever saw him so gravely troubled as on this occasion. He said to me then: It is of great importance to mankind that the true character of the German people, as revealed in Spiritual Science, should come to be understood in England. (He was referring to such truths as he had explained in his lectures on the nation-souls.) I think I know now what he had in mind. Without a deeper spiritual background, the Germans as a nation are in the long run an insoluble riddle to English people. I mean not individuals but the nation as such. What individual Germans have to offer, even if only on a modest scale, is generously recognised and thankfully received. The people as a people remain an irritating puzzle. One sees it in the memoirs of British statesmen and diplomats, notably those who are most trying to be fair – trying to arrive at a sympathetic understanding instead of merely judging from without. All this is connected with the destiny to which Rudolf Steiner was referring, which somehow withholds from the German people a self-contained and consistent national form, because in fact they have historic tasks of another kind.

For the summer vacation of 1922 a larger public conference was arranged, to be held at Oxford. It was entitled: 'Spiritual Values in Education and in Social Life'. We were trying to realise what Dr Steiner longed for in those years. Face to face with the urgent needs of the time, we should meet on common ground with men and women of consequence, who with all diversities of outlook had a feeling for spiritual activity as the creative factor in social reconstruction. Prepared for several months beforehand, the conference had two main organisers. One was Professor Millicent Mackenzie, who had in this the sympathy and support of her husband, the Hegelian philosopher J S Mackenzie, a former Fellow of Trinity College, Cambridge. The other was Mr Arnold Freeman, Warden of the Sheffield Educational Settlement. A younger member of the Fabian Society, he had been an active collaborator of the Webbs and others and was now intensely keen on the achievement of a threefold social order. The conference was mainly held at Manchester College, of which Dr L P Jacks, the well-known editor of the *Hibbert Journal*, was principal. In a book published not long before, he had expressed ideas not unlike those in *The Threefold State*, concerning which a substantial article by Dr Steiner appeared about this time in the *Hibbert*. Dr Jacks was there to welcome us on the first evening, and at his invitation – on the second Sunday of the conference – Rudolf Steiner gave an evening address in the College Chapel. It was a memorable occasion – the quiet dignity of the building, the evening sun shining in through the high windows, and Rudolf Steiner speaking, from the awakened consciousness of modern time, about the secret of the Trinity and the Mystery of Golgotha.

Among the lecturers at Oxford were the late Clutton Brock, C Delisle Burns, J S Mackenzie, and Dr Maxwell Garnett of the League of Nations Union. Mr H A L Fisher, a former president of the Board of Education, sent an opening address. In the mornings Dr Steiner gave an extended lecture-course on education followed by a shorter one on social questions generally. Frau Marie Steiner brought with her a group of experienced artists from Dornach. Eurythmy performances and demonstrations were given at Keble, where there was a larger stage. Lectures were also given by well-known teachers of the Waldorf School, Dr Caroline von Heydebrand among them. The Waldorf teachers who came with Dr Steiner to our conferences and summer schools were always welcome. Based on their practical experience and devoted work, their lectures – spiced now and then with wit and anecdote – were listened to with keen attention; sometimes with uproarious laughter. Rudolf Steiner, sitting there in the front row, was very evidently happy at these times.

Of the wider aims we set ourselves at Oxford – the movement for a Threefold Order above all – little would seem to have been realised. It was a time when intellectual idealists had not yet suffered the disillusionments of the succeeding decades; they did not feel the need for deeper spiritual insight. Yet the effort was not in vain, for in those post-war years it set the tone for our work, revealing as it did the open and worldwide scope of the Anthroposophical Movement as conceived by its founder. Moreover, it led to the beginnings of the Rudolf Steiner school movement in this country, some of whose ablest representatives found their way to us during the preparations or as an outcome of the conference. I think especially of Daphne Olivier (afterwards Daphne Harwood) who with her sensitive artistic nature, her candid enthusiasm and singleness of heart and mind, became Rudolf Steiner's devoted pupil. Several of those who have since become the bearers of the Anthroposophical Movement in this country became acquainted with it in the first place through her.

It was in those years that Rudolf Steiner met Margaret Macmillan. She had been one of the band of strong-willed, idealistic men and women who at the end of the 19th century founded the Independent Labour Party. She then became a national figure through her pioneering work in the Nursery School movement. At Ilkley in August, 1923 – through the initiative of a very energetic lady, Miss Nina Beverley, who also helped to develop the Anthroposophical Publishing Company in London – a further educational conference was held, at which Rudolf Steiner consented to give the main lectures. This was inaugurated by Miss Macmillan. Ilkley is near the industrial cities of the West Riding, notably Bradford, where she had begun her social work and where some of her closest friends became active in the Anthroposophical Movement. As often happens in the North of England, it still preserves the vigorous and elemental quality of the surrounding moors, the mighty rocks, the running streams of clear water. It is the country of the Brontes, and there are also memories of Druid times. I was particularly glad that after Stratford and Oxford, Rudolf Steiner should also experience this aspect of the English scene. His arrival having been delayed, I was at Harwich to meet him in the early morning, and we travelled straight across England instead of going via London. The train went through the fen country – Ely and Cambridge. The Isle of Ely could be seen in the distance, the great cathedral glistening in the morning sunlight. I spoke to him about Cambridge, and he told me of his friendship with Bertram Keightley, a much older Cambridge man, whom I was also to meet in later years. With a position of high responsibility in the education department of the Indian Civil Service, Keightley had been an active associate of Colonel Olcott and H P Blavatsky in the earlier stages of the Theosophical Movement. He had been Dr Steiner's host when the latter came to the theosophical congress in London at the beginning of the century.

While we were passing through Leeds – the crowded factories, the black and dreary streets with back-to-back dwelling-houses – Dr Steiner kept looking out of the carriage window, expressing his horror of what he saw. 'Do you not see these thought-forms?' he exclaimed. 'This is hell on earth!' He made me feel that we in England, with our developed sense of political liberty, of tolerance, fair play and respect for adversaries, had been far too complacent towards the social miseries we tolerated. Here was social inequality and material degradation in a degree scarcely known in the countries from which Dr Steiner came. As regards social conditions, Britain was anything but democratic at that time.

Yet there were always the champions of social justice and human betterment, prominent among whom was Margaret Macmillan, who welcomed us that evening at Ilkley and presided at the opening of one of the most remarkable of Rudolf Steiner's many lecture-courses on education. It is the one in which he traces educational methods from Ancient Greece through the Middle Ages into modern time, characterising the ideals of the 'gymnast', the 'rhetorician' and the 'doctor'.

In later years I visited Margaret Macmillan at her Nursery School and training centre at Deptford in the East End of London. She told me of Dr Steiner's visit, how in walking with her round the school he kept telling her, very concretely, of the spiritual presence of her sister Rachel with whom she had begun this work – whose death not long before had been a very heavy blow for her. She looked up to Rudolf Steiner as to a wise man whom she fully trusted. Shortly after the conference she writes from Deptford to her friend Margaret Sutcliffe: 'He came here and everything seemed new and wonderful as he entered the room. His science outruns the most advanced work of our day... The strange thing is that no one need tell him anything about themselves. He seems to see one. He knows already when you come near, and yet he never condemns or criticises or has bitter thoughts... The whole world is a whispering gallery to him, and vibrations reach him for which we have no name.' And Rudolf Steiner himself, on his return to Dornach and to the Stuttgart School, spoke and wrote of Margaret Macmillan with warm appreciation. On one occasion, I am told, he said that if she and he had met ten or twenty years earlier they might together have founded a worldwide educational movement.

I have left all too little space to tell of the memorable summer schools held during Dr Steiner's last two visits to this country. The first was at Penmaenmawr on the north coast of Wales, immediately after Ilkley. Here Dr Steiner was able to visit the cromlechs in nearby Anglesey and the stone circle on Penmaenmawr mountain. Next year, in August, 1924, we were at Torquay, whence Dr Steiner visited the ruins of King Arthur's castle at Tintagel. What he experienced at these places played a not unimportant part in his spiritual revelations during the last two years of his life, and we owe much to the spiritual insight and certainty of purpose of those who invited him there. He was there brought into immediate connection with the old Celtic spiritual stream, of the importance of which in the origins of European culture he had so often spoken.

Towards the close of the 19th century the 'Celtic revival' in Great Britain and Ireland – like the Wagner movement in Germany – gave expression to the longing for a rediscovery of deeper spiritual sources. Those who were looking for a knowledge of the elemental world of Nature and – what went hand-in-hand with this – for a more cosmic form of Christianity, were inevitably drawn to the old Celtic traditions, and a connection very naturally arose between this movement and the one led by Rudolf Steiner, new and for the most part untraditional as the latter was. The poetry of Fiona Macleod (William Sharp), for example, found beautiful expression in Rudolf Steiner's eurythmy; his widow presently became a member of the Anthroposophical Society. But it was D N Dunlop above all who linked this Celtic stream with Rudolf Steiner's work. With his very able helper, Mrs E C Merry, he was the initiator of the Anthroposophical summer schools at Penmaenmawr and Torquay. Dunlop's encounter with Dr Steiner was among the most important events of these later years. Born and brought up in a lonely district on the west coast of Scotland, he knew something of the spiritual and elemental world by direct experience. He had a deeply religious nature, an unquenchable enthusiasm, a strong and silent, seemingly gentle, yet all the more effective will. A life-long friendship linked him with the Irish poet A E (George Russell). Together in their younger years they had conducted a Theosophical Lodge in Dublin. Dunlop was also a man of affairs, with organising ability and the power to inspire others. Mystic though he remained, he could impress the hard-headed businessmen among whom he moved throughout his later life. At the time of his first real encounter with Dr Steiner – in London in the spring of 1922 – he already occupied a position of great responsibility. Rudolf Steiner met him with warm affection; together they discussed the worldwide and far-seeing aims in the pursuit of which Mr Dunlop, shortly after Dr Steiner's death, was to inaugurate the 'World Power Conference' – a periodic event which played a prominent and helpful part in international affairs during the succeeding years. Dr Steiner in his turn enlisted Dunlop's help. He introduced him to Ita Wegman, MD, in collaboration with whom he was at that time developing especially the medical side of the new spiritual movement. Dr Wegman was with Dr Steiner on his last two visits to England; lectures were also given to invited groups of doctors. Dunlop helped put the pharmaceutical side of this work on a sound business footing in this country.

Saying goodbye after their first meeting, Rudolf Steiner took Dunlop's hands in his and said repeatedly: 'We are brothers.' Of the summer schools which we owed to Dunlop's initiative, he said that they should be written in the 'golden book' of the history of the Anthroposophical Movement. Two of his deepest and most comprehensive lecture-cycles were indeed given at these summer schools; here above all he came to meet the need for detailed knowledge of the world beyond the Threshold and for a spiritual 'Cosmogony', in which he recognised the true and innate tendency of the Western spirit.

In Rudolf Steiner's encounters with men and women such as D N Dunlop and Margaret Macmillan, the worldwide character of his own task can be perceived. He himself represented a certain method of approach to esoteric knowledge – a method largely founded in the philosophic genius of Middle Europe. This in his hands made possible a genuine integration of the scientific spirit of the West with the deep realms of mystical and occult experience into which man enters when he transcends the Threshold. Such integration alone makes it possible for modern man to approach the hidden spiritual world without losing hold of the most precious achievement of the West – the inner spiritual freedom which goes with independent thinking, intellectual clarity and probity of thought. In the spiritual method developed by Rudolf Steiner we may perceive the genuine contribution of the German-speaking world to mankind's progress. Every such contribution is indispensable to the whole. Yet, sternly as he might insist on the methodic path he had to teach, Rudolf Steiner fully recognised the spiritual approach – often radically different – of those who took their start from other premises both of the East and of the West. His full life-story reveals how intertwined his destined mission was with other spiritual streams and with outstanding individualities of other countries and continents.

On the physical plane the 'spiritual guidance of mankind' works in manifold and seemingly contradictory ways, diversified by geographical and secular conditions. Yet it is there on every plane; it has its origin in regions far transcending the polarities and 'pairs of opposites' by which the physical manifestations of life are orientated, and in terms of which we have to form our standards of discrimination. The initiators of true progress know one another face to face, across the inevitable differences of spiritual pathway. Thirty-three years will soon have passed since Rudolf Steiner's death. From the eternal sources from which his life-work was inspired, the spiritual guidance of mankind works on; it will find access to human hearts wherever upon Earth they are open to receive it. Mindful of this, while faithful in the care and practical pursuit of what he has bequeathed, the Anthroposophical Movement will remain truest to its founder.

A Day at Tintagel in August 1924

Eleanor C Merry

AS AN INTRODUCTION to this piece, Mabel Cotterell wrote: Together 'D N D' and 'E C M' arranged the summer schools of 1923 and 1924, choosing the centres of Penmaenmawr and Torquay. We therefore owe to them Dr Steiner's two great cycles, *The Evolution of the Earth and of Humanity* and *True and False Paths in Spiritual Investigation.* This latter subject was chosen by Mr Dunlop to counter the growth of spiritualism in England. Dr Steiner too must have welcomed the chance of visiting North Wales where the rocky cliffs held Imaginations for so long, and where the Druid Circle above Penmaenmawr led to his descriptions of the Druids, etc., in lectures and writings. The visit from Torquay to the Cornish coast with the ruins of King Arthur's Castle and the interplay of elemental beings in the air and sun and sea-spray at Tintagel is described in Mrs Merry's delightful article below.

How well I remember that visit, crossing the rickety wooden bridge over the inlet, and mounting the rough steps up the cliff. Mrs Merry took Mr Dunlop, Mrs Pease and me in her small car and we followed the two large hired cars containing Dr Steiner, Frau Dr Steiner, Dr Wegman, Dr Vreede, Dr Wachsmuth with Mr and Mrs Scott-Pyle (née Mieta Waller, an artist and a great friend of Frau Dr Steiner; she was the first to offer the money for a building where the Mystery Plays could be performed). The article describes the drive over Dartmoor but omits to say – as Dr Steiner told us – that mischievous pixies and nixies appeared and made 'long noses' as he passed! Nor does it tell how afterwards we all rested in the big hall of the Castle Hotel with its Round Table inscribed with the names of the knights – the Dornach party somewhat apart from ours – and how Dr Steiner wrote a verse to Albert Steffen which he took round for us all to sign. The verse appeared later in *Das Goetheanum,* though of course without our signatures.

Rudolf Steiner appointed Mr Dunlop, with Mrs Merry, as representative of the medical work in England. Since D N D spoke no German she was always there as interpreter. It seems that at their first meeting Dr Steiner sat and held Mr Dunlop's hand while they talked, as if he had met a long lost friend. Dr Steiner knew, too, of Mrs Merry's presence in Austria years before she came to anthroposophy and spoke to her about it. It has been her destiny to outlive the days when she counted for so much in the work of our Society. Ill health brought retirement, but the days of work will come again.

'I WANT TO GO TO KING ARTHUR,' said Dr Steiner in a very resolute voice. It was very early morning, between 5 and 6 o'clock, I think, and I heard his firm footsteps coming to meet me in a dark passage of the hotel when I was on my way to waken Dr Wegman as I had promised. Dr Steiner was fully dressed, though we were not, as it was pouring with rain and misty.

I said: 'Do you really think we can go, in this weather?' He replied: 'Why not?' – and he added: 'A few minutes after 8 o'clock, the rain will stop.'

I hurried on to waken Dr Wegman, as I had promised, and to dress myself. By 10 past eight we had finished breakfast and, in typical English fashion, trooped outside to look at the weather; we saw that the mist had cleared, the rain had stopped, and the sun was shyly appearing. So the memorable drive of some 30 miles over the heather-covered hills began.

Nearly all the way, small fragments of rainbows seemed to descend to the sides of the road and hovered about us as though to make our journey a triumphal progress. It was a most wonderful sight. At last we came again to the sea, and straight ahead of us, at the top of a grassy cliff, were the last fragments of King Arthur's castle of Tintagel.

A deep rocky chasm divided this from a second rugged cliff, where other remains could still be seen. We all got out of the various motor cars and began to walk up the left-hand slope to the ruins. Dr Steiner was at first silently absorbed in the wonderful view; all around was sunshine, and fleeting cloud-shadows and little hurrying rainbows – and a stormy and angry sea.

Between the remains of the castle and the next promontory was a turbulent inlet of the sea. At first Dr Steiner stood, notebook and pencil in hand, near the site of King Arthur's scattered stones. 'Here,' he said, 'were the Kitchens, and over there the Knights' quarters.' Presently he said, 'A Knight is approaching us...' I looked in vain, there was apparently nothing there. It has passed from my memory what he said further, though he described the Knight, who, I think, was not riding but walking. He wrote other notes about the Knights' quarters and perhaps the banqueting hall; but for the most part he was silent and absorbed, though at the same time very positive and aware of everything.

Presently, most of us – and Dr Steiner – set out to scramble up the stony path of the opposite cliff, where there were more ruins. He said these had been the servants' quarters, and also the stables.

I do not think the cliffs can always have been divided by the chasm as now, though I do not remember Dr Steiner speaking of that. As we descended the cliff we went into what is traditionally called Merlin's Cave. Inside it there was a wonderful natural structure in which one had a good view of the shadowed rays of the sun – something like what can be seen in a Druid Trilithon, where the Druids obtained their knowledge in the shadowed shining of the sunlight.

So far as I remember, Dr Steiner did not speak about the cave, but I rather think it must have been in connection with it that he later spoke of Wagner and Merlin.

We then drove back to Torquay, and the visit to 'King Arthur' was over. But I have since felt 'in my bones' that there was something extraordinary about this visit. To what did it really refer? To England? I think not; King Arthur is too universal a figure for that. We have learned since, from Dr Steiner's lectures, that the name 'King Arthur' was the name, not of a single individual, but the name of the representative head of an Order devoted to the war against Evil, in the sense of an awakening of humanity to its inevitable and formidable presence.

There was not, of course, just one King Arthur as I used to think, but many, who were the Heads of a continuing Order of Initiates. The evil, and the social wrongs they fought against were, and are still, in another form, in our midst.

It is as though, in that expedition, we had been really taken into the past, and been able to realise some fragment of the enormous conflict which never ceases to assail mankind: that perhaps, in England, the typical Knight errant still remains real and tangible; and also that Arthur was one of the first stepping-stones towards the longed-for East, and the coming of the sunrise, whose first rays appeared somewhat later in the Quest for the Holy Grail.

The Origins of Michael Hall School

Helen Fox

THE FIRST TIME I heard Rudolf Steiner speak was the Christmas of 1921 in Dornach, when he gave a course of lectures on education rather specially intended for English teachers. The lectures were translated, almost verbatim, in three parts, by George Kaufmann (later George Adams), this being the first of over a hundred lectures which he interpreted in his way. Rudolf Steiner spoke of education as an *art*, a method rather than a programme; the teacher must first learn to know the true being of man – body, soul and spirit – and out of this knowledge he must discover how to meet the needs of the child at every age and in every subject. This was such a fundamentally different approach from what I had heard in my teacher's training course, with its programmes and educational maxims, that it left me somewhat puzzled, but after hearing Rudolf Steiner's Christmas Eve lecture in the great hall of the first Goetheanum, I came back to England eager to know more of his teaching. It was on the occasion of this Dornach course that Miss Cross, headmistress of a boarding-school at Kings Langley, offered her school to Dr Steiner, to be remodelled on anthroposophical lines. This developed later into the present 'New School' at Kings Langley.

During the next six months I began to study anthroposophy, and met others who were specially interested in education. In August 1922 Dr Steiner was invited to give his first public course of lectures in England. This was to be on education (published as *The Spiritual Ground of Education*), held at Manchester College, Oxford. Some of the Waldorf teachers were there and also a small group of eurythmists who gave the first public performance of eurythmy in England, with Frau Marie Steiner as reader. Most of the time between the lectures was filled up with personal interviews, and this was so wherever Rudolf Steiner went.

Thus I was fortunate enough to have a private talk with him, and on three or four subsequent occasions. In the space of a few minutes, one's questions and problems were answered – or rather, one was shown a new goal in life and how to set about finding the way to it.

During the next few months our little group of would-be teachers met more often, and gradually and hesitantly the thought was born in us: 'Could we not perhaps start a day school in London?'

Then, on New Year's Eve, 1922-23, came the terrible tragedy of the burning of the first Goetheanum. (The fire started in the room where we had had our lecture course a year before.) All the artistic and dedicated work of Rudolf Steiner and his many helpers was destroyed in a single night. I once heard a German teacher, who now holds a leading position in a school in north Germany, tell of how as a young man he happened to be in Dornach at the time and found himself standing next to Rudolf Steiner, watching the destruction. And then Dr Steiner turned to him and said: '*Nicht wahr, wir wollen weiter arbeiten.*' (We will go on working, will we not.) So the resolve for the future was already taken.

A digression: A few years ago I was asked to speak at a school for maladjusted children, on Rudolf Steiner's birthday. I told them this story, and when the talk was over I overheard one little boy retelling it with great gusto to his friends: 'And there stood Dr Steiner, watching how the whole thing was going up in flames, and – (with a jerk of the elbow) – he says to his mate, he says: ''Ere, come on, we've got to get on with it!' Apart from the humour, it was touching to see how a little boy's heart warmed to Rudolf Steiner's courage.

It was indeed fortunate for us that Dr Steiner's great carved statue was not yet in place in the Goetheanum, and so escaped the fire. Dr Steiner described this wooden statue (which now has a room of its own in the present Goetheanum), as the Christ-filled Man, holding the balance between the two great powers of evil in the world.

In the following August 1923, Dr Steiner was again asked to give a public educational course, this time at Ilkley, Yorkshire. During the conference we teachers came nearer to the resolve to try to start a school, and we decided to confer with George Kaufmann, who was acting as interpreter and a kind of young courier to Rudolf Steiner. He was himself pre-eminently a scientist, but education was one of the things that lay very near to his heart. I remember that it was almost impossible to find a quiet room for our preliminary talk together, so eventually we took some chairs into an old greenhouse, in which inspiring atmosphere our resolve to start a school came to life.

George Kaufmann arranged a meeting for us with Dr Steiner, Frau Dr Steiner and I think one or two other friends. We told him of our resolve and asked him if he would approve of such a step. Rudolf Steiner looked very thoughtful for a moment, and then said '*Ja!*' And when Dr Steiner said '*Ja*' in that full, rich voice of his, this was no mere acceptance; one experienced it as a *deed*. After this he spoke to us very quietly and seriously, saying how vital it was that if we did start a school it should be 'a *good school*', able to take its place beside other educational establishments in England, not just an interesting little experiment somewhere in a corner. We then asked Dr Steiner to choose the teachers, to which he replied: 'Who would like to undertake this work?' We indicated the four of us who were there, Miss Effie Wilson (who later helped to start and support the Ilkeston School), Miss Dorothy Martin (the late Mrs Darrell), Miss Daphne Olivier (Mr A C Harwood's first wife) and myself. 'But you should also have a man,' said Dr Steiner. We should indeed, and we did indeed, for Mr Harwood joined us some months before the school opened.

So the first step was taken, but only the very first. We had no prospect of children, no house, no money. Then a miracle happened. Our decision was made public at the Ilkley Conference, and immediately three anthroposophists, with incredible trust, came forward, each offering £1000 to buy a school house. These

were Mr Christopher Gill, a solicitor from Bath, who also gave us valuable advice
on business matters, Mr Edward Melland, father of Miss Ruth Melland (well-
known to all Old Scholars up to 1956), and Miss Elizabeth Stuttaford, a wealthy
lady who had been studying Dr Steiner's work for many years. Rudolf Steiner now
laid it upon her heart to take on the work of helping this new school as a task for
her later life. This she did most faithfully, also guaranteeing the teachers' salaries
for the first few years. Miss Irene Groves, a well-known anthroposophist from
Bristol, also gave us much practical help in those early years.

Another public conference was planned for the summer of 1924 at Torquay, and
we asked Dr Steiner if on this occasion he could spare the time to give us teachers
some talks to prepare us for our new work. This he gladly consented to do, and
these private lectures, for us and a few Waldorf teachers, were unique of their kind,
being the only ones ever given specifically for an English school – published as
The Kingdom of Childhood. Dr Steiner was now already beginning to look worn
and ill, but when he spoke his voice was strong and eager, and he seemed full of
vigour.

It may be of interest to mention a few of the thoughts that Dr Steiner gave us
in this course.

First of all, he described how at birth man descends from the heavenly world,
and how this process of incarnation during the early years is really a stupendous
task of the spirit, even a 'martyrdom' – often expressed in outbursts of temper
and the like. How important then is the loving understanding and support of parent
and teacher.

Then the child comes to school, to learn from his teachers about the earthly
world, about nature and all that concerns the life of his fellow human beings. Now
we must permeate our teaching with imagination, enthusiasm, humour and warmth
of heart, and Dr Steiner stressed the importance of taking all our examples from
real life, avoiding abstract and intellectual concepts. He told us how fortunate we
were here in England that our weights and measures and the money system – the
20 and the 12, the foot, the yard and so on – still stem from the lives and occupations
of the men of long ago. (Alas, we now have the encroachment of abstractions in
this sphere also.)

Fairy tales and folk tales, with their deep human wisdom, are a 'nourishment
of the soul' in the early years of school life. In one of the later lectures of this
course, Rudolf Steiner himself told us a fairy-tale which was perfect example of
how some of the deepest truths of existence can come to expression in the mind
of such a teacher. Briefly, the story was as follows: 'A little violet, newly blossomed,
looks up at the blue sky and is afraid. She asks a fierce dog what it is. The dog
replies that it is a great big violet which will come and crush her. The little violet
is more afraid than ever, and then a gentle little lamb comes joyously leaping by.
The violet confides her fears to the lamb, who then tells her that the blue sky is
the love of God, like a great big blue violet spread out over the world to protect
all little violets and all creatures on the earth.'

Such a story will awaken many questions which the teacher can speak about in his class, and perhaps later on, at the end of the Class Teacher period, he can refer to it again as a basis for discussion in the religion lessons.

In such ways as these Dr Steiner strove to inspire the teachers with a new educational impulse. At the conclusion of the lectures he said: 'From this first project the world must take notice that this is something . . . which arises out of a conception of the real being of man . . . And it is indeed the very civilization of today, which is now moving through such critical times, that calls us to undertake this task.'

Soon after the conference, Dr Steiner returned to Dornach. A group of us saw him off at Victoria Station, and went into his carriage one by one to say goodbye. When he shook me by the hand and with a kindly smile said '*Alles Gute*', I felt this was not so much a personal wish as a deep desire and concern that the work we were undertaking should succeed. Back in Dornach, Rudolf Steiner roused himself to an incredible task for the next month, giving three or four lectures a day and many interviews, though by this time he was gravely ill. His last talk was a short intimate address to the members on Michaelmas Eve, 1924.

On 20 January 1925, the New School (later Michael Hall) opened at Streatham with seven pupils and five teachers, a round dozen of us altogether. (We were not overworked.) Then on the last day of the first term we heard the tragic news of Rudolf Steiner's death, but we were grateful that our school, small as it was, had been established while he was still on earth.

Looking back, it is a delight to recall Rudolf Steiner's physical presence amongst us. There he stood, a commanding figure, with his black hair (which never turned grey) and eyes predominantly black, with a tinge of blue. His firm mouth expressed immense determination, courage and assurance (as one may see from the photographs), but never severity, and his whole face lit up with a smile when greeting his fellow human beings. He was of medium height, but had such poise and erectness of carriage that many people (myself included) imagined him to be taller than he really was.

Rudolf Steiner's sense of humour was delightful. He loved to tease people and tell witty little stories, especially at mealtimes (which he said should not be the occasion for grave and serious discussions). On one of his visits to England, Rudolf Steiner visited Stratford and saw a performance there. He laughed so loud and heartily at the antics of Falstaff on the stage that people began to look round at this distinguished-looking stranger who was enjoying himself so thoroughly.

And now a word or two about Dr Steiner's voice, a most difficult thing to describe. I can only say that it was capable of endless modulations; when he was lecturing, and perhaps speaking of the seriousness and urgency of the challenges that confront us today, then his voice would ring and echo round the hall, but in individual conversations it was deep and quiet, and when he was telling a humorous story it was light and free and had a whimsical tone.

There are many other features of Rudolf Steiner's personality that stand out in

one's memory – his universality, his forbearance, his patience and immense strength
of will. But there is one quality that I should like to speak of in greater detail,
namely, his reverence for the initiative and true freedom of every human being.
This was eminently clear in the sphere of education.

We may say that Rudolf Steiner himself began to be a 'teacher' at the age of
14, when with the warm approval of his teachers he helped the more backward
children in his class. This developed into a wide experience of coaching at the
university and elsewhere, and in his student days he had a very remarkable experience
with a 10-year-old boy. This child, from a well-to-do family in Vienna, was mentally
retarded, and so far no-one had been able to help him. At the request of the parents,
Dr Steiner undertook this task; he says himself that he was convinced that the
child had mental capacities which were in a state of sleep, and he set himself to
'draw the soul into the body'. This he did, starting with the simplest concentration
exercises and so on, and at the end of two years the boy was able to return to
school and pass the usual examinations; he became a doctor and lost his life at the
front in the 1914–18 War. The important thing to notice is that Rudolf Steiner
spent long hours of thought and preparation for what he did with the child, the
actual exercises lasting perhaps only a quarter of an hour. Thus through this deep
inward study of an abnormal child, Rudolf Steiner had begun to prepare himself
to be a 'teacher of the teachers'.

But it was not till 1907, when he was in his forties, that he gave his first lectures
on 'The Education of the Child' in various towns in Germany, and published a
book under that title. One might have expected that he would now start a school
somewhere and urge some of his followers to take up this work. But that was
seldom his way. To be fruitful and creative, such an impulse must come from the
workers themselves. So with infinite patience Rudolf Steiner waited another 12
years, when at last, six years before his death, his friend Emil Molt, director of the
Waldorf-Astoria cigarette factory in Stuttgart, asked him if he might start a school,
primarily for the children of his employees. That surely must have been a day of
very special happiness for Rudolf Steiner. This was the first of the 70 schools (for
normal children) which now bear his name.

In thinking of Rudolf Steiner and his work, the question naturally arises: 'How
was it possible for him to know so much, and of what nature was the deeper
wisdom which he was able to impart?' I should like to attempt an answer to this
question as a conclusion to these memories.

All through the ages there have been those who have been able to behold the
unseen realities of the spirit, and to impart these truths to those around them in a
form suited to the time. Moses and the Ancient Prophets, Buddha, Zarathustra,
Joan of Arc, Saint Francis, are but a few examples. But if such wisdom is to be
granted to men of our own day and generation, it must of necessity be founded
on clear, conscious knowledge, every bit as exact and comprehensive as what we
learn in our schools, universities and practical life at the present time. Rudolf Steiner
knew this; he tells us that as a child the world of the spirit had always been as real

to him as the physical world, but it was gradually borne in upon him that he must consciously lose this dream-like instinctive knowledge and develop in himself, step by step, a complete, detailed and conscious knowledge of the eternal world of the spirit, as revealed in man, in the stars, in evolution and in all the heavenly beings who guide our lives. This knowledge was then imparted, in written works, personal talks and some 6000 lectures, to all who wished to learn from him.

Rudolf Steiner undertook this completely selfless and sacrificial task out of his love for human-kind, and thus we may see in him an apostle of spiritual truth in the modern world.

Experiences in the Realm of Dramatic Art

Gottfried Haass-Berkow

WHEN I RECALL the inspiring suggestions given by Rudolf Steiner for dramatic art, they are inseparably bound up for me with the utilisation of them on the stage. A painter who wanted to show what Rudolf Steiner's indications had meant for him would perhaps paint a landscape; and what they have meant for me I can best express in word and gesture. For just as what Steiner has said about colour should give to the pictures of a painter a mark of genuine creation, so should everything that an actor has received from him come to view in the creative power of the actor's mime and in the vitality of his speaking. It is not possible for me simply to record that Rudolf Steiner spoke on several occasions in such and such terms on the subject of dramatic performance, and that he did this or that action or gesture in such and such a way. And if I am, notwithstanding, to make the attempt to put something down in writing of what an actor who knew Rudolf Steiner owes to impulses that came from him, then the reader must be asked to bear this in mind as he reads. With this reservation, I can assure him that it not only gives me great happiness to report on my experiences, but I am sensible of an inner obligation to do so, since what we were privileged to receive has too great a significance for our whole culture and civilisation for us to suffer it to be lost.

During the course of many years I had opportunities to put questions personally to Rudolf Steiner, and there were also questions that I put to him together with various members of the company I was leading at the time; and the answers to all these questions are not at all widely known. The treatment of problems in dramatic art does not of course admit of explanation simply in words, for everything depends on making the prescribed exercises live for immediate experience, and on demonstrating conclusively that what has been said can be made fruitful in persistent practice.

I should perhaps begin by speaking briefly of myself, so that my readers may know on to what kind of ground the seed fell. Acting has been my vocation ever since my 18th year, when I began my career in Austria. Four years later, prompted by the desire to explore new ways of cultural development, I entered the Jacques Dalcroze Institute for Rhythmical Gymnastics at Dresden-Hellerau. Having gained a Teacher's Diploma at Professor Eduard Engel's School in Dresden for Voice and Speech Production, I went afterwards to Berlin and had an appointment there as teacher in the Dramatic School run by Max Reinhardt and Maria Moissi. It was in Berlin that I first heard Rudolf Steiner lecture, and took part in the first lessons that were given there in the new art of eurythmy which he had created. In the summer of 1912 I was present at the performance of his Mystery Plays in Munich. At Christmas I was given the role of Herod in the Oberufer Christmas Plays which

Rudolf Steiner produced in the Anthroposophical Group in Berlin. At that time medieval Christmas Plays were quite unknown; we owe it to Rudolf Steiner that people's attention was drawn to them, and that today they are produced everywhere.

When at the beginning of the war the dramatic schools were closed, I asked Rudolf Steiner's permission to produce these plays, and the texts were sent to me. At first I worked at them with some students of Gottingen University; we took also other folk plays, such as, for example, the *Totentanz* (Dance of the Dead) which I had put together out of 15th-century texts. In 1910 I formed a permanent company, and for many years we continued to give performances in a number of towns in Germany and also abroad. For this we extended our repertoire to include dramas by standard authors. The 'Haass-Berkow Players' met with a warm welcome from young and old. In 1921, during the days of a *Hochschulkurs* (course for students) in Dornach, we put our questions to Rudolf Steiner, and his answers to them have since been published in a book entitled *Über die Schauspielkunst*. Three years later he gave, at the request of myself and others, the course of lectures called *Sprachgestaltung und Dramatische Kunst*, which has also appeared in print. At the conclusion of the course, we – that is, my company and I – were vouchsafed the opportunity to give a little demonstration of our stage work, after which Rudolf Steiner spoke to us, giving us what proved to be his last suggestions and advice for our work. This was almost immediately before he was taken ill.

Later on, after Rudolf Steiner's death, an intensive study of speech was begun in the section for the Arts of Speech and Music at the Goetheanum, under the guidance of Frau Marie Steiner. This was in the summer of 1925, and the study was continued for many years from the summer of 1926 onward. During this time a group of students was handed over to me by Frau Steiner for speech training. Quite a number of my actors remained on afterwards in Dornach, while I myself accepted an offer to undertake the leadership of the *Wurttemberg Landesbuhne*. So much for my own career, in so far as it has immediate connection with Rudolf Steiner and the Goetheanum. If now today, 30 years after Steiner gave his lectures on dramatic art, we want to face up to the question of where we are with the art of acting, I would like in the first place to quote from an article by the actor Ernst Ginsberg, which appeared in November 1954, in the *Deutsche Zeitung*: 'There is no denying it, the theatre is completely impoverished today. A zealous loyalty to his work in all its detail demands from the actor such a mastery of his craft as is hardly to be met with in our time... Artistic standards are sadly lacking today... One would like to say to the young actors: "Do take pains to learn once more how to breathe and how to speak! Study to be equal to all kinds of style in speaking, so that, for example, you are ready to speak with masterly skill classical passages which physically require you to hold the breath for a long time, and spiritually to sustain the mood throughout – instead of tearing it up into naturalistic shreds"... We should encourage actors much more than we do to work out of their own imagination.'

The present situation in regard to stage speaking was described at about the same time by the Darmstadt stage manager Rudolf Seller, one of the leading producers of our day. 'We cannot but have serious anxiety for the very existence of the theatre. The consolidation of the theatres by means of regulated dependence on the State has no sensible foundation... The kernel of all the problems concerned with form and style is the relation of the actor to speech... We must find new methods of working that will put the performer in his right place... Compared with the theatre of olden times, our theatre is to an extreme degree a personal theatre, a theatre of imitation, a theatre of the type. The actor in playing his part plays at the same time himself... Bent on producing a picture that is true to nature, he lets the word lose exactness and precision. The theatre must be born again out of speech. Will it ever succeed in bringing into this everyday kind of acting the ordering and dignifying power of speech?'

Rudolf Steiner has answered these questions. Thirty years have gone by since he pointed to new paths for the development of drama and opened up possibilities for that spiritual deepening of the art for which men are waiting today. We must, however, be prepared to find that the paths of development here implied are paths that each one has to discover – and tread and make fertile – for himself. We must also realise that any report of the answers Rudolf Steiner gave to the questions we brought to him could carry conviction only if at the same time it were possible to demonstrate them practically. All that I can attempt to do is to draw for you in writing an utterly inadequate kind of sketch, intended to suggest how such exercises can prove fruitful for an actor. And for this purpose I would like to single out two themes: first, conscious creative activity on the stage; and, secondly, the interconnection of gesture and word.

On the occasion of the *Hochschulkurs* of 1921, we asked Rudolf Steiner: How is consciousness related to dramatic activity? He replied as follows: 'Dramatic activity has a very special part to play in that enhancement of consciousness towards which man is moving in the present time. Again and again, in widely differing spheres of life, we hear it emphatically declared that this development of consciousness cannot but rob the artist of some measure of his naïvety and instinct. The faculty of immediate and vital perception, however, will most assuredly not be lost by such knowledge as we are pursuing here. One need have no fear of becoming inartistic through acquiring conscious control of one's medium... For mankind in general, and more especially for the artist, the process of becoming conscious is a necessity.'

These words I myself, along with many others who have travelled the same road, can fully confirm. Rudolf Steiner went on to say that Shakespeare had to a remarkable degree the faculty of beholding the characters of his plays. He could see them standing before him in imagination as objective pictures, and it enabled him to creep right inside them and know them from within. This faculty of the dramatist must, said Rudolf Steiner, extend to the actor. That is to say, particular care should be taken during his training to develop it.

And now Rudolf Steiner gave us an example for the development of consciousness which, as we try to follow it with sympathy and understanding, does indeed awaken within us the forces that can be creative in the realm of drama. He quoted to us the following words of the well-known Vienna actor Lewinski, one of our foremost character actors. When questioned about his relationship to his art, Lewinski said: 'I would of course simply not be able to play at all if I were to depend upon the little hunchbacked figure standing there on the stage, with his croaking voice and frightfully ugly face; he could never do anything! I help myself out of the difficulty in the following way. On the stage I am composed of three persons. The first is the little hunchback. The second is completely outside this hunchbacked figure, and leads a purely ideal existence; but I must have him there before me all the time. Finally, I myself creep out of both of these and am the third, who plays with the second upon the first – upon the hunchbacked Lewinski.' One might perhaps say, expressing it a little differently, that the artistically creative ego (No. 3) plays, with the imagined figure of his part (No. 2), upon the instrument of his body (No. 1). This division of oneself into three, said Rudolf Steiner, has great significance for the actor in all his work on the stage.

Rudolf Steiner emphasised also how necessary it is for the actor to know his body, before he can be ready to play upon it as on an instrument. 'He should have as thorough a knowledge of his body as the violinist has of his violin. He must come to the point of being able to listen to his own voice. He should also know how he steps, how he places the sole of his foot in walking how he moves his feet and legs, and so on.' The actor will, in fact make an intensive study of how people walk; he will learn the secret of different kinds of walking. He will observe that inconsiderate people walk on their heels – which corresponds to the gesture for K; or again that the more pleasant and agreeable person has an easy, flowing gait, which corresponds to the gesture for L. He will practise rapid walking, and then a mere shuffling along; or again, swaying to and fro as he walks, and then once more stepping out firm and straight. He will do best to practise especially the kind of walking that comes least naturally to him. If in a student we call into play merely what he brings with him by natural endowment, it will mean that we hold him fast in naturalistic acting – a procedure that is only too common in the film world. And it is a fact that even many stage producers, under the contaminating influence of the film, are tending to cast their parts on this principle. If, on the other hand, an actor's work is not restricted in this way to suit his more natural talents and disposition, he can develop such an alert ability for change that he can be perpetually turning into someone else. By submerging himself in many different 'imagined' characters, he acquires a rich store of possibilities of expression. Such an actor we shall want to see again and again, for on account of his unbounded versatility he will always remain interesting; whereas we shall soon tire of one who is for ever showing us what comes easiest to him. In naturalistic acting the actor is a prisoner; in fantasy he is free to change all the time. 'The actor should know whether he has himself a quiet walk or a quick, smart step – in ordinary life as well as on the stage; he should know how he bends his knee, how he moves his hands.' With these words Rudolf Steiner touched as early as 1921 the theme of the fundamental nuances of movement – a theme he expounded in greater detail in the Drama Course, showing their relation to the gymnastics of Greece. 'The actor,' he said, 'should make the experiment of trying to behold himself, in daily life as well as while he is studying his part. In this way he becomes able to stand right within the role he is playing.'

Once, when present at a rehearsal, I shut my eyes in order to be able to concentrate better, and found that I could hear from the way in which the actors were speaking what movements they were making; I could hear, without seeing, when their muscles were taut and when relaxed. My own experience is that the more I resolve myself into the movements of my part, gliding into its very being and becoming identified with it, the nearer do I come to understanding what the art of mime really is. Observation of life is of incomparable value for the actor. Imitation of life in its external appearance leads to naturalism; imitation, on the other hand, of the form that is beheld in imagination leads to style.

I would like to give you here two examples of how a cry of horror or dismay, which as a rule is rendered naturalistically on the stage, is lifted by a poet to the level of style. He accomplishes this by using the material that is given him in speech: rhythm, choice of sounds, alliteration, assonance, repetition, enhancement and so on. The first example is from the chorus in Schiller's *Die Braut von Messina:*

> '*Wehe, wehe dem Mörder, wehe.*   'Woe, woe to the murder, woe.
> *Der sich gesät die tödlichen Saat!*'   Who sowed for himself the fatal seed!'
> (From Act III, scene 5)

Notice, among other things, how d (or t) occurs seven times in the verse.

The second is from Goethe's *Pandora.* Epimeleia takes refuge beneath her father's cloak from the axe of the jealous Phileros:

'*Ai! Ai! Weh! Weh mir! Weh! Weh! Weh! Ai! Ai mir! Weh!*'

Many actors are completely at a loss how to render such passages.

I once asked Rudolf Steiner how spiritual science could help one to understand better the art of acting. He did not reply at once, but a few days later said somewhat as follows: 'Try one evening to build up a clear picture of some monologue or short scene. See the picture there before you. You will need to hold it there for about five minutes, no more. Next morning try to see it all backwards, to see it as a continuous series of pictures in the reverse order. This is a very good exercise, for it will mean you are no longer bound to the thread of the thought.' We all know what a dream is like, how it speaks to us in pictures. By means of such an exercise some part that we have to play is similarly converted into pictures. Gradually you find yourself becoming completely at home in the part; you are caught up into the fantasy of it. Gesture and word come alive for you, a dynamic makes itself felt in their antitheses, and you grow conscious of enhancements and of varying tempos not noticed before. In short, you become able to do your acting out of the picture that you have there objectively before you. Liberated from yourself, you begin to have positive joy in playing your role. Practice in this exercise takes one right away from any expression of self in the acting, right away too from naturalism, and teaches one to present the part objectively. When formed on the stage in this objective manner, even a cruel scene will win applause from the audience for its art, whereas the very same scene performed naturalistically and subjectively will arouse only abhorrence and disgust.

On the subject of the quick response of movement to tone and tone to movement, which can lead us to appreciate the close interworking of gesture and word, Rudolf Steiner said: 'If you want to represent human life artistically, try gradually to begin to notice that when, for example, you have a sentence to say that has an emotional quality, or again one that tends in the direction of sadness or distress, or when perhaps you have to scold someone – then on each single occasion you can feel that an absolutely definite movement of the body, and also a definite kind of slowness or quickness of speaking, belong to that sentence.'

Let me quote a few examples, although when they are written down, instead of being livingly demonstrated, they can give but a poor idea of the matter. Suppose we have the words: 'I've a perfect passion for skittles!' Let us imagine the situation. We are in a skittle-alley. A skittles devotee is standing there with the bowl in his hand, and behind him are his comrades in the game. He takes careful aim at the skittles at the other end of the alley and finally sets the bowl running. 'All nine!' shouts the boy in charge of the skittles. The man is delighted and calls 'I've a perfect passion for skittles!' – and goes off into a whole series of movements. The thing is done! From the sentence we have discovered the movements that belong to it.

Take another sentence: 'I am very sad!' I drop on to a chair and let my arms and legs droop. In this position, arms and legs hanging loose, I say the words: 'I am very sad!' The situation in which I find myself has to reveal to me the movement that fits the words; and then in the posture into which the movement brings me I find the right dynamic for the speaking of the words.

One more example. A peasant woman, so runs the text, has to say to her naughty little girl: 'You dirty little snuffler! You stupid, good-for-nothing child! Have you anything to say for yourself? I'll give it you!' It comes so natural to the mother, seeing before her this impudent little daughter of hers screaming and howling, to say: 'You dirty little snuffler!' and then to add in a hard, repellent tone: 'Stupid, good-for-nothing child!', and then with hands raised threateningly and in a voice trembling with annoyance to put the question to her: 'Have you anything to say for yourself?' Pause. The woman holds her clenched fists tight on to her sides and with the words 'I'll give it you!' treats her daughter to a smart box on the ears. There you have a succession of different movements, each in turn giving its particular nuance to the words.

And now we can go further and look at the relation between tone and movement from the opposite direction. Rudolf Steiner said: 'You should find a certain pleasure in moving your legs and arms, enjoying the movements simply as movements. Then, when you are studying, you should feel: The movement I am making at this moment calls for *this* tone of voice – another one for that other tone of voice.' Let us take an example. I am drumming on the table with my fingers, I am getting nervous. The sentence will form itself in a tone to correspond: 'He's not here *yet*!' With these words I am in the movement I am making with my hands. Or, I balance up and down on my toes, shrugging my shoulders. I shall then find myself saying with the corresponding modulation of voice: 'Well, well, after all, there's nothing to be done. He'll come all right. Let's wait a little longer.'

There are many other kinds of sentences one could take. But always the modulation and dynamic of the speaking will have to correspond with the movements. Two or more actors could make a game of it, one making the movement, and another having to find the right modulation of the voice. In this way one would arrive, without conscious design, at the recitation of a dramatic text by a separate reciter (the actor having then to find the corresponding movements) – a plan advocated by Rudolf Steiner again and again as an exercise of no little importance. In this way the actor becomes thoroughly at home in the whole play of movements, and learns also to find in the movements the right way to form his sentences.

Through the mouth of Hamlet, Shakespeare gives players instructions how to perform. It is interesting to compare these instructions with what Rudolf Steiner has given for the study of word and gesture. Hamlet says to the players: 'Suit the action to the word, the word to the action.' The first part of this advice is followed when the actor who is telling or describing elucidates and reinforces the word by his movements – as it were in picture; and the second when the dramatic action is the prominent factor. Take an example of this. You walk with quick resolute steps to an open door, shut it firmly and say in a threatening voice that goes well with your movements: '*There*! Now the door is shut and you can't get out!' Or, you take hold of the door handle gently, close the door with care, and your words have instead a reassuring ring: 'There now, the door is shut, and nothing can happen to you!'

Rudolf Steiner's indications on the subject of gesture and movement could well be followed up by experimenting, for example, with a well-known painting. Hold up before a circle of young players and students a picture, let us say *The Deluge* of Michelangelo, and cast the various parts. Each student will then proceed to make careful and exact inspection of the figure he is to present. After about five minutes the picture is taken away, so that the figures remain only in the memory. And now let the actors take up their positions in the group as they saw them in the picture. Then say to them: 'The flood is rising higher still, the danger is increasing, the little island on which you are taking refuge will soon be submerged!' At once all their gestures and mime are intensified. You then call on them to stay perfectly still, as they are. And now you have a picture absolutely in the style of Michelangelo, and so striking that it could well serve as a motif for a painter or sculptor. The actors feel this muscular tension by means of their 'movement' sense. (Rudolf Steiner describes man as having 12 senses. By means of this one he 'senses' his own movements.)

In a little while you indicate that the flood is subsiding. A feeling as of deliverance passes over the group In one and another, perhaps, it finds utterance in speech. Again you call a halt, and once more you have an impressive picture – altogether new and astonishingly lifelike. Experiments of this nature can be carried out with pictures by every variety of painter, and also with sculptures by Rodin, for instance, or Barlach. The actors learn what it means to live in imagined figures that they themselves have first to create out of the roles allotted to them – they learn to live in these figures and to take cognizance of themselves in all the different kinds of style that the pictures provide. Participation in such an exercise will also help to develop the faculty for *imitation of forms one has oneself created out of imagination*, in contradistinction to imitation of life in the world outside.

When asked what steps one should take in order to acquire a thorough grasp of a new role and make intimate contact with it, Rudolf Steiner made a special point of the interpretation of the drama as a whole through a preliminary reading rehearsal. This, he said, is a great help for the forming of the ensemble. The various characters will then become alive in all manner of ways for the imagination of the actors. He laid particular emphasis on the fact that if the actors have first found their way together into the piece as a whole, they will come more easily to an understanding of their individual parts than they do when each studies his own part alone for himself or when, as used really to happen in the days of 'written parts', the actor knows nothing of the play except his own part, bit by bit!

What should happen with all exercises – as experience will show – is that a new instinct should mature out of them. They must become second nature in the student – a complete matter of habit. They must never remain at the stage of being regarded as a lesson, or as a rule to be followed.

In a lecture given in 1909 on 'The Nature and Origin of the Arts', Rudolf Steiner spoke of how the art of mime proceeds from man's 'movement' sense, which he described as the sensation we experience when we move the limbs or members of our own organism. In the year 1921 I asked for exercises that would develop this sense. The reply was: 'Yes, they can't be given all at once, but I will look into the matter. Things of this kind, if they are to be of use, have to be worked out slowly and objectively, and no less so because they have their foundation in spiritual knowledge. I will make a note of the question and give an answer later on.' The answer came three years afterwards in the Drama Course. Rudolf Steiner pointed there to the gymnastics of the Greeks as a first foundation for the actor. Since the experiences these gymnastics afford, both external and inward, are fundamental, we will now proceed to consider them in some detail.

'In running, leaping, wrestling, throwing the discus, throwing the spear, the will that resides in the limbs expresses itself in its total relationship with the surrounding world and thereby brings to expression also the fundamental properties of stage speaking.' The essential mime movements or gestures that belong to the stage were designated by Rudolf Steiner as 'shadow-sketches' of the five gymnastic activities of the Greeks. Taking our start from stage speaking, we find, he said, that stage speaking should have the following properties: 'It should be able to be effective, and also thoughtful; it should be able to feel its way forward in face of hindrances, to show an antipathy that repudiates, to show a sympathy that gives reassurance; and finally it should be able to express a withdrawal into oneself or on to one's own ground. These properties of speech readily lend themselves to association with certain gestures, and the gestures again give rise to corresponding nuances in the speaking.' Thus in these six fundamental shades of expression in speech the actor has starting points for his artistic performance, much as the painter has in the fundamental colours, or the musician in the scales.

The 'movement' sense – the sense, that is, of one's own movement – is too little developed in man today. If it were in active use, how many and manifold discoveries it would lead to in life! In order to throw fresh light on these vitally important exercises, I would like now to give you some examples, taken from classical authors as well as from daily life.

1. 'The *effectiveness* of speech can be studied in connection with the "pointing" gesture and renders the word incisive.' The well-known words from *Julius Caesar* afford a good example:

'Friends, Romans, countrymen, lend me your ears!'

When the pointing gesture is made that corresponds to the sentence, then the gesture itself produces the incisively spoken word.

2. 'In *thoughtful* speech the inner processes of the soul are seeking revelation. The gesture will be a holding on to oneself, and the word will be fully formed.' Take the sentence in Schiller's Wallenstein:

> '*Solch ein Moment wars, als ich in der Nacht*
> *Gedankenvoll an einem Baum gelehnt,*
> *Hinaus sah in die Ebene.*'

(*Wallensteins Tod* Act 2, Scene 3. The whole passage in S T Coleridge's translation reads:

> 'There exist moments in the life of man,
> When he is nearer the great Soul of the world
> Than is man's custom, and possesses freely
> The power of questioning his destiny.
> And such a moment 'twas when in the night
> Before the action in the plains of Lützen
> Leaning against a tree, thoughts crowding thoughts,
> I look'd out far upon the ominous plain.')

You will see how in the sentence itself the gesture is already indicated: 'leaning against a tree'. It is a sentence that is called up out of *memory* and requires to be fully intoned, every consonant distinctly uttered and making its contribution to the picture. Or we could take something that happens in the soul, in the realm of feeling. 'Terrible!' Even as I say the word, I shut my eyes tight. And once more, this close holding on to oneself leads to a full intonation of the word. Or suppose you are chafing inside with pent-up anger. You will perhaps clench your fists and plant them firmly on your hips, and for action administer a box on the ears which you will thoroughly enjoy, pouring the enjoyment into the words: 'There now! I've paid him back!' A further nuance of this property of speech manifests in an inability to come to a decision: 'This expresses itself in the limbs being held still, and in a long-drawn-out manner of speaking.' Repeated questions directed to someone who is disconcerted or upset will perhaps evoke for answer nothing but a continual drawling murmur. This last is a nuance that was not so much in evidence 30 years ago as it is today.

3. 'The *feeling forward in face of hindrances*. This property of speech is to be studied in the forward-rolling movement one makes with arms and hands, producing a trembling or vibrating in the word.' Such a manner of speaking may occur in a question, or in an expression of doubt, or again in a wish. Romeo is standing beneath Juliet's balcony, where she is seen leaning her cheek on her hand.

> *Romeo*: O, that I were a glove upon that hand
> That I might touch that cheek!

4. 'The rejecting in a mood of *antipathy* is to be studied in the flinging forth of the limbs; it gives a hard tone to the voice.' Take the opening words of Faust:

'*Habe nun, ach! Philosophie*	I have studied, alas! Philosophy,
Jur sterei und Medecin,	And Jurisprudence, and Medicine, too,
Und leider auch Theologie!	And saddest of all, Theology,
Durchaus studiert...'	With ardent labour, through and through!

5. 'The expression of trust and confidence in a mood of sympathy manifests in a reaching out to touch the object, and the speaking becomes thereby gentle.'

> *Faust*: '*O sähst du, voller Mondenschein,*
> *Zum letzten Mal auf meine Pein!*'
>
> (Full orbéd Moon, would thou didst Shine
> Thy last upon this pain of mine!)

Note with what artistic feeling Goethe lets the sound O – so characteristic of sympathy – come three times in the verse.

6. 'The *withdrawal of man into himself* comes to expression in the thrusting forth of a limb that has first been held closely to the body. And this results in a short, abrupt manner of speech.' Take the last words of a dialogue in the poem of CF Meyer entitled *Die Fusse am Feuer*:

> '*Mein – ist die Rache – redet Gott.*'
>
> (Vengeance is mine – saith God.

Driven by a thunderstorm, a servant of the King begs a night's shelter in a castle. To his horror he finds in his host the Huguenot nobleman whose lady, three years before, he had foully murdered, because she would not betray her husband. Next morning the nobleman, after an agonising inner struggle, exchanges a few burning words with his enemy, and with this last solemn pronouncement sends him on his way.)

Everything that is brought to revelation in speech is comprised, said Rudolf Steiner, within these nuances: and one should make a thorough study of one's sentences in the typical gestures, in order to come at last to a natural and easy forming of gesture – for word, for sentence, and even for the whole character that one is playing.

Rudolf Steiner pointed also to further – and quite astonishing – results that can follow from the practice of the gymnastic exercises. 'In *running*,' he said, 'one practises stage walking.' We shall readily recognise that walking on the stage is not a thing we can do as a matter of course. In running, the foot is called into action just where it is most mobile – that is, in the front. The whole foot is more easily guided from there, the step is best begun and finished from the fore-part of the foot. Moreover, from running one learns to walk so that the walking articulates the word. For example, from Goethe's *Achilleis*:

Hoch zu Flammen entbrannte die mächtige Lohe noch einmal.

(High into flame burst forth once more the great conflagration.)

Down to one's very toes, one goes right into speaking, into the sounds, and learns how to work at them so as to develop them in full clarity. In ordinary life many people will set their feet moving when they want to bring their thoughts or their speech into flow. Any walking or running, but especially rhythmical running, will make itself felt in the 'feet' of the verse, in the run and flow of the language.

Another exercise that belongs here is writing with the feet. It is indeed true of this exercise, as Rudolf Steiner said: 'Man begins then to feel his own organism, and that is an incalculable gain for the soul.'

'Through the practice of *leaping*, one learns instinctively to modify one's walking – making it now slower, now quicker, to suit the character of the word.' Leaping also helps one to acquire readiness and vivacity in expressing one's thought, and a quick versatility in dialogue, both as speaker and as listener; and moreover the faculty of being able to change rapidly from one kind of speaking to another – for example, from thoughtfulness in speech to antipathy, to brusqueness, and so on. One becomes much more sensitive to the manifold nuances in speech and simply unable to tolerate a uniform, colourless dialogue that has no life in it.

'In *wrestling*, we learn instinctively what hand and arm movements to make while speaking.' The will goes here into the movements of the arms, goes into the hands, into the fingertips. We sense what our opponent is intending to do, and in our dealings with him, in our careful 'feeling' and 'touching' of him, in the play of forces between ourselves and him, we learn to feel ourselves – down to the feet in one direction and up to the head and the senses in the other. Alternate tension and relaxation; the mood that is all alert for action; pregnant pauses; echoes that linger on afterwards – all these we experience in wrestling; in short, we learn how to speak dialogue!

'In *discus-throwing*, the eye learns to fix its gaze exactly in the direction of the throw and then to follow steadily the path of the thrown object (a ball of some kind, or a little stone), to watch carefully also the movement of the hand – and from all this we learn the play of mime, the control of the muscles in mime, and moreover the 'look' in the eye. 'We are laid hold of by the object,' says Graf Fritz von Bothmer (who was chosen by Rudolf Steiner to be the first teacher of gymnastics in the original Waldorf School). Beginning from the eye, from the gaze in the eye, our whole organism feels itself caught up by the object. We can well understand that by means of such an exercise a thorough inner training of soul and body can be achieved. And it is also interesting to experience how by means of discus-throwing, speech is loosened, and the speaker is then taken hold of by the dynamic of the immediate sentence, so that each sentence – and this applies especially to dialogue – receives its own particular movement. Take, for example, the sentence: 'Look! There's a bird flying over the field!' The one who calls out these words is caught up by the movement of the flying bird; he has escaped from the prison of his subjective self. His speaking is right outside him; it is out there in the realm of the air.

'In *spear-throwing*, we learn the very foundation of all speech – namely, that it shall not come about as an expression of thought, but purely as speech. For speech is by this exercise drawn away from the intellect and enters into the speech organs and into the forming of them.' Fritz von Bothmer sums it up in the words: 'In the throwing of the spear, man masters the object.' The lifting of the spear for the throw will have its effect upon the inbreathing; the aiming of the spear will have its effect upon the holding of the breath; and then this right holding and measuring of the breath will have its effect upon the sentences, upon many sentences, upon a whole play. The actual throw goes together with a full out-breathing. Through this exercise one gains mastery of the breathing process and of its use in speaking, and also of the mutual relation of the sentences, one with another. Many experiences afforded by archery as practised in the Eastern Zen art are here confirmed, although there the approach is from an entirely different standpoint.

The professional actor can only be amazed – and filled at the same time with deepest gratitude – when he experiences again and again what love and what intensity of insight Rudolf Steiner brought to the whole domain of dramatic art.

If the art of acting is studied and practised and developed further in his spirit, then it will be possible for the ideal set up by Rudolf Steiner to find fulfilment. Dramatic art, he said, should be 'a necessary addition to every human existence worthy of the name'.

How Rudolf Steiner Taught Us to Paint

Louise van Blommestein

IN OUR CONTINUATION SCHOOL at the Goetheanum we have several pictures which Rudolf Steiner painted in our presence. Every one of them is dear to us, but there is one which is dearest of all. We always refer to it as 'Our Madonna', though Dr Steiner called it simply 'Mother and Child'. It breathes such tenderness and sanctity that we feel something very holy in it, and we think it well worthy of the Divine Mother and her Child. Again and again it fills our souls with its magic presence. I will briefly relate how the picture came into being.

Rudolf Steiner often visited us in our wooden shanty next to his studio. We knew him to be especially fond of our little school. How often he came and sat still in the class while the lessons continued. Often he devoted one or two mornings to us in succession. He would help and encourage us with his overflowing love, giving us new guiding lines again and again to awaken our self-confidence. Those were true festive days for us, when he arrived.

In our school especially, he laid stress on the cultivation of artistic subjects, and in the painting lesson, with which the curriculum concluded every day, he often painted for us. So it was again on the 28th February, 1924. A happy excitement and expectation prevailed among the pupils. The hands of the boy who had to pin the paper to the board were shaking, so that he constantly dropped the drawing pins and was laughed at by his fellows. Rudolf Steiner turned round very quietly and said with astonishment: 'Why are you laughing? What is there to laugh at?' Then he picked up the chalk and said: 'Now I will paint something for you, right out of the colour. Thereupon he set to work and placed two patches of colour side by side – a tender blue, drawn upward and slightly bending over, and side by side with it a patch of yellow. 'Look,' he said, 'here are two different colours – blue and yellow. See how beautifully they go together. They are pleasant to see. What would go well beside them now?' Among the coloured chalks, (for the picture is done in chalk) he then looked for a colour which he could not find. Thereupon he mixed it for himself, laying on a very tender rose-colour mingled with white, a gentle violet and a little yellow, one over the other and rubbing them together with his finger. 'I was looking for a gentle lilac colour,' he said as he did so. So there arose another little patch beside the yellow.

'There now,' he said, 'You see it goes very well together. These three colours together form a triad, just as in music – it is a real chord. It is united, it is one, harmonious whole, and you need add nothing to it. It is complete in itself. But now we will paint on. We must select a colour which does not belong to this triad at all.'

He picked out a very fresh and tender green which he laid right around the other colours, almost entirely filling the sheets of paper. Only on the left-hand side, towards the blue and flowing on beneath it from left to right, he added a rich violet colour. Then he said to us: 'And now you see down here' (below, on the right-hand side) 'a little patch has remained white. This we must fill in with one of the colours of the triad so as to hold it all together. You can feel how necessary it is for the composition.' So then he filled in the remaining patch with blue. 'Now,' he said, 'Now it is finished. The whole sheet is beautifully filled, it is a symphony of colours, beautiful in itself. But now let us try and see what we can make of it. Let us paint something into the yellow. Yellow in yellow would be invisible, so we must take a rather reddish shade.' And he began to draw something in with orange-red. He did so with a great deal of love and care, bringing out the highlights, rubbing away with his fingers, re-shaping it again, suggesting the form with great delicacy until at last a face arose. While doing the eyes he said: 'The eyes, these you can draw, quite properly,' and he did so as we watched him. Then in the lilac colour he painted a smaller head, the head of a child, indicating it with the same red, and working on it for a long time. The highlights were attained by rubbing-out, or covering with white and then rubbing again. The shadows were gently suggested, the whole was treated like a breath of air. 'So now,' he said, 'What can we make of it now? Let us say "Mother and Child." But we still need a connection between the Mother and the Child.' And he set to work and painted an arm and a hand in golden orange, and suggested the little arm and hand of the child in red. The arms and hands, in meeting, united the two figures. Now he began to bring out the blue dress, and on the other side of the face, the forms of a dress in yellow. The folds were painted in a darker blue; the whole was worked through and brought into connection. Finally, taking a broad piece of yellow chalk, in bold, broad strokes he overlaid the green of the background with yellow raying down from above – far over the blue of the veil about the head – saying again and again as he did so: 'This is the Light that comes from above. It must be made to *ray*, it is the light that comes from above.' Thereby the whole was lifted from the green to the golden yellow, from the earthly into the heavenly sphere.

Thus we were allowed to witness how the picture came into being. Glad, excitement, breathless attention, wonder and silent reverence were the changing moods with which we followed the process, stage by stage. The finished picture speaks to the onlooker like a delicate and holy poem. Untold love and inwardness ray out from it. The touching earnestness of the child is like a resigned acceptance of its fate. So we could witness how Rudolf Steiner listened to hear the language of the colours, leading to a motif which grew to form under his hand.

When it was finished he said: 'If you will prepare me a paper and get the colour ready, tomorrow or one of these days I will come again and paint it in water-colours.'

Day after day we saw him pass, but we waited in vain. Yet he never forgot it. At a far later date, when he came for the last time to our end-of-term festival (it was the 18th July, 1924) he said of his own accord: 'Oh yes, the picture. I had wanted to paint it again in watercolours. Unfortunately I was unable to come, I had so many other things to do.' And he added: 'But I will still do it some time.'

Unhappily, this was no longer given, for Destiny willed otherwise.

(By kind permission from the *Goetheanum Weekly*, Vol. 6, No. 25).

The Angry Young Men

Alfred Heidenreich

IN OCTOBER, 1919, I returned from a British prison camp in France to an impoverished and dispirited Germany. I had two years of study, law and economics, to my credit – on paper. In reality I had never been inside a university. In November, 1919, I went to Munich. The student body was torn by political passions. The trial of the young Count Arco, who had murdered the Bavarian Premier Eisner, aroused wild emotions. Most of my friends of pre-war days had nationalist leanings. I felt myself humanly more at home among young Communists, whose brotherliness and internationalism attracted me: the shadow of Moscow was to me not yet clearly discernible.

Although officially a law student, I attended classes of many kinds, including philosophy and chemistry. It all seemed rather pointless. At the end of my first term I took my bicycle and my rucksack and cycled through the whole of Germany to the university town of Rostock on the Baltic (where, as I learned later, Rudolf Steiner had taken his doctorate) and continued there. It soon seemed equally pointless. I had no difficulty in following the prescribed course with a minimum of effort. But most of my time I tramped through the country in search of – what?

During the summer vacation I spent three months as a farm labourer on an estate near the Polish frontier and saw people and conditions I had never dreamt existed. After looking briefly into the universities of Berlin and Breslau, I returned to Munich and changed my subject. History and languages took the place of law and economics. I had good friends and a happy social life. But the university was as disappointing as ever. Was it all my fault? Was I the incurable 'odd man out'? Or was something wrong with the world? On one occasion I gave a talk on 'The Dignity of Man' (the first of the interminable series of talks and lectures which I was to give in years to come!). But my best friends shrugged their shoulders.

About this time I received an invitation to the first anthroposophical *Hochschulkurs* (course for students) which was to take place in Germany. I did not particularly like the enormous claims which the prospectus made. I can still see myself throwing it into the waste-paper basket with deliberation. It seemed to me a typical example of overstatement. Besides – Rudolf Steiner? I had some curious memories of his name from childhood. There was a cousin, much older than myself, who at the beginning of the century had studied architecture in Munich. He was brilliantly gifted in painting and music, but for me as a little boy he had the particular attraction of being able to whistle out of the corner of his mouth. He died young from consumption, but it was said in the family that he died 'from Theosophy'. For he was one of the first ardent followers of Rudolf Steiner among the young generation at that time. Later on I inherited his notebooks, in which he had taken down with great care many of the early talks given by Rudolf Steiner in Munich, beginning with 1903. (These irreplaceable notes were later destroyed in an air-raid before I had time to transcribe them.)

My cousin's sister, who was deeply devoted to her brother, followed him in his interests. In the summer of 1910 her disapproving family sent her on a holiday tour with my father and my sister and myself. On the second morning of our journey she did not appear at breakfast. During the night she had gone off to Munich to attend the first of Rudolf Steiner's Mystery Plays. From these few incidents it will be understood that 'der Steiner' was not an unknown name in our family. But I had personally never taken the slightest interest in what seemed a very odd body. And now came this invitation, sent from a friend whose judgement I had every reason to trust.

I made up my mind to take a sample. I went to an anthroposophical lecture in the very luxurious headquarters of the Anthroposophical Society in Munich. The name of the lecturer shall be passed over in silence. I had fortified myself by taking a few friends, and for part of the evening we couldn't help shaking with suppressed laughter. It was a hopeless affair. But I bought Rudolf Steiner's 'Three Lectures on Adult Education' which had just appeared, and read them right through during the following night. It was just as well, for the next morning the detailed syllabus of the *Hochschulkurs* arrived by post with my friend's marginal note: 'That you may know what you are missing!' I sent in my application to attend.

It was during the opening lecture of the main morning series on *Mathematik, wissenschaftliches Experiment, Beobachtung und Erkenntnisergebnis vom Gesichtpunkt der Anthroposophie* that I saw Rudolf Steiner for the first time. I sat in the front row of the balcony at the back of the hall opposite the platform. The place was filled to capacity; there must have been about 600 people, if my memory serves me correctly. Let me confess at once that I did not grasp a single sentence of what Rudolf Steiner said. But the human picture was fascinating.

There he stood, a rather elegant figure with fine features and jet-black hair, wearing a long black frockcoat which on him did not at all look old-fashioned or peculiar. He spoke in a measured flow of words which seemed to come from a centre different from those from which other people usually spoke. He made wide gestures with his arms, but they were not commanding or compelling; though sweeping, they were rather delicate, seeming to indicate the wide range of his argument. He closed his eyes most of the time. He did not speak at the people, but seemed to pronounce truth as such. I repeat, I did not grasp a single word of what he said, but by the end of the hour I had lost the last trace of the cynicism with which I had come.

I attended nearly every session of the course. Most of it was conducted in the form of a 'Seminar'. Apart from his principal lecture course, Rudolf Steiner attended these seminars in turn and took part in the discussion. I remember a characteristic incident. In a session of the philosophy group, a young university lecturer said that he had come to assume a stage of pre-logical consciousness in the history of humanity. Rudolf Steiner stopped the discussion, walked straight to the back of the meeting room and shook hands with the speaker who happened to sit next to me. This was my first 'close-up' of Rudolf Steiner.

One day, halfway through the course, while we were walking down the innumerable steps from the Waldorf School to the centre of the city, I said to my friend, 'If I stay to the end, I shall be converted'. It was not all plain sailing, though, particularly in my own subject where I fancied that I knew something. I remember tossing about at night in our very primitive quarters, where we slept on two-tier structures, consisting of metal frames with a groundsheet suspended on them, hammock-fashion.

There came a next step. Among the young people present were some who, like myself, had been members of the *Wandervogel*, the original pre-1914 German Youth Movement. It is very difficult to convey an adequate picture of that Movement, as it was in its spontaneous origin at the beginning of the century, before its forms were taken over after the First World war by the political parties, the churches, and nearly every conceivable organisation; and only very one-sided histories have been written of it.

Perhaps its most curious feature was that it was a revolution of high school boys and girls which flared up as if by magic all over Germany. They simply had to find a different way of life from that of their elders who worshipped Caesar and Mammon. It was a jolly fight for going to school hatless, with open-neck shirt and shorts. It was a spontaneous urge to dig up the priceless treasure of medieval German folk songs. And above all the Movement found its characteristic expression in the practice of turning to the open country, of walking the countryside at weekends as well as during long holiday weeks, camping, sleeping and living with the peasants, helping with the harvest, reading and studying the living history in church, castle and village.

No adult leaders were tolerated. These groups developed their own code of ethics – teetotalism was taken for granted – and they gradually organised themselves into a kind of federated new society. No holder of the VC can ever have worn his decoration more proudly than the members of the *Wandervogel* in these early years wore their badges in their buttonholes, in spite of school regulations forbidding them.

Now, as I have said above, there were present at the *Hochschulkurs* some 'Old Wandervogel Scholars', as one might have called them. We thought we had rather special questions to ask – we had in fact an inkling that there might be a curious link between what the *Wandervogel* had tried to do instinctively and what anthroposophy was trying to do consciously, and on behalf of our group I asked Rudolf Steiner for a special interview. He showed neither surprise nor annoyance, but took out his notebook and pencil – a gesture of assent I was to witness very often later – and offered a meeting on the following Sunday afternoon, which happened to be Palm Sunday.

On that day, March 20, 1921, for the first time a group of some twenty young people sat with Rudolf Steiner round a table and had him to themselves. He received us in one of the committee rooms of the Anthroposophical Headquarters (in the Landhausstrasse) in Stuttgart; he sat at the head of the table, the rest of us all round the sides. I sat next to him (still with open neck, shorts, bare knees and all), and after having welcomed and thanked him, I took down what he said. These notes were published in the collection *Die Erkenntnis-Aufgabe der Jugend*.

Rudolf Steiner knew how to place our movement into the world-wide historic context of the time. 'If one approaches the Youth Movement with spiritual-scientific historic knowledge, it becomes clear that it has its roots in the historic turning-point which strongly impresses itself upon the Initiate as having occurred at the end of the 19th century, and which is an inward turning-point affecting all humanity.... There is nothing against the Youth Movement finding its way into Spiritual Science. One can even speak of a certain predestination of the Youth Movement for Spiritual Science...' Such were some of the highlights of the talk.

At the time it was not so much what Rudolf Steiner said, but the impression of his personality, which gave us the sense of an historic occasion. The difference between the altitude on which his mind and our minds moved made an immediate contact of minds almost impossible. But there was no difficulty in the contact of hearts. One could not say that there was any 'personal magnetism' in Rudolf Steiner on such occasions. He was, in a sense, cool and detached. And yet to have met him for the first time as a human being, to have sat at a table with him for an hour or so, was an experience which had a curious effect. We were so stirred that after the meeting we began to dance in the street in front of the house, to the astonishment of sedate Stuttgarters (Palm Sunday afternoon!), and to the annoyance of eager motorists.

During this time at the end of the *Hochschulkurs*, Rudolf Steiner gave a deeply moving lecture on the cause of the war and on the question of 'war-guilt'. How far he was out of range of the ordinary academic historians! How topical he could be, and at the same time with what perspective he was able to look at contemporary events. Some of his views on these matters afterwards became public, as will be remembered, in an interview with Jules Sauerwein in *Le Matin*. Perhaps the most astonishing fact for us to realise was how close Rudolf Steiner himself had been at times to the actual centre of world events, and how full of first-hand information he was.

After the *Hochschulkurs*, an announcement was made that a four-week special course would begin after Easter to train leaders of anthroposophical student groups. Any volunteers? – I volunteered. Some 30 of us met with Rudolf Steiner on the last evening to discuss the forthcoming course. The discussion went on late into the night.

Dr Steiner suggested that during the Easter break we should study, as a preparation, the collection of his essays on the Threefold Commonwealth (*In Ausführung der Dreigliederung des Sozialen Organismus*), which had just appeared. Could we get hold of copies before we left Stuttgart? It was by then 2.30 a.m. Yes, go down to the 'Kommende Tag' (the then publishing company) and get some copies right now. So someone else and I went down, woke up Herr Fried Geuter, who

was then an employee of the Kommende Tag, extracted some 50 copies and returned
to the meeting. When the meeting finally broke up at dawn, I was in such high
spirits that I climbed the facade of a three-story building, jumped down onto the
balcony of my friend's room and woke him up to join me on the train home.

The *Presskurs* ('High Pressure Course', as the special training course came to be
known) was a great delight. We were at it for a full month, from 8 a.m. until late
at night. The rising young star lecturers of the Society – Dr Stein, Dr Kolisko,
Dr Hahn, Dr Schubert – were our teachers. Rudolf Steiner himself came only for
a short spell.

Very soon after this, in July, 1921, I was to hear and meet Rudolf Steiner again.
Among the students of the Technical Academy at Darmstadt a lively group of
young anthroposophists had succeeded in arranging a substantial conference. I was
by now so deeply in the stream that I could ask Rudolf Steiner's advice as to what
I should do about a job. He seemed pleased at the idea that I should join the
College of Teachers at the Waldorf School, but he advised me to finish my formal
doctor's degree. In the course of the conversation he suggested, as a subject for
my thesis, a comparison between the rhythmical principles of ancient Greek poetry
and those of ancient and medieval German poetry. I found later that this was a
problem in which Rudolf Steiner himself took great interest. But at the time I felt
too diffident about it. It would have meant further study, and I was desperately
keen to get the university behind me.

Meanwhile, our rounding-up all over Germany of 'angry young men and women'
– or, as I should rather say, of Old Wandervogel Scholars – for the newly-found
world view continued. Goethe's lines 'Why did I seek the way so full of longing,
If I am not to show it to my brothers?' were our motto. My own efforts led to
the publication of my first small book, *Jugendbewegung und Anthroposophie*, which
appeared in February, 1922, in the Kommende Tag. Its edition of 5000 was sold
out within less than a year. To this day I meet people, now in their fifties and
sixties, and some of them prominent leaders in the anthroposophical movement,
who tell me that this youthful effort of mine was their first contact with
anthroposophy. I had been too shy to show the manuscript to Rudolf Steiner and
to ask his advice. But afterwards he said I should have done so. He would always
be at the disposal of people who wrote in the service of anthroposophy.

Our endeavours to bring Youth Movement and anthroposophy together reached
a certain climax and first fulfilment during the Anthroposophical Congress which
was held in Stuttgart from August 28 to September 8, 1921. For the first time an
appreciable number of Old Wandervogel Scholars were assembled, perhaps 100–150,
and they held several special meetings in one of the assembly halls of the Waldorf
School. It was decided to form a special body within the anthroposophical
movement. A first committee of three members was elected and I became the first
chairman. It became my duty to announce these facts to a meeting of some 1200
members of the Society, which was held during the congress (on September 4) in
Dr Steiner's presence.

In bringing these brief reminiscences to a close with the story of this meeting, I cannot resist the temptation of describing how all this was brought vividly back to my memory not very long ago. During my visit to South America in the summer of 1956, the friend with whom I stayed in Rio de Janiero read in the local German paper an advertisement which said that a series of bound volumes of *Das Goetheanum* were for sale in the course of winding-up an estate. When my friend returned from calling at the address given, he brought not only the bound volumes but stacks of other papers. As we sat on the floor to sort them out, I fingered through a very faded and crumpled brochure, and to my amazement read my name. 'Herr Heydenreich,' it was spelt. And there was recorded in the published proceedings of that special meeting (*Mitteilungen des Zentralvorstandes der Anthroposophischen Gesellschaft*) my first speech and announcement, as leader of the angry young men and women within the Anthroposophical Society.

I remembered then the curious circumstances. I still wore open shirt, shorts, bare knees, and so on, and when I sent my name in to the chairman, I noticed that the solemn gentlemen at the executive table viewed me with grave suspicion. Dr Friedrich Husemann, the leading psychiatrist among the anthroposophical doctors, was sent down to test my intentions. Apparently he was satisfied, for I was allowed to speak.

It was wonderful how Rudolf Steiner reacted. In his concluding address he said: 'A representative of the Youth Movement has spoken here. A whole number of representatives of student bodies are sitting here. My dear friends, the fact that members of such movements, members of such bodies, have come to our Anthroposophical Society, is something we must consider as epoch-making in the history of our Anthroposophical Movement. We must find ways and means to do everything which from those parts can rightly be expected from the Anthroposophical Society.'

At the end of the congress, Dr Steiner agreed once more to a special meeting with the ex-Wandervogel. A record of this meeting, on the basis of my verbatim shorthand notes, is included in Rudolf Steiner's *Die Erkenntnisaufgabe der Jugend*, but I refrained then, unfortunately, from taking down some delightful asides. Dr Steiner amused us greatly by telling us how at one time in Berlin he was a member of a kind of dining club called *Der Verbrechertisch* (the 'Criminals' Table') and that he took a great delight at the time *die Philister zu argern* (in annoying the Philistines). And at one moment, of which I cannot recall the exact circumstances, I had the temerity to ask him why there were so many elderly ladies in the Anthroposophical Society, a fact which we young people found difficult. 'They were the first people who were willing to listen to me and to make financial sacrifices for the Anthroposophical Movement,' was Rudolf Steiner's perfectly quiet and simple reply.

With the developments set in motion by these meeting and discussions, a process was well started which in the following years broadened out and culminated after the Christmas Foundation Meeting in the establishment of a special Section at the

Goetheanum, *für das Geistesstreben der Jugend* (Youth Section). In the course of this process, the stature of Rudolf Steiner began to appear more and more clearly before the younger generation. At first it was the exciting human being, the man who had the answers, who attracted us. Gradually the teacher of inner development, of spiritual discipline, became discernible, the great Teacher of the esoteric path for the West, who helped the 'angry young men and women' to become workers for the future.

How the Waldorf School Arose from the Threefold Social Movement

Herbert Hahn

THE FREE WALDORF SCHOOL was founded in Stuttgart in the year 1919, hence at a time of abysmal darkness in Middle European history; and it yielded the first gleam of light for a completely new path.

Some words in Goethe's *Fairy Tale* hold good for this time of the birth of a new art of education: 'One alone can do but little, but he can avail who in the right hour unites his strength with many others.' But in saying that these words hold good, I must make one reservation. It was indeed the right hour, and many united their efforts. But the essential help came from one individual – Rudolf Steiner. When, on the foundation of the energy and initiative of another of whom we shall be speaking, he called the Waldorf School into being, a cycle embracing some 150 years was brought to completion in the cultural history of Germany. For Rudolf Steiner gave the guiding principles of this new art of education in the midst of the storms and crises of a vigorous current in social life which called itself the 'Movement for the Threefold Social Organism'. The importance of this movement can be truly assessed only by recalling ideas and impulses that were astir at the end of the 18th century, but were destined to be covered with a layer of wintry snow.

Here we must think, first and foremost, of the young Schiller, whose medical studies at the Karlsschule in Stuttgart culminated in the writing of two treatises. One – it has survived as no more than a fragment – was called *Philosophy of Physiology*; the other, *On the Connection between the Animal and the Spiritual Nature in Man*.

Both treatises represent a new and significant germinating impulse in Schiller's life, a beginning that was not to find fulfilment until much later. For within a pronounced dualistic tendency, prone to antitheses in thinking and in style, they represent an urge, sometimes more tentative, sometimes more violent, towards a third, as yet unknown, principle. In the first of the two writings, Schiller is seeking, more from physiological aspects, for an intermediary force. In the second treatise the essential quality of precisely what is to constitute the link between the animal and spiritual nature in man remains undefined; it is summoned forth with a certain inner audacity. This seeking and probing, this challenging summons, are not only a significant prelude to the whole of Schiller's life-story; they are of interest also for the history of cultural development.

An essential part of the development of Western culture, from before the beginning of the second Christian millennium and even earlier, is dualistic through and through. In his whole existence, his whole path of destiny, and in his struggle between necessity and freedom, man is involved in opposing principles. Torn hither and thither between body and soul, he stands perpetually before the abyss yawning between the world and God, between this side and the 'Beyond'. True, the light of modern Western consciousness is kindled by these opposing principles, but the soul is impoverished in respect of its deeper, creative talents, and, with the gradually increasing dominance of a material culture, is drawn into slavery. The soul becomes a prisoner of the body.

It was therefore a moment of evident importance when in his mature years Schiller turned again to the theme he had set himself in his youth merely as a prelude, and brought it into definite shape. This was when he wrote his *Letters on the Aesthetic Education of Man*. Through a remarkable chain of circumstances, the basic thoughts in these *Letters* were conceived in Stuttgart.

In this work, where Schiller's thought reaches a peak, a threefold membering of man's inner life is shown to arise out of two contrasting functions, which partly merge into a third and partly press on to new creative activity. Schiller speaks, to begin with, of two urges: the urge of reason through which a place is assigned to man among the form-giving forces of the world of spirit; and the urge of matter, through which nature, in the abundance of her prodigious but at the same time unseeing life, breaks in upon him. If a man follows one of these two urges only, he cannot be truly free. Indeed, saturation in the one will usually throw him, enfeebled and devoid of will-power, into the clutches of the other. This holds good both for the span of an individual human life and for the successive stages of humanity. With regard to what man can achieve in the way of self-development and the education of others, Schiller strives, therefore, to find a third state. He calls this the 'aesthetic' state. Here he perceives the sway of a third urge, an artistic urge which he calls the 'play impulse' (*Spieltrieb*). As this play-impulse unfolds and takes effect, the warm surge of life continues to flow in from the side of nature, but it is divested of its blind, importunate violence; the form-giving impulse coming down from the side of the spirit spreads abroad its beneficent clarity but loses all inflexibility, every element of compulsion. And so, in thus making himself free, man becomes for the first time Man in the fullest sense of the word.

In the child at play, in the artist at his creative work, in the man absorbed in contemplating a real work of art, Schiller recognised the signs of this true manhood. And he is led to affirm: 'For to say it once and for all, man plays only when in the full sense of the word he is a man, and he is wholly Man only when he is playing.' And in another passage: 'It would be expedient to remove the former (the natural character) still farther from matter and to bring the latter (the moral character) somewhat nearer to it – so as to create a third character which, related to these other two – the physical and the moral – might pave the way for a transition from the sway of mere force to the rules of law, and, without impeding the development of the moral character, might serve rather as a sensible pledge of a divine morality as yet unseen.'

What Schiller established through his clear mental grasp of this third sphere in man cannot be valued too highly. He sets free the primal forces of the life of soul by not allowing the soul to be thrown hither and thither between Nature and Spirit, and by placing it, instead, in a condition of fruitful tension where it moves forward, conscious of itself. He was at the threshold of an age which, under the pall of an increasingly superficial civilisation was bound to bring in its train an enfeeblement of the life of soul, his aim was to rouse the soul to stronger and purer activity.

Did Schiller also divine in advance many things that the coming phase of evolution would inevitably bring? Again and again one conjectures this in following the trains of thought in these noble *Letters* – now entombed, alas, merely as literary tradition. These thoughts seem often to have been uttered far more for the 20th century than for the early 19th.

In speaking at some length about Schiller, I have not deviated from the basic theme of this essay. I hope it will become evident that in fact I have been leading up to it, and that the gateway through which the art of education revealed by Rudolf Steiner found entry into our age will be all the more clearly disclosed. At the very outset an essential question must be asked: How came it that all these significant thoughts of Schiller had so little effect, broadly speaking, upon the character of the following century? In other words, how came it that they could be entombed as mere literary tradition?

The age before whose portal Schiller had voiced his memorable thoughts, turned – as if in obedience to an irresistible, inner command – more and more resolutely and one-sidedly to the given phenomena of nature. The accepted rule was that each particular phenomenon was to be grasped through its sense-perceptible aspect alone. Applied to the human being, this meant the triumph of tangible substance over the imponderable soul. It was more interesting to get at the detailed physiological facts than to be guided by an idealistically orientated psychology. This was the fate of the basic thoughts voiced by Schiller in the *Letters*. True, in these thoughts he had paved the way for the threefold perception, but this was purely in the psychological domain. If the thoughts expressed in his *Philosophy of Physiology*, in the form of mere fragments, had been enriched by his new psychological insights and voiced in terms of a more comprehensive physiology, the material basis would have been provided for the threefold principle actually expounded in the *Letters*.

Because Schiller, dying all too early, was unable to carry his work through to that stage, his most important spiritual impulses remained without the bodily vehicle demanded by the age. And so, tragically swept aside by the dominating tendencies of the new century, they sank into an enchanted sleep.   They became active again when the young Rudolf Steiner brought them to life during his student years in Vienna and endowed them with a quite new freshness and energy. Later on he spoke of the delight which the dynamic conception of the life of soul presented in Schiller's *Letters* had given him. But even then he regretted that Schiller's treatment of them soared too far into abstraction. On the other hand, he was charmed with the artistic portrayal of the same realities in Goethe's *Fairy Tale*. Whatever metamorphoses these germinating thoughts might undergo, the basic motif of threefold man was there and could not be submerged.

This motif recurs again and again in the fundamental writings of Rudolf Steiner. But it appeared in a particularly conclusive and revealing form when in 1917 – during the First World War – his book, *Riddles of the Soul* was published. The essential principles of the threefold nature of man, in the physiological as well as in the psychological and spiritual domains, are outlined in the fourth chapter under the heading: 'Brief Supplementary Remarks on the Theme of the Present Volume.' In deliberate contrast to the philosopher Franz Brentano, Rudolf Steiner starts by distinguishing the three interrelated functions of thinking, feeling and willing. The physiological correlates of these psychical processes are presented with precision and exactitude. He then endorses the views current in the first third of the 20th century by seeing the 'bodily counterparts' of the psychical activity of ideation (thinking) in 'the processes of the nerve-system with their outflow into the sense-organs on the one side and into the bodily inner organisation on the other'. In the passage following, which deals with the bodily counterparts of feeling and willing, a completely revolutionary step is taken. The primary importance hitherto attached to thinking, in consequence of which feeling and willing are regarded as secondary functions subordinate to thinking, or as merely accompanying it in a particular way, is set aside. And there, too, the notion that the basis for investigating the physiological substrata of psychical processes is provided entirely by observation of nerve-processes. In the exposition given by Rudolf Steiner in 1917, feeling and will are, it is true, presented as organically linked with thinking, but as self-centred, autonomous functions. The physiological correlate of feeling is said to be the 'life-rhythm' centred in, and connected with, the breathing process. And now Rudolf Steiner shows that the rhythm of the breath must be followed 'to the outermost peripheral parts of the organism'. In a similar way he shows that willing is based upon processes of metabolism, the ramifications of which are to be observed over the whole organism.

Through these new conceptions – which are indicated here in a very elementary way and on the subject of which a great deal of literature has meanwhile been produced – the nerves-and-senses system, with its centres situated mainly in the human head, ceases to be the most important instrument for the life of soul. The whole body becomes the instrument of the soul-and-spirit. And this comes about, not through a static departmentalisation of particular functions, but through a dynamic process which plays into the whole organism from each of the three autonomous spheres, and which in its wonderful interplay of functions, mutually attuned to one another, first makes possible the phenomenon of human life.

Rudolf Steiner was fully alive to the fact that before complete confirmation of his views could be reached, physiological data would have to be followed up in a direction that is still an unfamiliar one today. This realisation, however, did not detract from the inner certainty and exactitude of his spiritual-scientific concepts.

A further aspect of the threefold nature of man presented by Rudolf Steiner in the same chapter of *Riddles of the Soul* is of far-reaching significance. He points to the different levels at which thinking, feeling and willing lie in the field of human consciousness. Man is fully awake only in his life of thinking; in feeling he reaches merely the intensity of dream; while even during the waking life of day, willing takes its course in that deeply obscured state of consciousness into which our whole being passes during sleep. We shall see later how these seemingly simple principles became fruitful to an undreamed of extent.

On the physiological side, however, to which the young Schiller had been able to point only tentatively, the clear light of consciousness now illumined the presentation of threefold man. By integration into the bodily, organic functions, by emancipation from the purely psychical – by this means the spiritual was for the first time given full scope for activity. It was *this* conception of threefold man that alone had every prospect of becoming fruitful in the 20th century, notably for education.

However, this particular fruit had to wait for two more years. The impulse of the threefold perception was first to take effect in a quite different direction. It led Rudolf Steiner to a diagnosis, as profound as it was all-embracing, of the present state of the social organism. Here again there is a remarkable parallelism with the life and work of Schiller. For Schiller, too, the recognition of the threefold principle, even though rudimentary, had become an instrument for diagnosing the great social problems of the time. It enabled him to make predictions, astoundingly definite and all too soon to be confirmed, of the denouement of the French Revolution.

Rudolf Steiner's diagnosis was of a quite different order: it pointed simultaneously to the great remedy for which the age was seeking. Amid the forebodings of a catastrophic outcome of the First World War that were already stirring in the heart of Europe, he appeared – first in small circles and then before the public – as the bringer of new, far-reaching knowledge. The essence of this was that just as the threefold nature was laid into the human being by Divine Powers, and is a reality, it behoves men today to carry into effect a threefold principle that is at present only latent in the social organism. He saw the devastating catastrophe of the times approaching from the side of the single, separate states that had crystallised out of the commonwealth of peoples as a whole. The vista before Dr Steiner was that of the unitary states, incited by their traditional but narrow interests, clashing with one another in defence of egoistic economic interests of every kind, and of forms of culture in reality fossilised and outworn. Through its inventions and discoveries the age has created a new picture of the earth; in the forming of this picture – and its detailed elaboration – man has acquired a new consciousness. Just as he himself, if he rightly understands his own being, is torn out of the old, static conditions into new, dynamic ones, so, through the worldwide expansion of trade, modern society has grown out of patriarchal forms of economy towards the problems of a global economy. This global economy tends everywhere towards emancipation from the tutelage of the State. In order to have a true economic character, it strives for autonomous forms which will develop on associative lines.

One of the three principles of the modern social organism is delineated here. Another will consist in a spiritual life deriving substance, impetus and configuration out of its own sources – which can only be sources of freedom. The creative impulses which, even in administrative matters, must be given freedom, will impart forms to the spiritual life which are in keeping with the status of man who has now become a self-conscious and independent being. Schools and institutions for higher education, the religious life, art and science – these can thrive only in the airs of freedom. They need the support and guarantee of the State for the maintenance of their rights, but they can and must dispense with the tutelage of the State. Rudolf Steiner saw the third member of the social organism in an Equity State, a life of Rights, in which, following the principle of equality applied in all its ramifications, every citizen has an active and fully responsible share.

It is of the essence of this Threefold Social Order that, as with the human being himself, it admits no rigid separation or loss of contact between the three spheres. Just as all the three organic functions are united and work together in one and the same human being, so in the Threefold Social Order man himself is the binding unit. One and the same man can, as a citizen with equal rights, rely upon the democratic observance of those rights. He can do this while at the same time he thinks and acts as an industrialist far beyond the boundaries of his country in association with others; and, acting ever and again out of the wholeness of his being in a free spiritual life, he can give effect to the impulses of his individuality side by side with the other men – sometimes different men, sometimes the same men, whom he meets in the other spheres.

Even while the First World War was still being waged, Rudolf Steiner summarised these basic thoughts in memoranda which were in the hands of the Cabinet in Vienna and also of government circles in Berlin. How much could have been done to solve the problems of Austro-Hungarian relations if, in accordance with the principle of a free spiritual life, it had been decided to concede full cultural autonomy to the 13 nations of the Danubian monarchy. And what new prospects there could have been for the peace negotiations at Brest-Litovsk, where Rudolf Steiner's memorandum was also available. Among other things, the whole absurdity of small nations each having its own separate economy could have been avoided; the seeds of the Second World War were nurtured within the border states, right up to the Baltic, from the very first day these states and their 'national economies' came into existence. But ears in Vienna were as deaf as were those in Berlin or Brest-Litovsk. The First World War came to its tragic end. Under the ruins it left behind, the fire of the second catastrophic world war was already smouldering.   In the spring of 1919 Rudolf Steiner drew up his basic thoughts on the Threefold Social Organism in a terse, concise form, making a powerful appeal to the conscience of Middle Europe in his *Call to the German People and to the Civilized World*. In the same year his fundamental book on the Threefold Social Order had been published: *The Threefold Commonwealth*.

I cannot regard it as chance that Rudolf Steiner's *Call to the German People* was sent to me from Stuttgart by a friend living there. I received it in Westphalia in strange circumstances. As a military interpreter with the rank of subaltern, I was engaged at that time on affairs connected with the winding up of a large hospital previously used for prisoners of war. Together with a friend who was later on a colleague in the educational movement, I read the lucid, monumental sentences in which Rudolf Steiner outlines the destiny of Middle Europe from 1871 until the end of the First World War. These thoughts struck into our conscience like sparks of fire. Young as we were, we were not able to assess their importance to the full, but we glimpsed something of the historic significance of the moment. My friend had not yet seen Rudolf Steiner, and I felt that this was the right time to tell him about my earlier meetings with this absolutely unique personality. All the desolate dreariness that had oppressed us in the barracks and their surroundings, like a fog, was dispersed. A ray of sun from the wide universe had penetrated to us. We felt it as a ray of sun coming from the future.

The accompanying letter written by my friend in Stuttgart mentioned a name hitherto unknown to me, that of the industrialist Emil Molt, director of the Waldorf-Astoria cigarette factory and also one of the leading figures in the *Treuhandgesellschaft Goetheanum* (Goetheanum Trust). My friend wrote that he knew Molt well and that he was one of a circle of men in Stuttgart who were 'preparing something of great importance'. It was not clear to me from the letter just what this was, but in the mood induced by the reading of the *Call*, I immediately had faith in it.

The name of Molt had already passed from my mind when, a few weeks later, it was vividly recalled to my memory. Through my friend in Stuttgart again, I was asked, to my astonishment, to go there for an interview with Emil Molt. There was a plan that I should take over work connected with projects set on foot by the Movement for the Threefold Social Order.

In Stuttgart, Emil Molt gave me more detailed information about the task in mind for me: I was to take over the direction and arrangement of educational courses for workers, to be given in as well as outside the Waldorf-Astoria factory.

My heart-beats quickened at the prospect of this new and fascinating task which gave my life some real meaning once more. I undertook it gladly: chiefly out of confidence in Rudolf Steiner but also out of confidence which arose, almost instantaneously, in Emil Molt. I found in him an unusual and happy blend of qualities not readily combined in one person. He gave evidence of a clear and practical mind together with great warmth of heart; his will was impulsive, impetuous – but any particular action was always performed with great calmness and after deep deliberation.

When I began this new work there was no talk as yet of the founding of a school. As well as brief lectures on social and educational matters given to workers in the various departments of the factory during fully paid, half-hour intervals, and a few foreign-language courses for members of the staff, my work included some educational help to the workers' children. In the afternoons I helped about 40 of these children with their homework. They were a haphazard little company, drawn from all the eight elementary school grades in Stuttgart. Later on I saw nearly all of them again in the lowest classes of the Waldorf School. At that time, when I helped them quite without any system or guiding educational principles, it would never have occurred to anyone to imagine that they represented something like a beginning of the first set of Waldorf School pupils.

The new tasks were therefore very varied and left me little free time. But such hours as were free were taken up with intensive study of the Threefold Social Order and with earnest discussions often lasting far into the night. There was an unforgettable atmosphere of enthusiasm and expectancy, both tense and fruitful. We were waiting for the day when Rudolf Steiner himself would come to Stuttgart.

Before this happened, voices which in retrospect seem full of significance had become audible among the workers at the Waldorf-Astoria. One heard it said: 'Yes, it is really a splendid thing for us older people to have these courses and lectures – but it comes a bit late. Our children should have something of the kind! They ought to be able to find in a school something that was denied to us when we were young.' It is of importance, historically, to realise that these thoughts arising in the hearts and minds of the Waldorf-Astoria workers during the period of the Threefold Commonwealth activities became one of the spiritual factors in the subsequent foundation of the Waldorf School.

But it is certainly no less important to realise that the workers had the courage and desire to express thoughts such as these only because the same thoughts had already been harboured for a long time by Emil Molt. And this is the point at which to think of the unique relationship existing between Emil Molt and the workers and staff of his factory. On the one side it was a relationship of fatherly care. One would have to write at length to convey what it signified in the human sense when Molt passed on his daily rounds through the rooms in the factory. In good Swabian dialect he was called the *Vatter* (father). Only the other day I heard that during the war he had provided a cow in order that some workers whose health was gravely endangered could get extra nourishment.

But Emil Molt's relationship with the workers was not merely one of fatherly solicitude – by no means so rare in Swabian industrial life at that time. For years he had carried in his heart the thoughts of Rudolf Steiner. Above all, he was vitally interested in Rudolf Steiner's lectures on social matters and on education. Through rigorous and indefatigable self-education, Molt had set about closing the gaps in his own schooling, and this helped to give him a ready ear for the educational problems of the time. In early days he had read Rudolf Steiner's book, *The Education of the Child from the Standpoint of Spiritual Science* – a little volume compiled from shorthand reports of lectures. This book included the following words: 'Spiritual Science, when called upon to build up an art of education, will be able to indicate in detail all the things that come into consideration here, even specifying particular forms of food and nourishment. For it is realism, it is a thing for life itself; it is by no means grey theory – as it might appear to be today according to the mistaken conceptions of many theosophists.'

When called upon to build up an art of education... Thousands must have read this passage, but they had overlooked its importance. It had not dawned upon them that in reality this was a challenge to put a question – a question for which the spiritual scientist, as an undeviating guardian of human freedom, is obliged to wait. Deep down in Emil Molt's soul this passage worked on unceasingly. And when the catastrophe of 1918–19 arrived, he divined that in reality it was a catastrophe due to faulty and neglected education. Education would have to be given a new basis. This insight led to lively consultations and discussions with representatives of his workers and staff, and to the organisation of the educational courses for workers. They were a first step, behind which lay far more than Emil Molt himself at first realised.

This unexpressed 'more' was to be stimulated into great activity when Rudolf Steiner was able for a short time to free himself from his manifold obligations in Dornach, and came to Stuttgart. For Stuttgart and Wurttemberg this was the beginning of the classic period of work in connection with the Threefold Commonwealth Movement. Its effects spread far into the other provinces of Middle Europe. One of its most unforgettable and also most effective preludes was the lecture on the Threefold Social Order given by Rudolf Steiner in the Tobacco Room of the Waldorf-Astoria Factory to all its employees. The active workers in the Threefold Commonwealth Movement had been awaiting this lecture with tense excitement, and it was therefore all the more disconcerting to find that to the first part of what Rudolf Steiner said the workers listened with obvious reserve. I still remember well how near I myself was to giving way to a certain feeling of disappointment. But then, from a side that could not have been foreseen, came the breakthrough.

After speaking by way of introduction of certain other great motifs of contemporary history, Rudolf Steiner went on to characterise the basic mood and frame of mind of the proletariat. He laid bare its deeper, spiritual origin by presenting it as the direct consequence of a catastrophe in the whole of Western cultural development. Millions of young people, he said, are wrested away every year at about the age of 14 from the real process of cultural development and are thrust into economic and industrial life in one form or another. True, in most countries they receive further training – this means that they are given technical instruction, with as much essential theory as they require. But they get no education that is worthy of the name. And it is this realisation of inadequate, curtailed cultural development that embitters the souls of the proletarians to their very depths; it is this that induces them to rebel against the existing forms of civilisation. Here, deep in the human heart, lies a permanent crater of smouldering revolutions.

'All of you sitting here,' said Rudolf Steiner, 'from the 16-year-old girl apprentice to the 60-year-old workers, are suffering from the fact that your real cultural development was obstructed, because from a certain moment onwards there was for you only the hard schooling of life, but no school in the true sense of the word.'

This was said with such warmth and came from such a profound understanding of human nature that it struck right into the hearts of the listeners.

All at once it was no longer the great sociologist and philosopher, introduced by Emil Molt, who stood there; it was a doctor who with clear perception, but also with a delicate, sensitive touch, was uncovering a wound he wanted to heal. All prejudices which had risen up at the beginning were swept away as if by a magic hand. Every one of us present experienced in common the liberating and at the same time challenging power of a truth uttered by a man who knew. A body of mere listeners became, in the best sense of the word, a gathering of human beings in whom something began to stir – the resolve to help to prevent the cultural development of man from being further obstructed at such a critical moment of time. In the middle of a lecture on the Threefold Social Order the vista of a wholly new kind of education was opened up. Mindful of the fact that this would never have come into existence but for the workers' decisive wish for it, it is this hour that I should like to name as that of the actual birth of the Free Waldorf School. At this point I must speak particularly of one man who had no connection whatever with the Waldorf-Astoria Factory, but had listened to this lecture with keen interest. He was E A Karl Stockmeyer, who played an essential part in the birth of the new school. Stockmeyer, who at that time was still teaching at a high school in Baden, had been acquainted both with Rudolf Steiner as a personality and with his teachings from the early days. By dint of strict mental discipline, he had mastered the fundamental principles and method of anthroposophical Spiritual Science. A strong, innate urge for research and inquiry had led him not to adopt a purely conservative attitude to Spiritual Science, but to develop and elaborate certain aspects of it, in particular that of philosophy applied to the theory of knowledge. Hence his personality was marked by a refreshing independence and firm inner poise. It was just this type of man that Rudolf Steiner particularly valued among his pupils.

After the end of the First World War – indeed, even before that – Stockmeyer had been occupied in his own way with plans for school reform. Finding in Stockmeyer's ideas something that tallied with his own inner aims, Emil Molt had persuaded him to come to Stuttgart and was engaged in lively discussions with him. This exchange of ideas had to do not only with education but also – as was only natural in view of the whole situation – with the principles of the Threefold Social Order in general, of which Stockmeyer had an excellent understanding. And so not only did he become an important collaborator in the founding of the Waldorf School; the untiring activity in the planning of the social work at that time cannot be imagined without the presence of his striking personality.

It was on April 25th, 1919, in the very late evening, that the decisive discussion about the founding of the Free Waldorf School took place. Rudolf Steiner, after giving a great public lecture to the employees of the Daimler Works, had come to the house in the Landhausstrasse belonging to the Stuttgart Group of the Anthroposophical Society, where he was accustomed to stay during his visits to Stuttgart. Emil Molt, Karl Stockmeyer and I were waiting for him there.

The basic ideas put forward by Rudolf Steiner in the ensuing conversation on the subject of the new school varied in many details from what was eventually embodied in the constitution of the Waldorf School. But the whole talk, both in its substance and in its tenor, was a source of veritable inspiration. Rudolf Steiner very soon threw off the last traces of the tremendous strain that had preceded the conversation. What he had to say to us flowed with increasing eloquence and vigour. And it was connected not only with the concrete plan for the founding of the Waldorf School, but also with social and cultural education in the widest sense.

I shall speak here of three motifs which to my mind form a basic and essential part of that conversation. Among other questions, I asked Rudolf Steiner from which point one would have to start in order to lay the foundation of genuine social feeling in the communal life of men.

Although the question in this form was very general and vague, he went into it willingly. He said that one could naturally speak for hours about such an all-embracing domain. On the other hand the matters that came into consideration could also be expressed quite simply. And then he went on to speak of the threefold nature of man, of the different degrees of intensity in which thinking, feeling and willing work in human consciousness: thinking alone is fully wide-awake, feeling has the intensity only of a dream, and willing rises as if out of a condition of deep sleep. Our cultural life in its present form could have been produced only by clear, wide-awake thinking. This has brought man a clear-cut, vivid realisation of his own personality. It has individualised but also 'de-socialised' him: it has torn him out of the natural connections of social life. In its intrinsic nature our ordinary conceptual thinking is antisocial – Rudolf Steiner underlined this. 'You may hold great congresses,' he said, 'where the deliberations from start to finish are concerned only with social questions, but as long as the approach is a merely intellectual one, the effect of such congresses upon social life will be nil. They will tend far rather to disintegrate it.' 'The true social life,' he went on, 'must be built up out of those deeper strata of consciousness which are the realms of the dreaming feeling and the sleeping will. Artistic capacities and faculties, which are identical with the primal forces of the religious life, must be summoned into activity – but not in such a way that the clarity of consciousness in the man of the modern age is ignored. If that were to happen, it would be at the cost of human freedom. Clear, independent thinking must not be sacrificed in order to set in flow the process of social reform. But this thinking must imbue itself with new substance coming from deeper strata of the life of soul.'

Rudolf Steiner went on to say that there is a method and a way whereby the foundations of social feeling may be laid. The abstractness of human thinking has led to far-reaching differentiation and specialisation in the labour process; it alone has made possible the technique of modern industrialism. But at the same time it has also removed the worker from the wider relationships in which he originally felt healthy and whole. He can experience himself now only as a part of a part, and what he produces only as the splinter of the part of a part. Together with the narrowing of his field of work, his consciousness has narrowed. The former must be accepted as a fact bound up with modern industrial methods; the latter, as an evil that is *not* inevitable, must be overcome.

At this point I looked at Rudolf Steiner very dubiously. The possibility that the essentially proletarian attitude could ever be overcome in the consciousness of the proletariat seemed to me to border on the miraculous.

As always, he perceived the eagerness of the question arising in the heart of one who was taking part in the conversation, and he spoke with all the greater emphasis. The essential thing, he said in effect, was to create for every worker and employee a picture of the whole of his work and also of its place and setting in the world. He started with the situation as it was in the Waldorf-Astoria Factory. All the employees, male and female, should be told about all the work done in the other departments. They should also be given a picture of the tobacco plant itself, of the regions where it is cultivated, of the civilisation in the countries concerned. Over and above this they should be told about the whole process of the distribution of the finished product and the economic and financial factors involved. Similarly, the salesmen should be made conversant with all the practical work that had gone into the finished product. When anyone who is engaged on some productive work has a picture of the whole process involved, his consciousness is widened and his human interest kindled. He may continue his work in the narrowest of sections, but he feels spiritually linked with all the others. The social connection then becomes real to him and the feeling of detachment is no longer there.

Rudolf Steiner thought that this widening of consciousness might be achieved by means of lectures and introductory courses. Something like a syllabus of production should be worked out for each industrial firm. He also had in mind that individual workers might be invited to visit other departments of a factory; they could go first as observers and later on be given opportunities for practical participation.

From the point of view of social history, it is important to underline that these things were said by Rudolf Steiner in April, 1919 – hence very shortly after the end of the First World War – and that in the very same year they were being put into actual practice in the Waldorf-Astoria Factory. As the result of the overpowering pressure of bigoted counter-interests, working now from one side and now from another, they were soon suppressed in Central Europe – to appear once again after the Second World War as an alleged 'new impulse' from beyond the seas.

It may perhaps be a cause of surprise that matters of this kind figured in a talk concerned primarily with the creation of a new school. But what was so characteristic of conversations with Rudolf Steiner was that he never kept systematically, let alone pedantically, to a set topic, but took hold of what came to him at the moment from the vital interests of those taking part.

I recall a third motif in this conversation, to the effect that it was now important to build a bridge from one people to another by means of a folk-psychology based upon spiritual realities. Rudolf Steiner regarded instruction in foreign languages, particularly in the so-called modern languages, as a way to this. Every language, he said, preserves quite definite conceptions of beings and things, and these conceptions come to expression in images, in pictures. It would be important, together with the foreign language itself, to convey such pictures and words to the children and young people. Rudolf Steiner called them 'linguistic values'. He then spoke of the lecture-course on folk-psychology he had given in the summer of 1910 at the Nobelhaus in Oslo: *The Mission of Individual Folk-Souls in connection with Germanic and Norse Mythology*. While referring to these lectures he became deeply earnest. He said: 'The intention behind these things was that, if rightly understood, they might have been able to help to prevent the catastrophe of the World War. But there were no ears to hear...' And then he spoke of how he had recently sent a copy of the Oslo lecture-course, with a commentary of his own, to Prince Max of Baden, the eminent German statesman, in the hope that the German government of the day would allow itself to be enriched by new ideas, by a new field of knowledge. And with unforgettable pain, he said: 'But there were no ears to hear. People did not want to hear, and so the catastrophe befell.'

We sat silent, and there was a pause. With a strong, solemn emphasis on every word, Rudolf Steiner concluded: 'Far worse catastrophes will follow the present one if ears continue to be deaf to these things.'

I have spoken at length about these three motifs of the conversation because they only seem to lie outside the sphere of Waldorf School education. Anyone who studies the latter thoroughly will be astonished to find that each of these motifs is most intimately connected with the principles and practices of Waldorf Schools. And so here, too, we have an illustration of how Waldorf School education was born out of the great diagnosis of the age and of civilisation made by Rudolf Steiner at the beginning of the Threefold Commonwealth Movement.

From April until August 1919, the preparations for the founding of the new school went forward in their own way. To begin with, the organising and explanatory work connected with the social-economic sphere of the Threefold Commonwealth was in the foreground. The courage and the fire, the intense devotion with which Rudolf Steiner endeavoured in lectures and discussion evenings to show how the great social demands of the time could be met, left unforgettable impressions.

Without having rested, and exhausted by conversations that might have taken up the whole of the preceding night, and then by conferences lasting from morning until evening, he would come into the lecture-room, sometimes a dreary hall in a factory, sometimes a tavern. The listeners, most of them industrial workers, sat with their mugs full of beer and cider in front of them. Smoke mingling with the fumes of the drinks soon penetrated into every corner of the room. This affected the vocal chords and made speaking very difficult for Rudolf Steiner, who had been a non-smoker and a non-drinker for decades. His voice, never known to be other than full and resonant, was often completely hoarse at the beginning of the lectures, but with wonderful strength and self-mastery he got the better of this, too. I was never present at a discussion-evening when, even if it took half an hour, he did not finally succeed in getting his voice clear.

He also had the wonderful art of responding to the idiosyncrasies of every audience. Here, too, his profound and instantaneous understanding of men – but equally, I believe, his human love – came to expression. He did not press anything ready-made upon his listeners, but developed his thoughts as it were out of their own experiences and insight, their own sufferings and joys. Hence one always felt free while listening to him, even when he spoke with intense fire. And in these gatherings, where the problems of community were being discussed, one felt challenged as a single person, as an individual.

In the discussions with the workers, with their strong party affiliations, the great difficulty of contending with ingrained prejudices and dogmas was soon apparent. Again and again they spoke of their hopes, seldom of their achievements. Phrases such as 'if the Threefold Order is introduced' were constantly to be heard. On such occasions Rudolf Steiner would cry out with a voice of fire that no human being could 'introduce' the Threefold Order; that it behoved everyone to work with untiring personal activity in order that what was everywhere being prepared in the womb of the times should gradually come to birth.

A strange and grotesque objection, shedding garish light upon the attitude of many minds, was prone to crop up: 'Yes – but if the Threefold Order becomes a reality there will be no longer any class war...' This was usually said with an undertone of profound regret – as if humanity would be deprived of something valuable if class war were to cease!

There were others again who took exception to the fact that Rudolf Steiner gave no sweeping definitions and also refrained from presenting detailed programmes. People had grown too accustomed to bold catchwords, aggressive epigrams, and so-called 'burning protests'. I remember how a worthy speaker in a discussion accused Rudolf Steiner of making statements that were as 'mushy as a plum'. Rudolf Steiner bore this remark, as well as previous utterances, with the greatest equanimity and composure; he merely jotted down one or two words in his notebook. Then he answered the various points briefly, in order. When the objection just mentioned was reached, he spoke to the following effect: 'One of the respected speakers complains that my remarks were as mushy as a plum. What am I to say to that, gentlemen? Perhaps that I have always tried to be very exact in observing nature. So I think too, that the plum should also be observed very carefully. And then I find that soft plums are juicy, sweet and ripe, but hard plums are tasteless, unripe and...' He did not get as far as the obvious word 'indigestible' because the large audience broke into delighted applause. The 'respected speaker' had been dealt with in the kindliest way, and the sympathy of the listeners made them more receptive to all that was said on this occasion.

On another occasion he turned aside a compliment that seemed to him too cheap; it was always his habit to reject admiration in any form. The chief engineer of a big firm came out with the words: 'Yes, Herr Doktor, it is because you are such a great philosopher that you have these important things to say about overcoming the crisis in our civilisation!' Rudolf Steiner answered dryly: 'Philosophy has little to do with these things. If I am able to contribute anything useful today, I ascribe it primarily to the fact that from my earliest youth I learnt to clean my own shoes!'

The kernel of an 'Industrial Council' took shape in Stuttgart at that time as the outcome of countless meetings, consultations and discussions. Rudolf Steiner considered that in an area of the size of Wurttemberg it would be possible to carry out the experiment of an industrial economy based on associations. A number of speakers travelled all over the region at that time in order to make known the contents of the book on the 'kernel of the social question', which had meanwhile been published.

I myself was one of these speakers, and I well remember an evening at the Mauser Works in Oberndorf. After particularly animated and even heated discussions, the endeavour to persuade the board of this enterprise to link up with the general council in Stuttgart had succeeded. I had already realised that my remarks that evening were being strongly supported by a man I took to be a skilled worker or a foreman. When the meeting was over this man came up to me and told me that many years before he had attended courses and lectures by Rudolf Steiner under the auspices of Liebknecht's Workers' Educational Institute in Berlin. 'We workmen liked listening to him,' he said, 'because what he told us was so entirely different from what the other speakers said. Among ourselves we often said, "Something great will come from Dr Steiner one day..." And so this evening I was particularly happy. I believe that what we surmised then has now been fulfilled!' Rudolf Steiner laughed when a few days later I told him of this episode. But he was also obviously pleased that such an enthusiastic witness still survived from those years which had been for him a period of hard spiritual struggle.

What he experienced in those weeks and months of practical activity in connection with the Threefold Order was not always so encouraging. He saw with great anxiety that these great and helpful ideas had to be presented by people who were very far from being up to the tasks devolving upon them at the decisive moment. With the wide-minded, cordial, and at the same time utterly uncompromising sincerity that was innate in him, he would talk again and again with the individual speakers. One day I said to him that it depressed me to be faced at such an early age with a task of this importance, I was afraid I was totally inadequate for it. He looked at me kindly, saying with warm emphasis: 'Yes, but you may also be sure that the spiritual world accepts enthusiasm as a substitute for maturity.'

In the economic and political field, the whole period here under review did not fulfil the hopes cherished by the pioneers of the Threefold Commonwealth Movement. Already in the year 1919, reactionary currents began to assert themselves everywhere. Hide-bound thinking and dogmatism won the day. It was as Rudolf Steiner had said immediately after the war, with grave, profoundly sorrowful emphasis: men had not learnt how to learn. And so under the pressure of dark powers of opposition, the Industrial Council which had represented a new seed in the economic field was crushed before the end of the year. What remained was the consciousness that valuable seeds had been scattered abroad and that a group of

men had exercised and steeled their forces in a struggle which for the present had
no prospect of success. But who can say whether, after all, a great deal more had
not been accomplished? Many a lightly sounded theme seems to die out in history,
thereafter to form the leading motif in a future age.

The question remains whether, when he inaugurated a social movement of such
promise, Rudolf Steiner knew that it was destined to have so little immediate
success. From the reports I had of many things he said, mostly in personal
conversations, I can only assume that he foresaw exactly the course things would
take. All the more worthy of admiration was the indomitable enthusiasm he showed
in the many activities of the movement, the way he had of presenting things as
being so urgent that there was not a moment to lose, as if they ought to happen
the next day. Not until years afterwards did I hear of illuminating words of his –
that there are 'prematurities' in history. They occur of necessity, in order to die
like grains of wheat out of which good, fertile seed is to grow. Extreme renunciation
is demanded of those who are the human bearers of these 'prematurities' –
renunciation that is not resignation but the silent soul of an activity enhanced to
the utmost. And so a life that is dedicated to them is necessarily a life of heroism.

With this inner attitude, hardly perceptible in outward appearance, Rudolf Steiner
bore also the wrecking of the attempts which, in the sphere of a free spiritual life,
were striving to find new forms for the autonomous development of culture –
attempts to establish a council of culture and similar institutions. In this sphere
everything was wrecked by hide-bound prejudices, by a passivity that had become
a rule of life. One might well be reminded once again of Fafner's words in Wagner's
Ring des Nibelungen: 'I lie and I possess, let me sleep!'

The principal of a High School in Leipzig was, for example, asked one day:
'Surely it would be easy for you, who are so convinced of the necessity for a free
spiritual life, to arouse enthusiasm in your staff for a new kind of collaboration?'
'My staff?' the principal said bitterly. 'What are you thinking about? Apart from
their teaching, they are interested at the very most in questions of pay and position!'
What was there to be done with such a generation of men? Seen against this
background, the founding of the Free Waldorf School, upon which all the energies
of the movement for the Threefold Social Order were now soon concentrated,
becomes an event of real significance in the social history of our time.

It will be obvious from the foregoing paragraphs that in founding the Free
Waldorf School it was not Rudolf Steiner's aim merely to add another school to
the good schools, private and modern, already existing in Middle Europe. His aim
was to build up a real science of education, and it was only as a seed born from a
free spiritual life that the Waldorf School interested him. It was not a matter of
particular reform or of supplementing good existing methods, but of creating a
new atmosphere and a new ground for education in the widest sense. Whenever I
encountered Rudolf Steiner in those days, with his utterly uncompromising, spiritual
resoluteness, I could not help thinking of an utterance that had come to my
knowledge shortly before my arrival in Stuttgart. It was a saying of Alfred

Lichtwark's, reported to me by Hermann Itschner, the educational reformer, with whom I was in close contact at that time. 'A merely *partial* reform of existing conditions does nothing but *strengthen the existing tendencies.*'

Already in 1910 an attentive observer of the times might well have become conscious of a striking contrast which even today is not obliterated but has become even stronger. It applies, on the one side, to industry; on the other to the cultural life, particularly to education. As is apparent everywhere, industry, vigorously carried forward by the spirit of the age, is at least on the way to achieving new forms and conditions of labour. By its very nature industry is progressive, and its pioneers realise quite clearly that humanity is in the throes of a change of consciousness. More insistently, however, than people are willing to admit, cultural life bases itself on forms of thought which in widespread areas of the West do not differ essentially from the spirit of the 18th century. And again, the reason why so much is wanting in European education is often because only a few perceive that things which in the Middle Ages were unconditionally to be regarded as good, and even inspired, are working on in a diluted and sterile, but also a tenacious and unyielding form. Rudolf Steiner's aim was to imbue cultural life and education with the progressive forces of the age. It was a question of rousing them out of static rigidity and of leading them into the dynamic movement of free, spiritual development. That this could be achieved only on absolutely clear, objective foundations was proved by the great introductory course [published as *The Study of Man*] he gave for the College of Teachers of the Waldorf School in August, 1919. In the course of a review of bodily, psychical and spiritual phenomena, these lectures built up a knowledge of man which affords entirely new starting-points for the education of the child at each stage of its development. They showed how the principle of threefold man could be the basis of an educational method genuinely congenial to the child: one which does not persist in applying to a child's early years the categories which are suitable at most for the adult life of soul.

An atmosphere of festival prevailed during this course, which was given in three sections: 'General Knowledge of Man' was a foretaste of what was to be learnt and experienced later on 'Didactic Methods' and 'Educational Practice'. In an age when learning is split into sections, with its branches unrelated to each other, here there was organic universality, embracing the whole scholarship of the times. This great knowledge, permeated with an equally great artistic power, was crowned by an even greater humanism. Here there was no trace of self-consideration or of vanity, no trace of satisfaction in dominating other human beings through the power to convince. One felt: in humility and as a server, this man stands at the great well-springs of spirit which have opened themselves to him, and he respects and protects every single individuality who comes before him. Rudolf Steiner possessed the rare art of lowering his own greatness to the level of the one to whom he was speaking – not out of condescension, but out of an attitude of human understanding and inquiry. In his presence one breathed freely, even when he was presenting things of the utmost greatness. One felt that one was being addressed in one's own language, and experienced the joy of an entirely natural converse between man and man. So it was, too, during this course of lectures. One felt confirmed in a hundred things hitherto only surmised; but admittedly one clung to the pleasant dream of having surmised them.

Some years afterwards, during a searching study of the lectures heard at that time, it was easy to realise how alarmingly little one had assimilated at first. And new perspectives open out every year as the interval of time lengthens. Yet the sheer enthusiasm with which one listened, with which one participated in the educational practice, was certainly responsible for part of that miracle in the year 1919. Here, too, the words that were said to me in the midst of the struggle to bring the Threefold Social Order to fulfilment hold good: the spiritual world accepts enthusiasm as a substitute for maturity. On 7th September, 1919, the Free Waldorf School came into being. This day, too, was a festival from morning until late in the evening. In the house in the Uhlandshühe in Stuttgart, in the former restaurant that had been rebuilt into a school, there was no suitable lecture hall. So the actual inauguration ceremony took place in the Stadtgarten-Saal; it was opened by Bach's *Prelude in C major*, played on the piano by Paul Baumann, our first music teacher. Frau Marie Steiner recited, and children demonstrated certain examples of the young art of eurythmy inaugurated by Rudolf Steiner. But the crowning point was Rudolf Steiner's address, in which he characterised once more the great social perspective in which Waldorf School education was now taking its first steps. Science becoming alive, art becoming alive, religion becoming alive – these he declared to be its well-springs. How easily these words might be repeated as phrases. The essence of the matter is that for Waldorf School education they have a spiritual, concretely real significance, down to the very details of practice.

In the afternoon the different classes were introduced to their teachers in an atmosphere of happiness and vivacity. In the evening the whole College of Teachers was invited to a performance of Mozart's *Magic Flute*. Rudolf Steiner, sitting by Emil Molt, pointed out to him with eager alertness where the teachers of the new school were sitting, all over the great Opera House. The delight and childlike joy with which he did this, before the performance began, revealed once again the sweetness of spirit incarnate in this great Friend of Man.

Widening the Art of Healing

Grete Kirchner-Bockholt

WHEN RUDOLF STEINER began to give out his world-conception and an ever-widening circle of people gathered round him, there were more and more requests for his advice on possible ways of restoring health and overcoming illness. It goes without saying that a great initiate such as he is also a great healer. He gave advice of this kind very readily, as often as he was asked, and in the early days recommended for the most part old remedies which had come originally from instinctive perceptions; they had been revived by M E A Ritter and tried out upon herself. Later, however, when medical doctors joined the Anthroposophical Movement, Rudolf Steiner preferred to give his advice to members of the medical profession, starting at the same time to suggest new remedies, or even whole courses of treatment.

At Dornach there was already a little laboratory where vegetable colours were prepared for the paintings in the cupolas of the first Goetheanum. Dr Schmiedel now began to prepare medicaments there as well. When, in 1920, a considerable number of doctors were gathered together, Dr Steiner gave them the first doctors' course. Some of them wanted to found clinics where anthroposophical knowledge of medicine could find practical expression. Thus there arose in Stuttgart a Clinical-Therapeutic Institute run by Dr Palmer, Dr Friedrich Husemann, Dr Peipers and Dr Noll. Dr Ita Wegman acquired a house in Arlesheim and had it transformed into a modest little clinic.

About this time, in August 1921, I too came to Dornach. But although I already had my medical degree, my concern was the new art of eurythmy, as I had the idea of studying curative eurythmy later; indeed, I came near to giving up medicine for eurythmy. Had I known of eurythmy two years earlier, I should certainly never have completed my medical exams. I now studied for a year under the tuition of Frau Marie Steiner, who accepted me as a pupil in the kindest way. I made her acquaintance when I had just arrived in Stuttgart and was arranging the chairs in the lecture-room at the house in the Landhausstrasse. She herself proposed that I should learn eurythmy with a view to practising curative eurythmy, and she invited me to Dornach. It was during the period of inflation, and a stay in Switzerland at my own expense would have been impossible. This generous invitation, coming as it did out of the blue, very much surprised me; I accepted it with the greatest joy. In order to be able to give at least some practical help in my odd moments, I learned to type, though I fear I was never much good at it; nevertheless Frau Marie Steiner comfortingly assured me that the goodwill of others does not as a rule get even as far as that.

After a year of training in eurythmy I had a talk with Frau Dr Steiner, telling her how difficult it would be for me to go on as a student and how I craved – after studying medicine for so long and then eurythmy – at last to have a profession. She listened most sympathetically and proposed that, with Frau Fels, I should direct the newly founded School of Eurythmy at Stuttgart. It was a hot day in summer when this conversation took place in a room behind the stage in the Schreinerei. Just at this moment, before I had time to reply, Dr Steiner walked into the room. He gave me his hand and said, emphasising each word, 'Well, Doctor, how are you?' Nothing more. Yet these words went right home. It is impossible to explain by what means I instantaneously grasped what he wished to say. The emphasis on the 'Doctor', the question spoken so deliberately, the carefully chosen moment – within me there was no shadow of doubt how his words were to be taken. They were meant to say: 'Shoemaker, stick to your last.'

How the interview with Frau Marie Steiner ended, I no longer remember; in any case nothing was decided, and soon afterwards Dr Ita Wegman wrote to ask me if I would go as assistant in her Arlesheim Clinic, which had then been running for a year. The head assistant, Frau Dr Walter, was ill, and Dr Norbert Glas wanted to start a practice in Vienna. This letter was written in August 1922. Dr Steiner was on a lecture-tour in England, Frau Marie Steiner was with him; thus, whether I liked it or not, I had to make a decision without being able to consult either of them. At that time we were not in the habit of telephoning all over the world; perhaps it was not even possible. On the other hand, the position in the clinic allowed of no hesitation. Dr Wegman was momentarily without a single assistant and had a good number of patients. I therefore went to the clinic. I had, it is true, to make the condition that I should occasionally attend to the sale of books in the Schreinerei, for I had promised Miss Mackenzie to deputise for her, she too having gone to England.

When, among the customers to whom I sold Dr Steiner's lecture-cycles or books, there were people I had shortly before examined medically, this occasioned some surprise. But it was I who was surprised when one day, as I was trailing along through the Schreinerei with a package of books, I ran across Dr Steiner. He had just returned from England and he stopped me to say: 'You have been to see Frau X today?' 'Yes, it seems to me that the trouble is so-and-so,' I answered. Dr Steiner nodded – all was right, treatment included. He then turned left into his studio while I, with my pile of books, continued straight on to Miss Mackenzie's little room... It was then the thought first came to me that I should have told Dr Steiner about my starting work at the clinic. 'Dr Steiner, I have not yet told you that I am working at the Clinic now,' I called after him. As he went on he said something that sounded like, 'Yes, that's good,' and only afterwards did it occur to me that this was no news to him.

There now began a great period of learning. Dr Steiner often came to see patients at the clinic and each time his coming was an event. Generally, during these visits, Dr Walter and I were allowed to be present in Dr Wegman's little consulting room.

Dr Walter took shorthand notes of what was said, and afterwards we worked out her notes together, so that we still have a copy of the instructions given. Before each of his visits everything was carefully prepared – analyses, results of examinations, all lay ready. Dr Steiner gave everything the most minute attention. But when he had the patient in front of him, his method was completely different from the traditional one. He looked at the patient with the utmost concentration. his gaze turning towards the various members of the patient's being; for him it was possible to investigate the cause of illness with a clairvoyance that was exact. For him, the symptoms were concentrated into a complex of causes which, as a totality, could be easily surveyed; the passage of time became one long present. Thus on one occasion he was able to say of a patient, who for years had suffered from eczema, that the cause lay in his having taken poison as a child. At first the patient was unable to recall anything, then it came to him suddenly that in about his ninth year at school he had inadvertently swallowed some hydrochloric acid in the laboratory. The 10-year-old cause of the illness had been perceived by Rudolf Steiner in the man then standing before him. From this it will be readily understood that most of the ordinary diagnoses fell to the ground; for what revealed itself to perception of this kind was always the picture of a quite special case of a quite special illness. In the light of such knowledge the treatment was immediately forthcoming. Whereas today we describe and determine the typical manifestations of definite illnesses, which one might say we look upon as detached from the person who is suffering from them, this method was completely the reverse.

One day we took a patient, a woman, to Dr Steiner. Her illness had already been diagnosed in other clinics; we agreed with this diagnosis and considered hers to be a characteristic case of multiple sclerosis. After looking at the patient, Dr Steiner said that hers was a constitutional weakness of the *medulla oblongata*, so that the connection between the spinal cord and the central nervous system was disturbed; moreover, this had been aggravated by an accident. On being questioned, the patient said that once in Paris, when she was about 18, she had fallen from a tram, but at the time was unaware of any real injury. In her 28th year there had come upon her this illness, which gave a picture of multiple sclerosis.

As soon as Dr Steiner had established the exact state of an illness, he went on to seek the treatment, and we can say that for this the whole world was at his disposal. In his all-embracing survey he looked upon the human being as born out of the macrocosm and bound up with nature, with plants, minerals, metals... Even if within man the processes are changed, they still show affinity with the corresponding processes in external nature, and in the case of illness the kindred forces of nature can be drawn into the service of healing.

For the faculties of knowledge possessed by Rudolf Steiner, the processes of nature were an open book. What he knew was, for us young folk, positively overwhelming. Whether it was a question of minerals, metals with their countless salts and combinations, or a question of plants, his choice was always sure. From the algae and fungoids, up to the most highly developed plants, remedies were taken from every kingdom. Sometimes he considered it necessary to change the air for a patient. One patient had difficulty in waking, and often it was nearly evening before he was really capable of doing anything. The prescription was that he should wake up in air with a large content of carbon dioxide, so that the waking process might be intensified precisely through overcoming this difficulty. Thus we added carbon dioxide to the air through the keyhole of the patient's room – no simple process, chiefly on account of our having to seize the moment before he began to wake of his own accord. In any particular treatment there were always variations and fresh plans, the details often being carefully given by Dr Steiner himself – for example, that a metal should first be reduced to a vaporous condition, in order then to let it settle as a sublimate.

There was only one method of healing to which Rudolf Steiner never had recourse: the direct use of his own powers, which would have been, in a certain sense, magical healing. Certainly for him, who had all the forces of the surrounding world at his disposal in the highest and widest sense, it would have been easy to effect cures by this means. Yet from his knowledge of man's evolution, he had to refrain from such a proceeding as not being in accordance with the age. For him, the highest ideal in our cosmic age was the struggle for freedom. He had no wish to figure as a healer with phenomenal powers. He wished to found a school, and all the methods of healing which he gave were capable of being looked into and learnt.

It would be quite wrong to imagine that learning under the guidance of such a teacher took its course without many surprises and questionings of heart. What was shown here in the way of spiritual revelations and insight into the being of man often brought one to the very limits of one's powers of understanding and endurance. What confronted us in the way of knowledge concerning nature and the cosmos was a unique phenomenon, yet all the time we had to struggle with the question how one's own inadequate self was to attain to such knowledge and capacity.

Considering the charitableness and kindness one knew to be in Rudolf Steiner, his verdicts upon people, too, often came as a surprise. Once when I was treating a patient who was a sub-tenant in a certain house, I asked Dr Steiner what had to be done, since the patient showed no improvement. He replied, 'Yes, it isn't easy to get well if one lives in the same house as such a poisonous fellow'. His wisdom always hit the nail on the head; there was no sentiment in the sane way he faced up to facts. What he said was the very breath of truth, and because it was so, one lived in an atmosphere of complete confidence.

It was this confidence alone that made it possible to learn in a way which differed so essentially from that of one's university. When we did not understand Rudolf Steiner's instructions, we never rejected them, but made every effort to enhance our powers of understanding. In this way our own activity was stimulated to the utmost. When we were working on our patients in accordance with his directions, either by medical treatment, curative eurythmy, massage, baths, or anything else, we tried to understand in each case what he had told us about the connection of the various members of the patient's being and the causes of the illness. If Rudolf Steiner said, 'Here the astral body has not entered fully, do so-and-so,' we learned from the very questions that arose in us as we went about our work. We were all the time sensible of the goading of these questions; thus it was not a taking-in of knowledge in terms of thought, but a learning through the activity of this inner questioning, which led finally to a process of cognition. In our struggle for the answers, we had to change ourselves in order to bring to full understanding what was often alien to us; and if after a time we had the impression that we understood something, unexpectedly a light would arise, illuminating whole fields.

There was one case which occupied my attention for a long time, a patient who came to us with abdominal and intestinal symptoms. Dr Steiner said that this man's thoughts were actually poisoning him, and prescribed compresses of burdock root. This root contains a quantity of oxalic acid, which always has the effect of giving fresh life. After a little of this treatment, the patient, who had been looking very dismal, felt better. If this case is understood with all that has to do with it, including the remedy, it can give the answer to many questions. To learn in this way is possible only when we constantly experience afresh how justified is our unbounded confidence in our teacher. How quickly today medical books become out of date. Remedies that to begin with make a great stir often lose their significance after a few years. Dr Steiner's recommendations are a lasting treasure of knowledge.

I must here put in a word that has to do with Dr Wegman – namely, that nothing I have said about learning holds good for her in the same way. At that time she was already a ripe human being, having had in her work up to then an extraordinary faculty for entering with her feeling into the very being of the patient and into the manifestation of the individual illness, besides which she had acquired great medical experience. The way in which she gave her whole soul to each individual case allowed her to find the right medicament through what Rudolf Steiner called a power of medical Inspiration and Intuition. Naturally, she did not possess his clear vision or his great insight into all the forces of nature, but she could live herself with such intensity into what we might call the picture of an illness that Dr Steiner's instructions appeared to her a matter of course.

It makes a great difference whether we pass on a recipe to a good cook or to one who has little understanding of the art. The good cook will know at once what to do and will not ask how to beat the eggs or brown the butter... Dr Wegman understood in the profoundest sense all that was involved. Out of her deep connection with Rudolf Steiner, which was a matter of destiny, Ita Wegman took her stand, called as she was to found together with him a new source from which healing was to flow.

Out of such inner conditions she was able, after the burning of the first Goetheanum, to ask him: 'Can we not renew the Mysteries of medicine in a Christian sense?' As leader of the Medical Section at the Goetheanum, and working in collaboration with Rudolf Steiner, she was destined to make this a reality. 'All that she begins will spring up and blossom,' he had once said of her. We experienced the full truth of these words in those years of development and growth in the whole of the medical work. An ever-increasing number of patients had to be taken in and cared for, new remedies constantly worked out even if the manufacture of them often made chemists tear their hair. It was my duty at this time to look after the patients in the newly acquired 'Sonnenhof', and also to give special attention to developing curative eurythmy. During the course for doctors in 1921 the principles of the new art of therapy were given, and since then Rudolf Steiner had been furthering and completing his instructions. The year I had devoted exclusively to my training in eurythmy now became an organic part of my destiny. In the treatment of almost every patient there had to be curative eurythmy, often a trying-out of new suggestions. It was wonderful to see how these suggestions were always modifications of the actual sound-movement, to suit the form of the illness and the patient's capacity for movement.

For example, spastic children, such as those with Little's Disease, had great difficulty in making a wide movement because it was then that the convulsions started. I was advised to let them make all movements with the upper arms firmly pressed to the body and to carry out the movements only with forearms and hands. Then everything went splendidly. Curative eurythmy was certainly not an art of modified movement alone; each single movement was prescribed with physiological precision as to its effectiveness upon the existing state of the illness, and thus it became a remedy. Art and medicine in a sublime union.

Dr Steiner required of us complete absorption in our work. He often trusted in us more than we did in ourselves, and this trust awakened forces. Thus, for example, when I had been practising curative eurythmy for a bare two months in the clinic, a request for a lecture on this subject came to us from England. It seems that Dr Steiner had recommended me. I made it clear to him that I was not competent, since I had been practising curative eurythmy for so short a time and also lacked sufficient command of English. His answer was: 'But you are capable of curative eurythmy, and your English can soon be improved.' Some little time after this I concluded that I ought not to be practising curative eurythmy exclusively, but ought to make a greater study of the use of remedies, and I said so to Dr Steiner. 'Have patience, that will come of itself,' was his reply, 'but your destiny is curative eurythmy.'

This medical work of Rudolf Steiner's, which was something so new, embracing as it did the whole man, aroused in a great number of young students eager questions and intensive searching. It was a way of healing entirely in keeping with their own inner conception of their calling. But how was it to be learnt? It was not only a question of adding new methods to those already learnt, but of bringing healing forces to life within one. This was a goal that called for special methods of training and practice. The young doctors sought not merely a deepened knowledge, but inwardly developed powers which could give depth and renewed life to the whole art of doctoring. To the stammering questions they brought to Dr Steiner, he gave answers which can be summed up in the words: 'You are seeking to make medicine more human.' As he always wanted to be sure that everything proceeded concretely from man and was carried through by man, he gave this advice to his questioners: 'Gather together 30 or 40 young doctors who think in this way, and I will give you a course of lectures.' The first to approach him were the medical students Henk and Maddy van Deventer and Helene van Grunelius; we in the clinic took the greatest interest in what would come of this. In January 1924, in direct connection with the Christmas meeting for the founding of the General Anthroposophical Society, the first course for young doctors was held – the first course within the newly founded Medical Section at the Goetheanum. For the whole day and a great part of the night, those attending the course were together, discussing and taking counsel with one another concerning what Dr Steiner had said in his lectures. The whole house rang with fresh, enthusiastic voices. Much as I delighted in it all, secretly I was disturbed lest with this extra work we were not doing justice to the patients in the Sonnenhof and clinic. I confided my fears to Dr Wegman, and the next day through her received a message from Dr Steiner that he was glad the Sonnenhof afforded a meeting place for the young doctors; glad too that I was actively engaged with them. This is mentioned as one example among many of how he had in mind not only the whole but the individual details of it.

Dr Steiner now appeared in the clinic almost daily, generally in the morning. And in difficult and acute cases he was ready with his help at any hour. For a time we had with us a little patient of nine suffering from severe asthma. This youngster went to school at the Goetheanum and was so pleased about everything that he said he was glad to have asthma; otherwise he couldn't have come to Dornach. The asthma improved apace. But one evening – it was his birthday and he had been over-excited by all the love shown him – he had an attack which left him unconscious. We three doctors were busy with him and Dr Steiner, when telephoned, came immediately. He stayed at the clinic the whole night and with the three of us tried to bring the boy back to life. In addition to artificial respiration he constantly advised new measures which we tried at once. It was only at 6 o'clock the next morning – the dawn of an autumn morning was breaking and the window looking east was opened – that we relinquished our efforts; then Rudolf Steiner spoke to us of how it was impossible for the boy to continue his life on earth for reasons which lay in his whole organism. Our work being ended, I offered to bring him coffee, which in his kind way he declined. He went home and was off to Basle station the same morning. He was travelling to Vienna where, in the autumn of 1923, he was to give his lecture-course, 'Anthroposophy and the Human Heart'. Never was he known to spare himself. At times there were very difficult cases which it was necessary to receive because Rudolf Steiner made a point of such patients not going into other hands. I remember a case of mental illness so exacting that it was almost beyond our strength. Rudolf Steiner had promised us help if we were driven to extremities and no longer able to deal with the patient. One evening things arrived at that point. I went to the Schreinerei, where we knew him to be still in his studio, met at the door a strong young Goetheanum watchman, and asked Dr Steiner if we might take this friend down with us to the clinic. He quite agreed, but, in spite of the urgency of the moment, gave us a lesson on always respecting the authority of others. He said he had given over the organising of the watch to Dr Wachsmuth, and we must therefore ask Dr Wachsmuth whether this would be convenient. In the summer of 1923, after seeing the patients, Dr Steiner called Dr Walter and me and told us that in future he would have to put more responsibility for the clinic on our shoulders. This was necessary so that he could do more intensive work with Dr Wegman for the Anthroposophical Movement and for medicine. They had decided to write a medical book together. Dr Walter and I must have looked rather disconcerted, for he added, 'What – do you find that so hard? I thought I was giving you a piece of good news'.

After that the work took on a rather different shape. For the most part, Dr Wegman, after having discussed everything with us in the morning, went off to Dr Steiner in his studio, working there with him till about 11 o'clock. They then came together to the clinic in the little dark blue Ford, generally accompanied by a small shaggy dog given the name 'Mussolini' by Dr Steiner; this little dog was always reluctant to give up his place in the car. Then began the consulting hour.

The amount of work Dr Steiner did was inconceivable. What happened in a single hour was a constant source of astonishment to us, and without a pause in the work, one hour followed another. After the Christmas Meeting in 1923, when his health was already affected, we were always making vain efforts to spare him. The following situation is an example. One morning, already very late – perhaps nearly half-past one – I had still to report on a patient in the Sonnenhof, and I gave an account of several new symptoms. The patient's chief complaints were of pain in the head that ran down into her neck and arm, and a nasty-smelling discharge from the nose. Dr Steiner became more and more serious, finally saying: 'I shall have to see this patient myself.' Now the symptoms did not appear to me of very great importance; therefore my only thought was to spare him, and I said: 'But, Herr Doktor, surely that is not necessary; one really does not see anything.' He looked at me quite kindly but with some surprise, and said with emphasis: '*One* perhaps sees nothing.' Then he visited the patient and saw an extraordinary amount, namely a progressive lethargy of the forebrain, and by the exhaustive nature of what he prescribed, the serious illness was arrested.

I should like to end by mentioning one more incident, because it so often comes back to me when we are exercised in our minds about our young workers being tired. They may feel what I then experienced and have to recover without the encouragement of the teacher. During the Christmas Meeting in 1923–1924, every room, even every corner, of our house was occupied. The stream of visitors from all the various countries could hardly be dealt with. In the Sonnenhof, people were sleeping on any improvised structure, often several in one room. There were scarcely sufficient hands to cope with the most necessary tasks in the sick rooms and kitchens. Hot and breathless, we rushed into the lectures. One day, as I was going up along

the Bretterweg to one of the meetings, I thought to myself how terrible it was —
such a world-historic moment, and here was one of us, simply by reason of tiredness,
unable to bring to it all her forces and ideas. Feeling guilty and depressed, I toiled
up the hill and entered the hall of the Schreinerei. There I was stopped by those
standing around; they pointed in a certain direction, and as I turned I saw Dr
Steiner coming towards me with outstretched hand. After his handshake all tiredness
left me. With new energy and open-heartedness, one could again enter into all that
was going on.

The completion of the book, written in collaboration with Ita Wegman, was a
great joy to Rudolf Steiner. He received the proofs on his sickbed. The book —
called in English *Fundamentals of Therapy: An Extension of the Art of Healing through
Spiritual Science* — appeared after his death in 1925. A seed was here sown which
bore within it powerful forces of growth. Rudolf Steiner said of it: 'This book
will be able to give only the very first elementary beginnings; we shall have long
left the earth by the time it is accepted as a developed science... What is important
is that everything should have passed through human experience.'

In an age when even in medicine the materialistic world-outlook has more and
more to say, and man's perception threatens to be destroyed by technical and
mechanical diagnosis, Rudolf Steiner with Ita Wegman laid down the first principles
of the renewal of a medicine that has its starting-point entirely in the knowledge
of man. This knowledge does not take into consideration only man's bodily sheaths
that may become sick, but also what the eternal in man wishes to experience, has
to experience, in an illness. With the knowledge of reincarnation and karma as
background, the conception of sickness and healing given us by Rudolf Steiner
can be ever further developed.

The Initiate and the Teacher

Gladys Mayer

ONE HAS THE FEELING that anything one can write descriptively must seem naive and inadequate, everything one leaves out must seem a crime of omission, in recording experience of the great Initiate who lived amongst us, to whom we were privileged to speak, and who is now no longer on the earth.

How would he himself have me write of him? I think he would have me write not at all of him, but only of the work he came to accomplish. Yet in so doing, I must try to recreate the picture of the man, Rudolf Steiner, through whom so much was achieved.

I have in mind the picture of the last time he spoke to us in the Schreinerei at Dornach on Michaelmas Eve of 1924. Every seat was occupied, and we waited in silence, knowing that he was making a great effort, rising from his sick-bed, to speak to us once more. As we heard his steps approaching, about 800 people rose as one and stood in silence until he had taken his place at the lecture desk. It was a last tardy act of reverence and respect for the sacrifice of a life utterly devoted to the spirit. It was a small act, but significant.

Mine was a strange, perhaps unique, experience of him. It is of the Initiate I must write, for I came to him late in his earthly mission, and I was not permitted to speak with him in outer life, until I had recognised him, supersensibly, as my Teacher.

Shattering events in life brought me to Rudolf Steiner. I came, not for myself, but on behalf of others. I came with doubt in my heart concerning him, yet the events which made me seek his help were beyond the competence of any but an Initiate to understand. I needed the advice which I knew he could give, yet a demonic picture had planted doubt in me – doubt not of his powers as an Initiate, but doubt of his genuine goodness. With this demonic picture in my experience, although I never really believed it, I had to approach Rudolf Steiner, not knowing with certainty that I could trust him. For that doubt I can now feel some thankfulness, for this made it possible for me to gain ultimately an overwhelming certainty. I had seen an evil, lying picture of him. By force of circumstance, I still had to come to him for help. He could only help me when the evil picture was completely overcome. So this had first to be overcome by further supersensible experience, before any fruitful relationship could be established.

To begin the story I must go back to 1915, when, among many other books of an occult nature, I read *The Way of Initiation* in the British Museum Library. This was the only one that made a lasting impression. I had a curious feeling as though I knew all its contents already; it was utterly familiar. After seven years packed with intense life-experience, I met this book again, on the book-table at Stratford-on-Avon, during the conference on 'Drama and Education' in 1922. It was Rudolf

Steiner's first visit to England after the war. I picked up the book, and realised in that moment why I had come.

I watched him from a far seat in the great Hall in Vienna a few weeks later, as he was giving the East-West course of lectures. Hearing only an uncomprehended flow of words, for I knew little German then, I could see with a painter's eye the power which streamed from him in his gesture, and saw how the thousands of listeners were roused to enthusiastic response. I took a German copy of *Knowledge of the Higher Worlds: How is it Achieved?*... and lived with it in the mountains of the Tyrol for some months. Friends outside the movement asked me with curiosity what I thought of Rudolf Steiner. I could give no answer. Something new and immense was before me, for which I had no standard of measure.

It was a time of intense spiritual preparation amongst the peace and solitude of the mountains. Returning to England, I was soon plunged into the great karmic crisis of my life. I have to explain this a little in order to make subsequent events intelligible.

The months of intensive study of *The Way of Initiation*, the seven years previous in which it had slumbered in me, had prepared me for what now happened as a kind of Threshold experience in the outer life, of a kind symptomatic of our times. On not only one occasion, but three times in the space of about six weeks, I had to face madness and impending tragedy in my own immediate environment. Twice in this period, on distinct occasions and amongst unrelated people, I had to intervene when a murder seemed imminent, and once to check an intended suicide. I began to ask myself: 'Is the world about me going mad?'

But *The Way of Initiation* had already begun to bear fruits in spiritual experiences which guided me through events of terrifying responsibility, from day to day, and sometimes from moment to moment. I knew the spiritual worlds as reality, and Spiritual Beings as my aid. I received pictured instruction, through which healing was brought to the madness of one friend, and through which I was able to save the life of another. At length, I received the instruction to go to Rudolf Steiner for further advice.

This was not very easy for me. Although my spiritual development was won through Rudolf Steiner's writings, although I knew his spiritual power, yet I had doubts of him. Occult training has its dangers. As Rudolf Steiner has himself so often said: 'Occultism is not to be played with.' My pictures had so far been true, and I owed my inner strength and certainty to them. I had battled with demonic forces in the outer world; now they were attacking my inner world.

As a newcomer to the Society, I had seen and misinterpreted something which took place between Rudolf Steiner and one of his pupils. With that kind of spiritual arrogance which was born of my newly won powers, I judged this incident, and a small doubt formed in my mind. The demons transformed by doubt into picture, and I saw, with apparently equal reality, a hideously evil picture of Rudolf Steiner's face, which was terribly disturbing. Although I never really believed it, yet I could not wholly reject it.

At this stage of seeing, everything depends on seeing rightly, on understanding the pictures and perceiving their source. A sense of truth and untruth is indispensable. I was faced with something like the test described by Rudolf Steiner, in Scene III of his first Mystery Play, when Maria's form is possessed by a demon; but I was not so far advanced as Johannes in spirit pupilship, and let the doubt remain in me as a question, never as an actual unbelief, but as an unuttered question. It was in this state of inner uncertainty about him that I gathered up all my resources to go and meet my Teacher.

I was to experience similar demonic pictures again later, after his death, when I saw them as delusory pictures actually destroying his work, attacking his closest friends and colleagues, and, at last, setting friend against friend. But now, at my first meeting with him, Rudolf Steiner showed how these could be dealt with in this particular instance.

I met him frequently for something over two weeks: each time I met him he greeted me with a smile and a warm hand-clasp. Each time I asked him, 'May I come and speak with you?' he put me off with the reply: '*Frage mir nochmal* (Not just yet).'

Friends in Dornach told me this did happen sometimes, and of course it had a reason. I was willing to believe there must be a reason, but was utterly baffled as to what it could be, for my doubts had by this time sunk into the background. Meanwhile, my spiritual instruction was going on, but it had developed a new phase.

Every night I awoke about two hours after midnight, and was aware of a continuous experience. At first it was a Star, very distant, that was shining on me: then it was gradually coming nearer, and at length it was a man with a lamp who stood by my bed. By the light of the lamp I was aware of another, greater figure, and from this other one, though I could not see him clearly, came words instructing me in the spiritual understanding of what was going on around me. I was shown, unexpectedly, the concealed suffering in the heart of a nearby friend: it was as though I were lifted up by the unseen Teacher to learn to know, through the Light of the Lamp, what was happening behind the veils of sense appearances.

At length, after about 14 days, I became anxious to know from whom I was receiving such teaching. I had become accustomed earlier to receiving instructions from an unseen Spiritual World. I had been made aware of the reality of spiritual discarnate Beings. But this Teacher was more concrete. I could see him unclearly towering above me, too great, it seemed, to be in any way connected with a human form. I could see the great form, but not yet the face of this Being.

At last, I could bear it no longer: I felt I must know more. I seized hold of him, as it were, with all my soul forces, and challenged him, saying: 'Who are you' Then, as there came no answer, I asked wonderingly: 'Are you the Christ?' '*Nicht so* (Not so)'. Then, because these were German words, a further thought came to me. 'Are you, can you be, he whom we known on earth as Rudolf Steiner?'

There was an instant stillness, and then the answer came softly, '*Ebenso* (Even so).'

I was still not satisfied. It seemed impossible for anyone so spiritually great to be also a human being. So I pressed further. 'Then show me your face,' I asked.

Immediately away to my left, where was situated the studio in which Rudolf Steiner lived and worked, I saw a tiny distant picture of his face and form resting with eyes closed, as is seemed to me, not in sleep, but in deep meditation.

I understood now why I had been kept waiting. I had doubted, and doubt came in through a false spiritual perception. It could be put right only by my seeing and recognising him in truth, in supersensible experience, as my Teacher. I came to him joyfully the next day, and asked confidently: 'Now can I come to see you?

I knew what the answer would be and was not mistaken. When we talked together, I felt that I had known him for all time. I told him of all the terrible and wonderful experiences I had gone through, where earthly disasters had been averted through spiritual enlightenment, yet had eventually left me with responsibilities I felt were too great for me to bear alone; and how these responsibilities had eventually brought me to him. He listened quietly, and one had the impression he made his whole being receptive, soul to soul. Then he explained my experiences with the simple words: '*Dies ist eine karmische Sache* (This is a karmic matter).' I felt enormous relief. Here, at last, is someone who understands, who takes all these astounding events calmly, and is competent to give advice.

He told me I had come another way; and that before he could advise me I must decide whether I would go further along my own way, or would choose to go the way of the Anthroposophical Society. He could help me further along either way, but I must choose first, or his help might bring a great hurt into my life. He told me to go away for a few days and think it over.

I could not easily understand his meaning. His own book, *The Way of Initiation*, and a steady practice of the exercises therein, had brought me to the experiences before the Threshold which are there described. Life had put me through tests of the utmost severity where I dared make no mistake. I knew that my experiences were real and true, and that their truth was not for me alone. How then was my way different?

I had only to put the questions in meditation and the answers came immediately. I saw my way as one in which I could receive the light of the spiritual worlds and direct it in full consciousness to the others, to light them through spiritual darkness; but yet could not clearly see the source from which it came. I saw the anthroposophical way as one in which observation and thinking were gradually raised into a clear perception of the living etheric world, so that thinking became true Imaginations, and feeling was raised to inspired perception in the soul world. This was shown to me in pictures, and I asked Rudolf Steiner if I had interpreted them correctly. When he assented, I made my choice.

It was a difficult choice. I had to sacrifice the further things now in order to retain power to help my friends. Rudolf Steiner gave me meditations to help this. Then he added: 'But I think the Way of the Anthroposophical Society is also yours.' I answered joyfully: 'I know it; I know this is my way, and as soon as my karmic task is complete, I must come to it.' I went back to England and completed my task; then sold up all I possessed and came back to spend all the time which was possible still with my Teacher. I could see it might not be long.

I came only once more to talk with him in those days when he was giving out so much to us all, and at the same time fighting a developing illness. I came to ask how best I could help in the work. He asked, did I want to help in painting? I was trained professionally as a painter, but the Dornach approach to painting through intensive life in colour seemed so far from mine that I doubted if my best opportunities lay there. Painting, writing, speaking – wherever could I best help? I knew only that I wanted to give my life to the Movement. He gave no conclusive answer. '*Arbeiten Sie tuchtig.*' 'Work very hard, then perhaps you can help,' was all he said.

But the experiences in the night continued, and now they were to teach me painting. I had shown a painting, created out of colour as I thought, to my Teacher, and I asked myself: 'How did it look to him?' I saw immediately my own picture, looking hopelessly muddy and grey. 'How should it have been?' I queried. I saw my picture transformed into radiant transparent colour.

I began to work hard at painting. There were few to advise, and Rudolf Steiner's own work had for the most part been lost in the fire of 1923, when the first Goetheanum was destroyed. But I was getting advice enough. What I painted by day was generally corrected for me at night. I discovered, out of my daily experience in painting, a rhythm of seven, in which my picture-imaginations developed out of the colour, and only towards the end of the series revealed their theme.

I did not in this time see Rudolf Steiner, except when he gave his lectures. Nor did I see him in supersensible spheres, but felt his presence continually as my Teacher. Once only, as our paths crossed in the Schreinerei, when he was hurrying by to his atelier, he turned tack to give me a glowing smile, with shining eyes of recognition. I mention this only because it brings me to the last days.

This last summer of his lecturing life was so grand, yet filled with a certain sadness. We could see Rudolf Steiner's physical body fading before our eyes. Yet as we listened to that tremendous cycle of lectures on 'Karmic Relationships', as he lightened it for us ever and again by rousing spontaneous laughter, even when unfolding the most tremendous themes, it was difficult to believe that this individual spirit, which was so amazingly triumphing over physical weakness, could ever really succumb. We did not want to think it. But the evidence grew clearer. I saw him once at dusk, stepping into a waiting car, with no-one near, and I could see the pathetic frailty of the body. I was shocked at its frailty. When he came to the lecturing desk, looking as though all his clothes had become sizes too large for him, one held one's breath, wondering: 'Can he?' Then in five minutes he was dramatizing the leading figures in the French Revolution, so livingly, so convincingly, in his own person, that it was hard to believe he was even ill.

When our Teacher passed through the Portal of Death, and his pupils were, in a way stunned by their loss, I was among those who filed through the death-chamber to take a last look at that well-loved face. I looked long, and memorized it carefully:

the dark sunken hollows of the eyes, the broad magnificence of the brow, the full upper lip with so much love in it, the firm strong chin, the great heart-breadth across the cheeks. I tried to memorize it so that I might never lose it.

That night, I awoke again after midnight from a clairvoyant dream. I had been sitting at an easel trying to draw a picture of *Das Viergetier* (the Fourfold Being of Man). I had been in difficulties over drawing the head. I was told, by a voice behind me: 'Try to remember it clearly.' I was awake now, and knew that the head I must remember was that of Rudolf Steiner. I made a strenuous effort and pictured it clearly. I was told again: '*Belebe es !*' – 'Enliven it.' I made it alive with an intense effort of recollection; I placed the living face, as it was when he had given me that special personal smile of recognition, behind the dead form I had studied. I brought the living form into the dead until they were one... Suddenly he was there in face and figure, a living form.

What he said was for me – a personal gift; but the joy which his presence gave can be shared, for it was one of overwhelming certainty that the Initiate does not die as other men die. He lives on and works on amongst us, sharing with us his abundance of the Spirit. We have lost only the presence of his outer physical form.

I had been on the Gempen hill the day before with some German friends. We had climbed the hill and were resting on the lower slopes; all had been filled with the sadness of those bereft.

Suddenly, after a long silence, sitting in the sunshine together, one stirred and spoke as to a sudden awakening. 'Now,' she said, almost in awe of the responsibility of which she had just become aware, 'Now it all rests on us.'

It all rests on us. It was heartbreaking to see and hear how little we were ready to take up the challenge. The demons grew bold. All our inner uncertainties of ourselves and of each other were exploited. Those who were a little clairvoyant saw the faces of others, even of our leaders, demonically transformed. Doubts were sown abundantly; there were accusations, recriminations; the opposing forces which Rudolf Steiner's living presence had kept in check were scattering confusion among his followers. Once in those first years I heard his voice again, in a kind of despairing wonder: '*Aber, meine lieben Freunde, was tun sie alle?*' 'But, my beloved friend, what are you all doing?'

It all rested on us, the cosmic task which was his task, which he bequeathed to us, and it seemed we were totally inadequate. I saw enacted in Dornach during the next years on a small scale the tragic drama which was later enacted all over Europe. Doubts, confusion, recriminations and suspicions, one of another, and then tragic separation into two conflicting groups. Only in Dornach it was not a war with physical weapons, but with spiritual ones.

I confided something of what I was seeing to Dr Ita Wegman. She listened sorrowfully, and confirmed much of what I was seeing, but she could do little, for she was a principal victim of attacks. But not the only one. I heard whispered around each leader in turn the stories which bred distrust, and which, frequently, I had seen earlier in pictures. It was a terrible time of testing. I asked myself: 'Why does not everyone see that it is the demon-world we should be fighting, not each other?' But the tragedy went on. We were like petrified onlookers, stupefied, as the world was, later on, when the Nazi horrors were taking place.

Occultism is not to be played with! How often do those words come to mind. 'Three steps in moral development to each step in occultism.' It is our own feebleness, our own errors, which we refuse to face, which the demons take hold of, and project distortingly on to the faces of our companions, so that we become blinded to the Divine Spirit which is there in each one of us, at work in transforming the earthly being, and we see only the evil and the failings. We become petrified in seeing the evils at work in the world, and lose courage to recognise that ours is the task to transform these evils.

What has our Teacher given as message from the heights, in the dawn of the Michael Age, into the chaos of the turning-point of the 19th and 20th centuries? As it seems to me, he has given *certainty* of the Spirit, *guidance* to the awakening faculties of spiritual seeing, and *example* of strength, courage and love to attempt the tasks of the New Age.

It all rests on us, and the darkness grows ever darker, the evil powers grow more potentially devastating, and their challenge more widespread. Again and again, our Teacher warned us of what was coming, of the challenge of the demons, which only the awakened powers of the spirit could overcome. It is now almost upon us.

But are we awake enough? The Teacher is there working with us and through us, but he waits always for our conscious co-operation. Never do I know this with greater certainty than when standing before a strange audience, on a public platform, with men who are waiting to hear his teaching of the spiritual world before me; with my own inadequacy strongly pictured in my mind, and the certainty of our Teacher's presence supporting me to do always a little more than I can. Because men are so very hungry for the certainty, the wisdom, and the good, which this teaching, entrusted to Rudolf Steiner out of the Divine Worlds, can bring to our suffering earth.

Religious Renewal

Emil Bock

IN CLEAR sunshine, early on a Sunday morning in August 1916, I was walking from Tegel into Berlin. For two years already the war had been raging; after recovering from a serious wound I was serving as an interpreter. Unexpectedly, I had been sent at five in the morning to one of the big factories in Tegel, where there had been sabotage by French prisoners of war who worked there. The hearings were soon over, and I thought the best way of using the early hour would be to go all the way home on foot.

My feelings occupied by the contrast between the golden solemnity of high summer and the tragic events of the time, I reached the centre of the city. Then I noticed surprisingly many people streaming into the 'New Church', the so-called 'German Cathedral', on the Gendarmenmarkt. I recognised a number of university professors; and it seemed to me as if from every direction representatives of the spiritual life of Berlin were coming together. With eager expectation, but with a touch of scepticism – since I had sometimes attended the sermons of well-known preachers in Berlin – I went in too. I could have no idea that through what I was to hear a curtain would be lifted for me upon a new world. With amazement I looked into a realm which was at once very strange to me, and yet on a deeper level entirely familiar. I had never heard such preaching. The south German voice gave full expression to genuine warmth of heart. But more important still: a comprehensive life of knowledge revealed itself in illumined clarity. A characteristic conception of the world, which could be felt in the background, became more concrete at certain points, in definite statements about Christ and the spiritual world. The sermon was not on a particular text, but gave something of an introduction to St John's Gospel in general.

On the way out I learned that fate had led me into the inaugural sermon by Dr Friedrich Rittelmeyer, who had just transferred his field of work from Nurnberg to Berlin. The question arose in my mind, with a mysterious, strong feeling, of things to come: 'May it, after all, be possible to find a religious message and method of work which would be honestly fitted for our time and strong enough to have a healing effect in our crises?' My working-class origin and education at a modern school, where mathematics, scientific subjects and modern languages were mainly taught, had prepared me for anything rather than the study of theology. I had indeed, while at school, made friends with a number of grammar-school boys for whom it was a matter of course that they would enter the ministry. And there had been no lack of well-meant advice, seeking to persuade me that I should prepare for the same calling. But it seemed to me more and more that it would be the most unnatural thing in the world for me one day to put on the gown of a Protestant minister.

I had no particular calling in mind. But from an early stage I had intended to earn enough for university studies by giving lessons. I hoped to find a place somewhere in the spiritual life of the time where it would be possible, in a world becoming more and more external, to do effective service for inner values. In a general way I dreamed of a renewal of culture affecting everything.

I soon came to know Rittelmeyer personally. The approach of the 21-year-old student in the grey army overcoat gave him, as he often said, a glimpse of his own future; the new generation was appearing, with whom he could begin a new work. I felt that something or someone else must stand behind Rittelmeyer, and I was waiting eagerly for the moment when, in conversation or companionship with him, this riddle would be answered. And then Rittelmeyer spoke of Dr Rudolf Steiner as the greatest, God-sent contemporary. At first this did not convey enough for me to see clearly all that was involved. I was faced by a host of questions. But I was deeply stirred when it occured to me that I had come across the name of Rudolf Steiner once before, in a very peculiar way. About a year before, I had had to examine, in the postal censorship office at the Silesian station in Berlin, the printed post for Switzerland. I had been struck by the innumerable books and lecture-series, bearing the name of one author, Dr Rudolf Steiner, which were sent by the Berlin Philosophical and Anthroposophical Publishing Company to Dornach, where the first Goetheanum was being built. Officially, it was clear, there was no reason for detailed examination of these parcels, or for objections to them, but I was attracted by the endless abundance of writings by this more than prolific author. And the titles indicated subjects not limited to the surface of life. So on several occasions I took such books or lecture-cycles home to my lodgings and read until late at night. I met in them an atmosphere which made me feel that they might open up new, wide horizons for me. Yet I had to say to myself: the time for this has not quite come.

When I again heard Rudolf Steiner's name from Rittelmeyer, the feelings I had had then were re-awakened. And yet – how could I connect the warm language of the heart, in which the sermons at the New Church spoke, with the language of knowledge used in these writings in an almost more than prosaic philosophical style? But my reverence and trust for Rittelmeyer could only be increased when I realised that he, who had been in his own way a master for so long, felt himself as pupil of a genius who was so very different.

I had to find my own approach – and so it must be for everyone, fundamentally speaking – to the new directions of knowledge opened up by Rudolf Steiner. Rittelmeyer attempted to convey to me, in the language of religion, ways of approaching certain fundamental elements of anthroposophical knowledge. Only with difficulty could I understand him. I was not concerned with particular religious problems. Either the field of world-knowledge would open out as a whole for Christian religious life, or everything was in vain. And, with a clarity beyond all expectations, this comprehensive, penetrating vision for world-knowledge was provided. This I found when, in the spring and summer of 1917, I was able to hear Dr Steiner himself.

Rittelmeyer made use of the permission given to him to bring guests to Dr
Steiner's intimate lectures, and took Eberhard Kurras, with whom he had already
corresponded from Nurnberg, and me, both still in uniform. The lectures were
given in the group meeting-room, consisting of three ordinary rooms joined
together, of the Anthroposophical Society headquarters in the Geisburgstrasse, not
far from the Nollendorfplatz. They were attended by about 100 to 150 members
of the Society. Nothing that Dr Steiner described was difficult or strange to me.
One cramping limitation after another, in my thinking and in my soul, fell away.
What a deep breath of relief I drew when Dr Steiner described the new real thinking
in the first lecture we heard.

The cycle then being given was called 'The Karma of Materialism'. It was the
time of the centenary celebrations of the Reformation; Rittelmeyer was giving the
great addresses which are published in the little book, *Luther Among Us*. How often
the thought stirred in the souls of us younger ones that, in the midst of the confusion
of war, a new Reformation was due. And Rittelmeyer, too, sought with us for a
new stage in Christian history. Among the climaxes in Dr Steiner's series belonged
the lectures in which he illuminated Luther's innermost character and destiny. We
began to discern the impulses for the renewal of civilisation which could proceed
from anthroposophy.

On one of these group evenings I could not leave the book table, where lay in
still greater profusion the series of lectures, some of which I had had to examine
as censor two years before. Obeying a strong inner impulse, I bought the Hamburg
series on St John's Gospel, though the last money I had was only just enough. I
have never devoured a book with such feverish enthusiasm as this. I had suddenly
found the bridge between Rudolf Steiner's lectures and Friedrich Rittelmeyer's
sermons. In a warm, golden light the field of religious life and knowledge lay
before my soul. From now on there was no real doubt about the content of my
work in my future calling. But only gradually could I survey as a whole the
unimaginably rich and wide foundations Rudolf Steiner had already given for a
cosmic and human knowledge of Christ and a Christian knowledge of the cosmos
and of man.

After the lectures given in the circle of members, Rudolf Steiner liked to stay
on for personal conversations. The circle was then still small enough to make this
possible. He usually sat beside Dr Rittelmeyer, and the conversation soon passed
from the content of the lecture to the tumultuous problems of day-to-day events.
Sayings which sprang from the greatest anxiety about mankind, and unsparing
descriptions of personalities who were reckoned as great figures in public life, made
a deep impression on us. During this time we could come to Dr Steiner for our
first personal conversations with him, and received advice about our studies, and
guidance for our innermost work upon ourselves.

From 1917 onwards Rudolf Steiner was always to be found in the front line of
a violent battle. Up to the outbreak of war he had used the temporary lull in world
affairs to build up a modern 'Theosophy', a comprehensive wisdom of the

supersensible, with its centre in the contemplation of the Being of Christ. In the midst of the age of triumphant scientific knowledge about nature, a modern spiritual science, in the most exact sense of the word, had quietly come into being, in creative abundance. Light was thrown on the whole mythological and religious history of mankind, with all its documents. And amazing contemporary events in the spiritual world were indicated, which were connected with the approach of Christ and His gradual new revelation in the realm of the etheric.

The outbreak of war had put an end to this quiet, creative, esoteric work. Rudolf Steiner turned clearly and decisively from inner to external things, from the esoteric to the exoteric. This became quite plain when, after the Russian Revolution and the entry of America into active belligerence, the war entered a peculiarly tragic and dangerous stage for all humanity. At the same time in the life-work of Rudolf Steiner, the point had been reached when the full development of theosophy into anthroposophy, of spiritual science into a renewed science of nature, became possible. It was now a question of making anthroposophy practically useful and fertile in the most varied fields of outer life. We younger ones, who had only just become members of the Anthroposophical Society, could become fellow-fighters in the struggle for the future of civilisation.

Rudolf Steiner came forward with the impulse of the Threefold Social Order, which had among its purposes that of rescuing the real mission of Middle Europe, then experiencing military defeat – the mission to show humanity a way into the future, guided by ideas which originated in the Spirit and were nevertheless practically realisable. We were witnesses of the tireless, self-sacrificing endeavours of Rudolf Steiner to awaken the circles of those responsible for political leadership in Middle Europe, and to inspire in them the courage to support real ideas. And after the Armistice he took on the superhuman labours involved in the Threefold Commonwealth movement.

The idea of the new Threefold Social Order could not then be given practical realisation. But from the mobilisation of every effort the new educational movement developed, headed by the Waldorf School at Stuttgart, and soon there were inspiring beginnings of entirely new knowledge, and new possibilities of work, in science, medicine, and several other special fields. On the day after the November Revolution in 1918, I entered the theological faculty. With a few theological student friends, I threw myself into the hope that the evangelical churches would now develop courage for a genuinely free spiritual life – for example, for the separation of Church and State – so that the way would be open for a new, free kind of religious work. We were able to arrange at this time for Dr Rittelmeyer to give frequent talks to student audiences, large or small. Only too soon it was evident that in the Churches everything would remain the same. All the more did we, who saw the approach of a new age of Christianity which anthroposophy could stimulate, search for the possibility of a new Reformation.

Independently of one another, several groups and individuals approached Rudolf Steiner with questions about a renewal of religious life. Not so much the plans of a group of Protestant ministers, as conversations between two young people and Rudolf Steiner proved in the event decisive. A German student, who had been an officer in the war and had been brought into great distress of mind by the course of European events, asked in February, 1920, whether after the Petrine and Pauline form of Christianity, the Johannine form could not now be brought into being. Dr Steiner's answer was that he himself had to bring spiritual science, and could not come forward in any way as a religious innovator. But 'if you, with a group of 30 to 40 like-minded people, carry through what you intend, it would have great significance for humanity'.

Two months later, when Rudolf Steiner was giving his first great course of lectures to doctors, a Swiss woman student, who asked similar questions, received the answer: 'It might well be possible to achieve something even within the churches, if a considerable number of young theologians took possession of the pulpits.' Rudolf Steiner's willingness to help was lively and active, and so the possibility of a course for young theologians was at once discussed: 'In such a course it would be possible to speak much more intimately than can be done at present with the doctors.'

Although Dr Steiner had made it quite plain that he reckoned with energetic activity – thus in the second conversation he had advised that contact should be made with the questioner of the first – both these persons, almost overwhelmed by the great possibilities opening up before them, considered practical steps only a year later, when they met in Dornach. When the Swiss woman student came to Berlin at Easter, 1921, to continue her studies there, what she related in our circle about the two conversations of the previous year kindled so much enthusiasm that we insisted that not one day more should be allowed to pass unused. There were in Marburg, Tubingen and Berlin, groups of young people who had long been burning for what now seemed to be on the way. In the name of about 20 friends, Dr Steiner was asked at Whitsun to give us advice and direction in a course of lectures. As if something for which he had long been waiting now at last came to him in tangible form, he met our request with the greatest willingness, and invited us to Stuttgart for a course, which was to begin in a little over two weeks' time.

From then onwards a wind filled our sails which carried the little ship powerfully onwards. We had to take Rudolf Steiner's words and bearing as implying that we had to catch up much lost time, and that it might soon be too late for the beginning we intended. It was important for us, and surely not without significance in the objective course of destiny, that we had to find among us younger ones the starting-point of our joint activity. Of the 18, with whom Rudolf Steiner met eight times that June, one was 30, all the rest between 19 and 27, half of them younger than 23. Only then, when we had to find in a little more than two months about 10 times as many like-minded companions and bring them together, did we begin to approach older people. Obviously, we were in the closest contact over everything with Dr Rittelmeyer, and reckoned on him as a leading fellow-worker when the time was ripe.

In spite of the almost insuperable exchange problems, at that time of inflation, Dr Steiner, relying on the willingness of friends to help, had invited the circle, which was to be so considerably enlarged by then, to come to the Goetheanum at Dornach for the month of September. Now hectic activity began. Our small circle separated in all directions, in order to get on the track everywhere, as far afield as Mecklenburg, of those who were ready, like ourselves, to devote themselves to religious renewal. And in fact, when in September Rudolf Steiner gave us 29 lectures, there was the most varied assembly of about 110 participants.

Naturally the transition into the inner necessities of a new age of Christianity, as this stood before our minds, could not be made without great difficulties. And so we had soon to overcome hindrances that were bound up with the history of spiritual life. Our aim would not be accomplished if a number of theologians now simply made use of the possibilities offered by anthroposophy for a new understanding of the Bible and of the mysteries of Christ. Rudolf Steiner had opened up for us the prospect that at a time when Christian life had taken the path of intellectual theologising, real religious substance could be quickened again only by a renewal of sacramental life fitted to the present time, and therefore only by the courage to found a new priesthood.

But among the participants in September there were a number of Protestant theologians who had no feeling for the fact that intellectual discussion, of the kind that had become their natural element, meant the death of religion. Through their questions, which were not genuine questions but themes for discussion, they occupied the whole field of our meeting; and so we felt with acute anxiety the danger approaching that we should be held back in intellectual preliminaries instead of going forward to build up a new priestly, sacramental form of religious work. We fought a despairing battle in the intervening meetings, when the questions to be addressed to Dr Steiner were worked out.

For our course the White Room had been put at our disposal, a room for eurythmy practice high up under the roof of the south wing of the first Goetheanum. Before each meeting I fetched Dr Steiner from his studio in the wooden workshop building called the Schreinerei, and accompanied him across to the Goetheanum and up the many stairs to the White Room. From the third day on I begged him constantly, instead of the so-called 'discussion hours' which alternated with the lectures, to give lectures then as well. But he said: 'Be patient; we must go through all this!' As though it were necessary, beyond the personal participation of those present, to give a new direction to a whole spiritual stream within humanity, he devoted himself with the greatest calm to questions which made the younger ones among us impatient and irritable. But we were relieved when after some days he acceded to our request, and, instead of holding discussions, gave lectures which were connected with the questions I had handed to him on the way over. Thus a number of fundamental, comprehensive lectures, inexhaustible in the perspectives they opened up, came to be given.

In the second half of the fortnight, although it was plain that by no means all the participants would have the courage to become bearers of the religious movement which was to be founded, what Rudolf Steiner gave us was an immediate preparation and equipment for priestly work, with sacraments renewed for our time. The future was more important than the present, and so he spoke over the heads of those still caught up in tradition and discussion (they had been given their full due), as if the only persons present were those who would really take up fully into their wills the intentions of the spiritual world and make them into earthly facts. Not that answers to theological questions were not given. The old Dr Geyer, Dr Rittelmeyer's close friend and ally at Nurnberg (Dr Rittelmeyer himself could not be present at Dornach because of illness), said he had always been astonished in what degree Rudolf Steiner was at home in the mathematical, scientific, and historical fields of academic knowledge; now he saw that he was a master in theology too, in every detail; he was really a whole university in himself.

For the circle of those who had made up their minds – we were to begin with not even 40 – a year of intensive preparation followed. Rudolf Steiner was at all times available to us as adviser. It was not quite easy to find the balance between the will of the younger ones, eager to rush forward, and the urging, chiefly by the older ones, that a firm foundation must be laid. In this, too, Dr Steiner helped. He accepted both attitudes as justified, but made quite clear to us that there was no time to be lost.

Among the undertakings through which we hoped to find and win for our work further companions eager for action, there was in particular a conference for theologians held in Nurnberg, on the initiative of Rittelmeyer and Geyer, at Easter, 1922. And in fact several valuable people came into connection at this time with the purposes for which we stood. Through everything that we undertook there went a strong wind of enthusiasm, which we ourselves felt as something given to us. At Whitsun, Dr Rittelmeyer made his farewell to his congregation in Berlin. We pictured that he, Dr Geyer (who was 10 years older) and I (more than 20 years younger), would have the task of leading our movement. And so the three of us tried to prepare the final emergence of the movement in detail. Many of the younger friends had already allotted among themselves the towns where we hoped to find congregations, and were looking round for people who sought what we were to bring.

In September, Dr Steiner was expecting the whole circle at Dornach, so that we might be finally prepared and equipped for our task. In order to achieve the right sense of community in feeling and willing among us, we decided to meet at a quiet place in August, and learn from each other the results reached during the time of preparation. Before these last steps the three of us, Geyer, Rittelmeyer, and I, were able to be in Dornach for a fortnight, to put before Dr Steiner the questions which were still to be asked, before the common starting-point of our work. It happened that this was the time, at the end of July and beginning of August, when the 'World Economy' course was given. We were allowed to attend this course as guests. These days were a rare opportunity to experience the worldwide breadth of view with which Rudolf Steiner suggested new directions for the most modern problems of money and world economy. We were able to have eight conversations of an hour each with him. He answered our questions in the most concentrated way, so that at the end it was as if he had given us a further course, very rich in content. Now everything was concerned with the practical religious work of forming congregations, on the threshold of which we stood.

It was a particular favour of destiny that led our circle in August, 1922, to Breitbrunn, on what was still the quiet shore of the Ammersee in Upper Bavaria. There Michael Bauer, through whom Rittelmeyer had found the way to Rudolf Steiner more than a decade before, and Margareta Morgenstern, the widow of the poet, were living. They had a specially heartfelt concern for our project, and with other friends had prepared everything for us. In a cowshed which had been cleared for our meetings, a room had been arranged and decorated with flowers.

A solemn and joyful sense of expectation united us with such elemental force that even the withdrawal of Dr Geyer could only be a cloud, passing over a brightly shining sun. Something was approaching us that could be felt as a woman may feel when she expects a child. Was not the stable a true element of Bethlehem? The spiritual power hovered over us, for which we were preparing to make an earthly dwelling and corporeal form. It seemed to be reflected in the archetypal character woven into the landscape: the blue lake nearby and in the distance the white-capped mountains. It was as if we had entered a universal Galilee. Further we felt that through Christian Morgenstern, who was near to us as inspiring genius, and also humanly through his wife, and through Michael Bauer, through whose almost completely shattered physique the warm gold of a soul permeated by Christ was shining, whole streams of human history, filled with longing for the Spirit and for Christ, were bringing their gifts like godparents at the cradle of a new Christmas event.

The expectation at Breitbrunn was followed, in the days from 6-22 September, by the fulfilment at Dornach. What happened there so quietly, unnoticed by the surrounding world, lifted us so much beyond ourselves that it is scarcely possible to describe in words the core of our experience. Our circle, consisting of 45 people, including three women, was with Dr Steiner twice every day, often for hours on end. Again the high White Room was allotted to us. But this time the essential was not the receiving of instruction. What Rudolf Steiner gave us was no theological course. In our midst the Christian ritual and sacramental life was born in the form corresponding to the present time, the age of the spiritual soul. Rudolf Steiner was among us with quiet humility and devotion, and at the same time with highest spiritual authority. The time was ripe and our hearts were open; and so he could bring down to us from heaven what the spiritual powers united with Christ, and serving Him, had intended as a gift of blessing for future humanity. We were to go out into the world as bearers of a new priestly mission.

During the evenings of these same days, in the great auditorium of the Goetheanum, Dr Steiner gave the lectures of the 'French Course' – 'Philosophy,

Cosmology, and Religion'. Here a great audience was gathered. Among the many French-speaking people was the aged Eduard Schuré, whom we often saw during the day walking up and down in front of the Goetheanum in friendly conversation with Dr Steiner. The lectures were translated into elegant French, each in three parts, by the well-known journalist Jules Sauerwein. It impressed us very much that every morning Dr Steiner gave him a detailed summary, on clearly written pages, of the lecture that would be given in the evening. We now saw for ourselves how full every day was for him.

There was for us something symbolic in the alternation between the White Room high up under the roof, where we passed the days, and the great auditorium, where we sat among the audience in the evening. Inwardly, we had also to be at home on different levels.

The wonderful structure of the first Goetheanum, having been seven years in the building, was in use for only two and a quarter years between its opening in the autumn of 1920 and its destruction by fire on the Sylvester night between 1922 and 1923. A quarter of a year after our great days, the annihilating fire was first noticed in the White Room. By the grace of destiny, two important stages in the development of our task fell within these two and quarter years. When, after the disaster of the fire, Dr Steiner wrote the retrospective account, 'The Goetheanum during 10 Years,' he mentioned these stages: 'At the end of September and the beginning of October [1921] a number of German theologians gathered at the Goetheanum, bearing within them the impulse towards a Christian religious renewal. The work then done here found a conclusion in September 1922. What I experienced in September 1922, with these theologians, in the small room in the south wing, where later the fire was first discovered, I must reckon among the festivals of my life.' (*Das Goetheanum*, 18.3.23.)

If today it appears to us like a miracle that the inauguration of the new ritual drawn from the spiritual world, and therewith the foundation of the 'Christian Community', fell within the short life-time of the first Goetheanum – all the more was it an invaluable grace of destiny that Rudolf Steiner was able to accompany our work with his advice and help for two and a half years before death put an end to his many-sided labours on earth in March 1925. He never denied himself to us, however great the burden of work which he had to carry, for example, during his visits to Stuttgart. So one or two or three of us, who were responsible for the leadership of the Christian Community, were able to report to him in many conversations about progress in finding congregations, and to ask his advice about the problems which arose out of the work. Through this period, above all, ran the golden chain of moments, when he transmitted to us as a gift of the spiritual world the words which completed our sacraments, as we had received them up to that time, and so made it possible for us to celebrate and shape afresh one great festival after another in the course of the year. When, early in 1923, I received from him in this way the Burial Service for children, he was himself radiant with thankfulness for this special form of creativity, which was at the same time the highest art of

receiving. Twice he came to me on that day – it was during a conference – with
the words: 'Is not the text beautiful!' In the midst of the mighty waves of events
during the Christmas Foundation Meeting in the last days of 1923, he gave us the
words through which the festival of the Epiphany could be shaped anew, and
during the agricultural course at Koberwitz, at Whitsun 1924, the words which
made possible the founding of a Christian festival for the summer solstice.

During the four meetings which the circle of priests were able to have with Dr
Steiner at Stuttgart in the summer of 1924, he was concerned above all to help us
in overcoming the crisis which had arisen for our work through the necessity for
differentiating it clearly from the specific work of the Anthroposophical Society.

Then, a year after the burning of the Goetheanum, came the great spiritual
breakthrough which Rudolf Steiner achieved in the service and through the power
of Michael, the Spirit of the Age and of which the name, 'Christmas Foundation
Meeting', is only an indication. A new impulse was to come into all the branches
of the efforts proceeding from Anthroposophy to bring about a renewal of
civilisation. Towards our work, too, Dr Steiner expressed once again great
willingness to help. He wanted to aid us towards the strongest possible connection
with the newly flowing stream. He said he would like to arrange it that our circle
should henceforth be invited not only once a year, as it had been until then, but
twice a year for a course at Dornach. When we asked for a course on the Apocalypse
of St. John, he agreed with spontaneous enthusiasm. The ideal of concrete
co-operation between the specialised movements, especially between teachers,
doctors and priests, shone before us, too, with a fresh light. Dr Steiner made an
immediate contribution to this by letting individual members of the circle of priests
take part as guests in the medical and other courses. Thus I was permitted to attend
the course which was held to found the work of Curative Education. And with
another friend I was guest at the great Speech Eurythmy course, in which all that
had been worked out until then in this field was summed up and developed further.
In this kind of connection it happened that at Easter, during a course for young
doctors, a request from our side was made to Dr Steiner that he would help us
with the difficult pastoral problems in which co-operation with a doctor seemed
advisable. He at once agreed to give, within the sphere of the Medical Section, a
course for doctors and priests on pastoral medicine. He added that there would
certainly be time then for a few, perhaps two or three, lectures on the Apocalypse,
as he had promised us.

There was something incomparable, almost breathtaking, in the abundance and
character of Dr Steiner's work during the months of 1924 when he was still able
to give lectures. One could see how sore already were his bodily sufferings and
struggles. Sometimes his physical strength seemed to leave him so completely that
his friends, for example in July at Arnhem, were appalled, and acutely anxious
about him. Those who knew of it were deeply struck by the courage – the courage
of a Michael warrior – with which he put before us the developing revelations of
the Karma lectures.

When, at the beginning of September, he returned from England, a large and interestingly composed audience had gathered at Dornach, full of intense expectation. Many special courses, due to take place simultaneously, had been announced. Several groups of actors, together with those concerned with speech production, were waiting for the Drama Course. Nearly all the anthroposophical doctors had come to hear, with the complete circle of the priests of the Christian Community, the course on Pastoral Medicine. Many other friends had come from all directions to share in the Karma Lectures expected in the evenings, and the special lessons for members of the School of Spiritual Science at the Goetheanum. So began the three weeks which, not only in the history of the Anthroposophical Movement, but in spiritual history in general, represented a unique event. Dr Steiner, who said to us on the first day, as if he had to apologise for it, that he had unfortunately come back very ill from the journey to England (he could move only with great physical efforts from the car to the rostrum) gave four, if not five, lectures every day. Finally, including the early morning talks to the building workers, he gave in this short period 70 lectures, each of them bringing in the most concentrated form so much that was absolutely new, inspiring fresh beginnings: so that what was given in these days alone contains substance and tasks enough for working on through many decades.

The overwhelming character of this pregnant development is something that we priests of the Christian Community experienced, day by day, in a particularly definite way, not only because we were permitted to attend all the courses and evening lectures. We had the impression that besides the course which we received with the doctors, Dr Steiner would say something to us about the Apocalypse, but only in a short, concentrated form. Yet our course on the Apocalypse began on the first day and was continued daily, even when the lectures on pastoral medicine were concluded. When we had received such rich gifts for nearly two weeks, I had to undertake the not exactly pleasant task of asking Dr Steiner how long the courses would still last. In many places we already had congregations which reckoned on Sunday services, and we had already once telegraphed to them that our return was delayed. The answer was: 'Be patient for a few days more; then it can be seen how long we shall continue.' In the end the Drama Course grew to 19 lectures, the course on pastoral medicine to 11, and our course on the Apocalypse to 18 lectures. Could we avoid the anxious question whether this might not be the farewell, during which Dr Steiner was endeavouring to give the uttermost possible?

In spite of his great physical weakness, Rudolf Steiner would not be prevented from receiving many of us personally, in order to give advice and help on the inner questions, and also with the questions of health, with which they had to deal. We were able, too, to speak to him several times about questions concerned with the leadership of our movement. He recommended us to complete our constitution by instituting the office of *Erzoberlenker* (head of the movement), and when we asked him to take part himself in the ceremony of institution, he said that he had limited himself consistently until then to advice and help, without intervening actively in what must be done entirely by us, on our responsibility. But since we specifically asked him, he would this time make an exception and himself take a direct part. And so we could fix the place and the time of the ceremony with him.

But it was indeed the abundance of a farewell, in which we had been allowed to share. Immediately after the last address, like a testament, which he was able to give on the eve of Michaelmas Day by summoning the remnant of his physical forces once more, illness laid him on the bed of suffering, and which six months later became his deathbed.

Concerning our ceremony, he sent a message that he would arrange everything for us, so that we could fulfil what was necessary without him within the circle of priests. But we replied that since we had his agreement to take part, which was so important for us, we would prefer to wait until his health was sufficiently restored. Some months passed, during which from all parts of the world anxious hearts sent their hopeful thoughts towards Dornach. Rudolf Steiner continued his work for his pupils and for humanity through the apocalyptic, guiding letters on the 'Michael Mystery.'

In the second half of February 1925, I was able to be for some days in Dornach, and through Dr Guenther Wachsmuth, who belonged to the Vorstand at the Goetheanum and the leader of the scientific section of the School, put to Dr Steiner some questions which had arisen in our work. When he learned of my presence he sent me a message, that I must not leave until I had received what he wished to give me. Two days later I held in my hands the sheets on which he had written the text of the ceremony that was to be held. I received at the same time the proposal that for the fulfilment of this we should call the circle of priests together in Berlin on the day before the conference that we were about to hold there.   The destiny that spoke in this last sign of Dr Steiner's concern moved us deeply, particularly as we were bound to feel, in the fixing of a date so near at hand, the breath of urgent time.

On the 24th of February, Frau Marie Steiner and Dr Guenther Wachsmuth were present in Berlin at our ceremony as representatives of Rudolf Steiner. The thoughts which we sent to the sickbed at Dornach were carried by acute anxiety; but inasmuch as the greatest thankfulness was united with it for all that we had received from and through Dr Steiner, and were still receiving, the radiant spirit-form shone out before us, which showed him to us as the Herald commissioned by Christ Himself. Dr Wachsmuth relates that on the next day, when he had returned to Dornach, he had at once to report, and Dr Steiner was deeply moved by the account given him.

A few weeks later came the incomprehensible news of his death. Never can those who watched during those days and nights by his bedside under the tall statue of the Christ, and who were present as Dr Rittelmeyer held the burial service at the open coffin, and Albert Steffen spoke of the 'Friend of God and Leader of Mankind', forget the earnest, clear reflection of the spirit upon the countenance of Rudolf Steiner. From then on we experienced our task and our missionall the more strongly as one that was accompanied and aided by higher powers.

The Rising Generation

Ernst Lehrs

S OMETIMES CHILDREN have strange dreams of professions and vocations which bring a smile to the lips of an adult, yet if one looks back on them in later years, they appear to be a childlike figurative expression of deeper relations of destiny. The ideal profession of my childhood was 'the Emperor'. I wanted to become an emperor, because I was convinced that being an emperor implied 'knowing all'. For I was unable to imagine that anybody could fulfil the task of a ruler without knowing everything. Even when I learned that only certain people had the prerogative of becoming an emperor, namely the eldest son of the living ruler, I continued to regard the emperor as the representative of the absolutely ideal profession. For I was still convinced that an emperor must know everything.

What I experienced as a young student in meeting Rudolf Steiner for the first time brought back to my memory that long-forgotten dream of an ideal profession which had accompanied my childhood. Here I faced the man whom I seemed to have sought in an instinctive divining of destiny, and who evoked in me the comforting experience that the human spirit is able to ascend to a sphere where it is possible to 'know everything', though, indeed, in a manner different from the usual conception.

Somewhat later, when I had become familiar with the nature of spiritual training in its historical development, I was able to understand why the idea of the all-knowing one had become identified with the emperor in the mind of the child. Echoing in it was something like a primeval memory of those times when initiates, in enhanced states of consciousness, had speech with the all-knowing gods and received their counsel, which enabled them, in turn, to become leaders of their peoples. 'A king should have nothing more at heart than to be as many-sided, as well informed and as free of prejudice – in fact, to be and to remain as complete a human being – as is possible.' That is how Novalis expresses the same primeval memory and the same hope in his essay: 'Faith and Hope, or the King and the Queen'.

It is necessary to indicate, if only in a few words, what impelled me, a student of physics and mathematics, to take part in the anthroposophical course of lectures for students held in Stuttgart in March 1921, when I first encountered Rudolf Steiner and his work. For only so can the decisive effect of all that took place during this course become comprehensible.

The conviction that I was living 'in the best of all worlds', which had become mine as a result of the conventional education before the First World War, had been thoroughly shaken by the experience of war in the front line. When I resumed my interrupted studies, another conviction was shattered: that the scientific method of cognition, as it had been developed by mankind in the course of the past centuries, could enable us to order and handle all human affairs for all times by means of exact thought. For not only had all the nations been drawn into the catastrophe of the world war in spite of their scientific achievements, but this war had also surpassed in cruelty all preceding wars by the application of those very achievements.

Albert Einstein's theory of relativity, then the subject of much discussion and sharp controversy among professors and students, became for me an eloquent symptom of the problems thus haunting me. For the relativism pervading this theory resulted in denying all reality of being and existence to man as man. Nevertheless I felt compelled to accept Einstein's method of thinking as a consistent development of prevalent scientific thinking, whereas all attempts to refute it appeared to lack this logical character. Thus the refutations appeared to me to be of no avail.

Arising out of these premises, a definite spiritual demand in relation to the further evolution of mankind shaped itself within me, clothing itself in the following picture: I saw before me a river, on the banks of which we, existent humanity, were standing. On the opposite bank lay the new land which was to be reached. The question therefore was: how to bridge the river? Knowledge of the laws of nature would enable one to begin to build the bridge, but, at best, to reach only the middle of the river. In order to build the remaining half, a knowledge of the forces and laws prevailing on the opposite bank of the river would have been necessary, and this could be obtained only over there. But how could one get there while the bridge did not yet exist? First of all, no doubt, some pioneers would have to cross the river by swimming. Where could the men be found who were prepared to equip themselves for such a deed? Where were those who could muster the courage for it?

What I read in the programme of the anthroposophical lectures for students in Stuttgart, pinned on the notice-board of the university where I was studying, appeared to me to speak of a willingness to carry out such a courage-demanding deed in the spirit, and so I decided to attend. I was led to recall in my memory these feelings and impulses when, on a later occasion, in summing up what he had said before in various ways, Rudolf Steiner told us young people: 'Anthroposophy is meant to be the great school of courage.'

Besides Rudolf Steiner's lectures and those of his co-workers, the course included daily discussions in the style of a seminar on various subjects. The content of these discussions cannot now be reproduced: apart from the fact that the memory of the beginner of those days fails me here (except for isolated details), there are unfortunately no shorthand notes of those impressive deliberations. However, what did leave an indelible mark was Rudolf Steiner's personal attitude. He was present at all the seminars, listening kindly without immediately taking part. Presently, however, a moment would come when he spontaneously entered the discussion. All that he then brought forward, in reply to a question or an objection, made the members of the seminar realise with astonishment that they were faced with a thinker who was not only fully versed in every specialised field, but could also amplify the existing body of knowledge by offering essential information drawn from his own knowledge of the spiritual side of man and the universe. Whether the question concerned some problem of science, higher mathematics, the history of art, philosophy or anything else, it was just the same: he invariably made his contribution in a quiet voice, instinct with inner assurance, as a friendly offering, thus giving the impression that it took no effort to know and master all this. Here one could recognise a mind which had reached this all-embracing knowledge in a different way from that of accumulating a mass of learned details, exhausting its vitality in the process. Rudolf Steiner lived, as I came to realise in the course of these days, on a higher vantage-point in relation to knowledge; from there he could dive down into a given realm and speak about it as though he had occupied himself with nothing else throughout his life. It can be imagined what this meant to a student who was thirsting for the truly human, and for an understanding of the real nature of man. In this connection it was a special experience to watch how very differently Rudolf Steiner would behave in situations apparently similar in character, taking into account the human background of those who had raised a question. Three examples will bring this out.

Among those taking part in the discussions there were some who tried to draw attention to themselves by praising everything brought forward from the anthroposophical side, but at the same time liked to mention some other spiritual teaching, with the 'good' advice not to neglect it, but to bring it into a synthesis with anthroposophy. There were others who felt the call to disturb almost every discussion, just when it had reached a generally satisfying conclusion, by raising an objection which appeared to be relevant but was not based on personal knowledge.

Towards the end of a discussion on the significance of mathematics for a natural science extended by spiritual science, the conversation touched on synthetic geometry, following a remark by Rudolf Steiner. One of those who took part in the discussion, a representative of the first group, remarked that he was not a mathematician and had no knowledge of higher mathematics, but on the subject of synthetic geometry, recommended by Dr Steiner, he would like to advise the anthroposophical scientists not to underrate the importance of the infinitesimal calculus.

Barely had this been said when Rudolf Steiner stood up with flashing eyes and thundered into the room: 'I don't understand how anyone who has to admit that he knows nothing of mathematics can venture to give us advice in these matters.' The adviser never made himself heard again during the whole course of lectures. Another man, representative of the other attitude, who had come to be quite a burden on all the open-minded members of the conference because of his futile or superfluous objections, raised his voice at the end of a history seminar which had been dealing with the spiritual differentiation of humanity into an Asiatic-Eastern, an Anglo-American-Western and a mediating European group: 'But what about

Czechoslovakia?' he asked. The discussion leaders, certain of being backed by all the open-minded students, were just about to ignore the remark and to close the seminar, when Rudolf Steiner quickly rose to his feet and pointing towards the audience, said: 'The gentleman at the back has raised a very interesting question which I would gladly answer.' He added that he would need about three-quarters of an hour for it, and asked whether this could be fitted in on the following day, which of course was agreed to.

At the appointed time on the following day, Rudolf Steiner addressing a packed audience, gave a survey of the history of the Czech people, going into amazing details, with the aim of making clear the special spiritual task of the Czech, as bridge-builders between the Central-European and the East-European-Slav spirituality. In the course of his talk he repeatedly turned to the man who had put the question, addressing him somewhat as follows: 'You may remember, in such and such a century (the exact date followed) such and such an event occurred with such and such significant consequences.' Or: 'Then your well-known writer (the name followed), in publishing his work in such and such a year exercised a powerful influence of such and such a nature on the evolution of the Czech people.' Listeners sitting near the man thus addressed saw him become more and more astonished. While leaving the lecture-room I passed him accidentally and heard him say, partly to himself and partly to the man walking by his side: 'No, never would I have thought that anyone could know so much about the Czech people.' His 'but' was silenced for the rest of the conference.

A third happening which threw a liberating light on the theory of relativity, so sorely troubling me, was the following. Some representatives of orthodox science took the opportunity of the conference to invite Rudolf Steiner to a discussion on a number of fundamental theses such as the electromagnetic wave-nature of light, the atomistic structure of matter and the relativity of movement. The invitation was accepted. One of the speakers tried to demonstrate the validity of the theory of relativity in a somewhat light-hearted way by first striking a match on a matchbox which he held motionless in his other hand. Then he lit another, this time holding the match still and moving the box across it. Whereupon Rudolf Steiner, quite calmly and with what seemed like a sly smile, replied: 'I would like to know how you would carry out your demonstration if I were to nail the matchbox over there on the wall?'

It was clear: in order to carry out the second method of striking a light, the person holding the match would have to take his stand somewhere outside the earth, at a fixed point in space, and from there would have to move the whole earth, with this building and the matchbox attached to it, across the match. In this way Rudolf Steiner illustrated the fact that, as he repeatedly expressed it, relativity theory operates with 'thoughts one cannot really think'. Among those who represented the views of science was a well-known theoretical physicist, today one of the leaders in this field, who was then at the beginning of his rise to fame. Not long before, I had myself attended, at my university, a course of lectures he had given on the theory of electrons. He now himself entered the discussion and advanced in favour of relativity the fact that for our observation there exists no standpoint from which a cosmic motion such as that of a planet can be observed, except in relation to the movement of some other cosmic object of observation, and that therefore we have no right to bring such a motion into our scientific considerations in any other way than as a relative one. To this Rudolf Steiner gave the following reply. He asked us to imagine two people sitting on a bench in a park, and therefore both in the same state of motion, outwardly; but differing in that one of them is breathing normally and has a normal complexion, while the other is deeply flushed, with his forehead covered in sweat, and is panting for breath. In such a case it would be evident, from observable differences in the physiological conditions of the two people, that one of them – though in this case at a time previous to that of the observation – had been in a different absolute state of motion from the other. And science will develop to the point of observing in a similar way, on the single planetary bodies, phenomena from which it will be possible to read their absolute state of motion.

For myself, this was a moment when a curtain seemed to lift, giving a glimpse into a realm of possibilities of knowledge such as my heart had yearned for. There was the joyful realisation: 'Here is genuine science. Here is no countering of one hypothesis by another; here, limited experience is answered by an actually – or at least potentially – wider experience.' At the same instant the physicist, greatly moved, sprang from his seat, and with emphatic gestures showing his emotion, exclaimed: 'Yes, yes, indeed. If some day that becomes possible, the theory of relativity will collapse!'

For a few moments all was quiet in the hall, then the discussion went on. Although at the time I was unable to give a clear account of it to myself, I had the impression that in the destiny of the physicist's entelechy something had taken place of far greater significance than his acknowledgment or denial of the spiritual-scientific statement. Through an intuitive recognition of his personality, Rudolf Steiner had helped him to gain this, just by refraining throughout the discussion from making the slightest effort to compel his opponents to acknowledge the correctness of his views and the error of theirs. Again and again he simply set forth, with quiet assurance, what a realistic method of observation had to say about the matter under consideration.

The concluding words of Rudolf Steiner's lectures at that conference must be given here verbatim, for one can hear in them a keynote which rang forth again 18 months later in a significantly altered situation.

'It is not my habit to use traditional phrases, even when they have acquired a hallowed character. I prefer to go back always to the unadorned truth. In our histories of literature and culture a pompous phrase frequently occurs, supposed to have been the last words of the dying Goethe: "Light, more light!" Well, Goethe lay in a dark corner of his small room and the opposite window had closed shutters. From all I know about Goethe, I have good reason to believe that these words were simply, "Open the shutters!" But in dealing so heretically with this pompous phrase in relation to Goethe, whom I love and revere, I should like all the same to invoke the simpler phrase, at the close of our study-course, by saying: To you, my dear fellow-students, now that we feel united in the room from which the windows open on spiritual knowledge, I would address this call... Out of the spirit which has brought us here together, I say to you: Open the shutters.'

A year and a half later, in October 1922, young people crowded round Rudolf Steiner – this time not merely to hear about the possibility of a spiritual renewal of science, but in order to receive an answer to essential questions concerning their own development as human beings. And in view of the chaos in human affairs which was then clearly beginning to manifest itself, they also sought guidance for the social tasks of the future. Again Rudolf Steiner contrasted the phrase attributed to Goethe with the real one, but this time in a somewhat different key, characteristic of his way of speaking to these young people: 'Perhaps the words Goethe really said are more apt than the phrase, "More light". The state of things prevailing at the end of the 19th century gave rise indeed, to the feeling, "The shutters have been closed by those who came before us". Then this new generation came along, and they felt hemmed in; they felt, "The shutters which the older generation has closed so tightly must be thrown open". Yes, my dear friends, let me promise you that, although I am old, I will speak to you in the next few days of how we can try to get the shutters open.' These were the words with which Rudolf Steiner concluded the opening lecture of that series of 13 lectures which we called 'Pedagogical Course for Young People', or, simply, the 'Youth Course', a name they have retained (published in English as *The New Generation: the Spiritual Impulses of the 20th Century for the Cultivation of the Inner Life and the Outer Deed*). In many respects this course was an unusual occurrence in the life of the anthroposophical movement, for it had come about through a group made up partly of very young people who had approached Rudolf Steiner directly, ignoring the functionaries of the Anthroposophical Society as well as the active members then living in Stuttgart. Besides this, these young people found themselves in a difficult situation before the course began. During the preliminary conversation between their representatives and Rudolf Steiner, he was told that in their opinion all the preceding conferences and lecture-courses contained too much of the element of programme, and that this was detrimental to the unfolding of individual creative powers. All this appeared to them to have too much of a 19th century flavour. Rudolf Steiner listened to all this with visible, positive interest and promised to arrange the lectures accordingly. Then these young people went off to travel round and kindle interest in the project among those of their own age. Great was their shock, however, when they heard shortly before the course was to begin that Rudolf Steiner, in reply to a query about the actual purpose of this course, had replied that he did not know it either. The representatives of the young people had brought him a variety of requests, but they had not made it clear what they really wanted.

One of us went to see Rudolf Steiner, hoping to hear from his own lips how matters stood. The answer was that as we had told him of our aversion to programmes, he had decided to give the course of lectures entirely without a programme. He had been informed that we proposed to arrange one or two days before the beginning of the course in preparation for our work with him; we ought to use that time for getting our minds clear about the subject of the first lecture. After the first lecture we could take what he had said to us and from out of it find the theme for the second lecture, and so on. 'In this way we will shape the course together, entirely without a premeditated programme.' At that moment we got a foretaste of the inexorable method he was following – throwing us back on our own initiative and waiting for at least a first step from us before stretching out his hand to give us further help and guidance. Never before or afterwards can human beings have been so grateful for Rudolf Steiner's *not* coming as were the young people then gathered together: in the course of two and a half days they received repeated telephone messages from Dornach to the effect that unfortunately Dr Steiner was still unable to leave. This gave us more time to wrestle with the formulation of a subject which would express our spiritual situation. Barely had we found it, when the message reached us that Dr Steiner had left Dornach.

Punctually, at the appointed time, he arrived. But when our subject was mentioned, he surprised us by not appearing to be particularly interested; he merely said kindly that he would first give a lecture which would be of the nature of a welcome and an introduction. In fact, this lecture contained in close-knit structure all the themes which had exercised our minds during the preceding days. Throughout the following 12 days we were never asked for another subject. Obviously in the days of our wrestling something had happened spiritually which sufficed to provide Dr Steiner with a setting for all he wished to say.

The arbitrary procedure of appealing directly to Dr Steiner arose from our feeling that our situation in the anthroposophical movement was a very specific one, forcing us to ask questions which could not be answered profitably by the older members. We also felt that we could not find the help we needed in the existing anthroposophical literature, whether books or lectures. We sought for clarity about our own aims; we wanted to know how we, as young people, could train ourselves in order to become creative co-workers in shaping the new culture which was demanded by progressive humanity. Above all, we wanted to know how one could proceed 'from speaking about the spirit to speaking out of the spirit'; how spirit could stream into the manifold professional activities which were coming to engage us. Then we were exercised by the problem of how a human community could be formed and nurtured in the spirit of our time. As a goal before us, we saw the creation of foundations for a modern 'cultural pedagogy', and particularly a pedagogy for the adolescent age.

Referring to those lectures, Rudolf Steiner remarked later on that, thanks to the character of his audience, he had been able to speak more pictorially than almost ever before. Indeed, lecture after lecture called up a whole series of pictures growing out of one another. He started by dwelling on the inner stress and strain experienced

by young people at the beginning of our century, because the older generation
confronted them with all manner of standpoints derived from this or that philosophy
of life. But all these points of view, he said, had by then acquired beneath them a
crust of ice. The spiritual ice-age had come. The ice was thin, but as people had
lost the sense of weight in their standpoints, they did not break through the crust.
Besides, being cold at heart, they did not thaw the ice. The young people stood
alongside their elders; their hearts were warm. Their warmheartedness was still
speechless, but it broke through the ice. The young person did not feel, 'This is
my standpoint', but, 'I am losing the ground from under my feet. My own heart's
warmth is breaking the ice'. The ice, he said, had been formed out of empty phrases,
convention, and routine – empty phrases, which intruded into spiritual life when,
in the last third of the 19th century, thoughts ceased to be permeated by the soul;
convention, which dominated social life, instead of a real human community coming
into being; routine, which in the practical life of men had usurped the place of
personal commitment.

When Rudolf Steiner used these images, he was not merely giving an artistic
clothing to a fact which could have been expressed in an unpictorial way. What
troubled the young people was essentially an emotional experience which they did
not fully understand. But the life of feeling takes its course on a level of consciousness
which is similar to dream-consciousness. Just as we dream in pictures, so, too, we
feel in pictures, although the latter may not always rise to the level of awareness.
Hence they can torment us. Rudolf Steiner raised these pictures into the consciousness of the young people, as, for instance, when he spoke of *Wissenschaft*
(untranslatable here: the word covers both science and the humanities) as a being.
When one made her acquaintance, when she has been repeatedly introduced to one,
then the recognition comes (in this degree it probably came only to Rudolf Steiner,
who even as a young man could consciously experience what we only dream) 'that
another being has stealthily crept away to one side in a shamefaced manner, feeling
that she was no longer tolerated. But she would still say ,if one felt goaded to talk
to her secretly in a back-room: "I have a name which may no longer be mentioned
in the presence of Objective Science. I am called Philosophy, Sophia: Wisdom. I
take my disgraceful first name from Love (*philo*), and I have something which by
its very name is bound to have something to do with man's innermost being, with
love. I dare not let myself be seen; only in a shamefaced way dare I move about.'''

With words such as these, Rudolf Steiner did not intend to make the young
people arrogant or supercilious towards higher learning and its achievements, or
to dissuade those who studied it from continuing their work seriously. Earlier on,
in fact, referring to a certain tendency in the first youth movement to treat thought
in its pallor in a contemptuous way and to flee from it, he had said: 'Thoughts
are necessary for living as a human being, and we can never dispense with the
thoughts given us by the last few centuries. However, they should not get stuck
in the head, but they should be conceived so strongly that they stream through
the heart and through the entire human being right down into his feet. For, truly,

it is far better if not merely white and red blood-corpuscles, but thoughts also pulsate through our blood. It is right for man to have a heart, and not merely thoughts. *But the most precious thing of all is for thoughts to have a heart.*' It was not science, but the way science was handled, that he had in mind when in this way he characterised the inner experience of the young people.

In the course of these lectures he spoke of the significance of the path leading to the strengthening of thinking, as indicated in his *Philosophy of Spiritual Activity*. In making the effort really to practise what is there called 'pure thinking', one comes to experience that this is a will-exercise, leading right into the centre of man's being. It shows one that ordinary thinking is indeed nothing but an activity of the head; you feel you are beginning no longer to think 'so high up there', but to think in the breast. 'You notice that as the process of thinking becomes more and more an activity of the will, it first wrestles itself free from the chest and then gradually from the entire body. It is as though you had to draw forth this thinking from the last fibre of your big toe.' In this way one comes to feel that 'a new inner man is born who, out of the spirit, can bring about the unfolding of the will'.

Throughout the Youth Course, Rudolf Steiner had repeated occasion to refer to his *Philosophy of Spiritual Activity*, because he wished to bring out the significance of moral intuitions which had to be drawn forth from every individual for the moral life of the present and the future, and because this book indicates the path to this intuitive capacity.

For the fourth lecture he appeared carrying a small notebook. Those familiar with his method of working knew that he possessed a great number of notebooks, dating from all his years of work, in which he was in the habit of putting down thoughts or making sketches. He did this, as he said, not for the purpose of looking up, later on, what had been written down, but because it is easier to remember something the spirit has grasped when it is immediately connected with a movement of the limbs. We young people were deeply touched when we realised that Rudolf Steiner had taken the trouble of going through his notebooks on our behalf in order to pick out one belonging to the year 1893. From this notebook he read us a review of Spencer's *Principles of Ethics* which had appeared in a German literary magazine of those days, where the reviewer had written that Spencer's master-work 'must silence, at least in the realm of exact knowledge, the last attempts to found ethical discrimination on intuition, inborn feelings, even self-evident axioms, etc'.

Then he began to describe how he had had to place his *Philosophy of Spiritual Activity* right into the ethical mood of that time – this book which shows that 'the whole future of human ethics depends on the power of moral intuition becoming stronger every day'. When he described from various aspects his own radical opposition to the prevailing views of that period, the inner struggle he had gone through at the time became more and more movingly evident. What can be read today in the clear and smoothly running report of this lecture should be pictured as having been uttered in tones of vibrant emotion. There he stood before us, once again a man of 32, who, out of a self-imposed duty of service to his time and because of his spiritual insight into its needs, faced his contemporaries in complete loneliness and boldly raised his voice against the ever-rising storm of materialism.

The inner drama he had gone through, while to outward appearance sitting quietly in a Vienna café – this came before us at that moment in bodily reality. There he was, standing at the balustrade of the platform, with shining eyes, his right hand holding his notebook, and hammering thunderously on the balustrade, while with a voice that filled the entire hall he called down to us: 'It was therefore necessary for me, my dear friends, to make the attempt to write a book representing, in a most determined way, the very standpoint which was described by men of learning, in an equally determined way, as one that should be finally silenced.' The 'search for the hero', so often mentioned in the youth movement here found fulfilment; here the heart of youth, oppressed by the troubles of the time, found its hero of the spirit.

We went home after this lecture without saying very much to one another; the experience had stirred us to our depths. Many among us may have pledged themselves silently to follow in Rudolf Steiner's footsteps in the unfolding of courage, in soul and spirit, on however humble a scale. Later on we were to learn more exactly the actual character of this courage. It was the courage to say to oneself, 'The life of the world must be made new again from its very foundations'. And certainly, 'Courage – one learns it very quickly, or not at all'.

Our question, 'How can we learn to progress from speaking about the spirit to speaking out of the spirit?' was answered by Rudolf Steiner during the Youth Course, and subsequently, by simply demonstrating it in practice. The word 'simply' is meant in the sense that he often took the apparently simplest examples, thus illustrating what in the 1924 lecture course, which laid the basis of curative education, he called 'reverence for little things'. Almost daily, too, he met us apart from the lectures, entering into the manifold needs of those taking part in the course. There were young sculptors who showed him samples of their labours, in order to seek advice for future work; poets who received from him individually the most varied indications concerning rhyme and rhythm. Daily he came to the recitation lessons provided by Frau Steiner, gave speech-exercises, explained the vowels and consonants, and on two occasions even recited to us himself. Because an interest in painting had arisen, he gave a few painting lessons. Finally, he was present at some of the discussions which the members of the course had arranged among themselves. During one of these discussions, a young farmer spoke as best he could about the being of the Christ. Although he expressed himself rather awkwardly, we listened to him with a certain respect, due above all to his subject. But as he went on and began to speak of what his experience in farming had taught him about manure, we turned up our noses with the feeling that Dr Steiner's presence should not be claimed for such 'vulgar' matters. The next day those responsible for running the course had an interview with Rudolf Steiner on some special points. He asked for the name of the farmer and said to our surprise: 'What the young man said about Christ was fairly insignificant.' Then he added, with friendly emphasis: 'But what he said about manure was excellent.' He would like to add something himself to it at the next meeting. (The course of lectures which founded biodynamic agriculture had not yet been given.) The following is an attempt to record not only what he said at this meeting, but also his manner of speaking:

'It was interesting what you said yesterday, as a farmer. I have no time to stay here much longer, so I will briefly add the following. In agriculture, too, the spiritual is being sought. There, too, it is believed that new methods should be found, right down into the handling of material substance. If you turn to modern materialistic science, you will not find much affection for agriculture. Modern science holds that in the case of a field needing so much nitrogen, one must put this quantity into it. The scientists are not aware that one need only plant sainfoin [*Onobrychis sativa*] systematically round the field in order to draw in the right amount of nitrogen by radiation. It would be enough to plant a single row of sainfoin all round the field.'

A brave man among us, who did not know what sainfoin is, asked about it. Dr Steiner immediately replied, and in such a way that we felt he was not speaking 'about' this plant, nor as though it were absent, but that through the intimate tone of his voice, the pondering attitude, the movement of his hands, the immediate spiritual presence of what he was describing could be experienced deeply and impressively. It was as if the sainfoin actually came into being through his words and gestures. Perhaps one might try to catch an echo of this experience from the following recorded words: 'Sainfoin... they are plants... they have flowers that grow in clusters... butterfly-shaped flowers... they are pinkish-red... the leaves are feather-like...' And then: 'This plant has the remarkable capacity to permeate the ground over a considerable area with what human beings are trying to introduce into the soil artificially. Do you believe this is nonsense? No. These are indeed things which can be recognised if one is able to penetrate into matter by means of definite spiritual knowledge right into the material realm.'

The scope of an essay such as this is limited by the space available. Much of what was experienced in connection with the great addresses to young people which followed in the years 1923–24, and during my own life as a Waldorf School teacher, must be left out. There is room only for a few aspects which are as valid today as they were valid then. Their significance for the young people now growing up, as well as for the coming generations of this century, will indeed increase continually.

The older generation usually tends either to criticise and reject the rising one, or else tries to win it over to its own side and for its own aims. When some of the young people brought their questions in a corporate way to Rudolf Steiner for the first time he responded so readily because the spiritual background lay open to him – the background whence the new generation had started on its way earthwards, and whence all the following generations would proceed. He saw that deep in the souls of these young people there was living something new in the history of mankind. He knew that what was 'rumbling' in them had great possibilities, but that it could also involve great dangers if the right guidance were lacking. His first step in this direction was to help the young people to become conscious of their own inward tendencies. He emphasised repeatedly that the opposition between young and old, which at the turn of the century had emerged for the first time on a large, organised scale, was different from anything of the kind that had arisen previously (referring to the German *Wandervogel* movement which arose in 1899 and, together with its successors, played a significant part among the rising generation up to the First World War).

As he told us in his address to young people gathered at Arnhem in Holland in the summer of 1924, it had been quite clear to him from the very beginning of the youth movement that 'in the deepest subconsciousness of the great majority of the young people of the present day there lives a tendency towards a remarkably thorough understanding of the fact that a great earthquake-like revolution in the entire development of mankind is bound to take place'.

We are in the habit of associating definite, clearly outlined ideas with certain centuries, as when we speak of the two phases of Renaissance painting, designating them simply as Quattrocento and Cinquecento. We speak of the 20th century and connect with it a certain way of thinking which differs from that of the 19th century. To the spiritual penetration of Rudolf Steiner the turning-point between the 19th and 20th centuries revealed itself in a far deeper sense as something very special in the history of mankind. This turning-point is connected with a unique change in spiritual conditions, not only on earth, but in the whole cosmos – that is, the world in which the human soul dwells before birth. It was this change which made it possible for Rudolf Steiner to begin his teaching work from the moment of that turning-point – as, in fact, he did. Naturally, it sounded presumptuous to the older people when the human beings born at that time described themselves as 'totally different people'; in reality it was a stammering, a begging to be taught to understand themselves, the human beings whom they felt to be 'totally different'. Rudolf Steiner saw what was trying to break through. Since the turning-point these souls had indeed been bringing down to earth, in the depths of their will-nature, an urge towards the spiritual – an urge which, if it fails to find its goal, is bound to manifest in pathological ways: in organic defects, in mental disturbances, juvenile delinquency, political mischievousness. Because Rudolf Steiner foresaw all this, he took every opportunity of lending his ear to the questions of the young people about their problems, of talking with them and addressing them in impressive fashion, so as to bring to their consciousness their historical responsibility. But as with him everything was kept in true balance, he allowed those who came to him to experience also a necessary damping down of premature aspirations, or, at least, a correction of their impulses. Some of the foregoing accounts provide examples of this.

There was still another anxiety which one could hear in his words when he spoke to the young people. The human soul is not given its character only by what it brings with it from pre-natal existence as unconscious memory and the subsequent impulse for earthly life. It is affected also by everything that comes to it from environmental influences, especially education and upbringing. Frequently Rudolf

Steiner had to help to clear away 'the senile foreground' in the souls, so that the 'juvenile background' might come into its own. When he experienced how young people, thinking that they ought to talk with special 'cleverness' in his presence, got themselves entangled in abstractions; when he felt that their souls were too heavily burdened and oppressed – and every soul suffers from this in one way or another today – his kindness was instantly ready to help in overcoming such hindrances.

It is against this background that we can understand on the one hand his great addresses, charged with stimulus, and on the other the humorous stories and anecdotes which were never absent from his talks to young people, sometimes occurring in the midst of the most fundamental expositions of world problems. They embodied some essential thought in a way that brought it into direct contact with life, making it the very reverse of an intellectual abstraction. How readily did he let his eyes twinkle in warmhearted humour – while perhaps at the very next moment he would seem to be gazing out with lofty earnestness, far over his audience, as into cosmic distances.

In the last lecture of the Youth Course, Rudolf Steiner gave to us – and thereby to the young people of our whole epoch – the crowning picture of the course: Michael's fight with the Dragon. It is the picture for the struggle of the spiritualised intelligence of man against the power of materialism and all its effects – killing men, devouring men. In older times, too, this picture was known and given outward expression, but in those days it had a prophetic character and was intended as a pointer towards what was to be expected in the future. Today the struggle has become acute. In theories such as that which recognises in man nothing but the final stage in the sequence of animal development, or in the theory of the conservation of matter and energy which prevails in physics, the spiritual signature of the Dragon of our time is revealed. For through these theories 'the way to the truly human is closely barred'. But 'the Dragon must be conquered, and therefore people must come to understand that the picture of Michael conquering the Dragon is not only an ancient picture, but a picture which has attained its highest degree of reality in our own time'.

Rudolf Steiner then transformed this into another picture which is entirely new – indeed, one can say that it inaugurates a new mythology for mankind. In the imaginative speech of old, the 'chariot' repeatedly played an important part. Elijah was seen ascending to heaven in a chariot of fire. The sun-god was experienced as driving across the sky in a chariot drawn by fiery steeds. And now Rudolf Steiner revived this image for what he wished to impart to the young people – the picture of a chariot, but of one coming from the spiritual world into the earthly world. Once more he spoke of the forces in man which he brings from his pre-earthly life into earthly existence, forces which work on the child and continue to work on him and to reveal themselves through him as he grows up. 'This is a reality which, if we cherish and nurture it, will become for Michael the chariot in which he will enter our civilisation. If we educate in the right way, we are preparing the vehicle for Michael, so that he may enter our civilisation.' To fashion the vehicle for Michael means being able to become a companion of Michael. 'And you will best achieve what you want, my dear friends, by becoming conscious that *you want to become the companions of Michael.*'

Thus the new generation of our time, the generation of yesterday, today and to-morrow, was given its sign – the sign from which the impulses for its spiritual tasks are seeking to flow.

One of the Young Doctors

Kurt Magerstädt

IN 1921 I HAD GONE TO STUDY in Tübingen. At that time there were few vacant rooms in German towns, or only very expensive ones, and as I could not spend much money I had taken up my quarters in a neighbouring village. I had to go on foot a fairly long way every day to the university, and as I walked along in the dusk between the lime-trees of the avenue, I put a question to a quite definite star which I did not know at the time to be Sirius. I asked: 'If there is a spiritual world I should like to know something about it.' I was interested at that time in Swedenborg's writings, especially his Heavenly Jerusalem, and this may have ultimately prompted the question.

One evening – deep snow had fallen, the stars glittered in the sky and I had stayed late in the university library because I had no coal at home – I put my question more intensively than usual and in the night I had a dream. I heard these words spoken by a member of the family who was dead and whom I had deeply revered: 'Pay attention to the next three days.' With these words I awoke.

Two or three days later I was in a group of theologians – how as a medical student I came to be there I no longer remember – and heard a tall young man give a lecture. It was on anthroposophy and new theological knowledge; it appeared, moreover, that there had been two Jesus-children. The speaker was named Emil Bock, and the student who sat next me and then lent me Rudolf Steiner's *Philosophy of Spiritual Activity* was Kurt von Wistinghausen. Inwardly I pricked up my ears; was it to this that I had to pay attention?

About a year went by. I moved to the Rostock University and was one day called upon with another student – as was customary with the seniors – to attend a Polish peasant woman at the birth of her child. The child did not come; a whole night was spent in waiting, and during the night my fellow-student – Heinrich Hardt – told me about anthroposophy. We struck up a friendship and a few days later he said to me: 'We will go presently and meet a colleague who has just been in Dornach.' As we stood on the platform after our work, the man we were expecting got down from the train and Hardt introduced us: Manfried v. Kries – Magerstädt. 'What is your name?' asked Kries in astonishment, 'Magerstädt? You are the one I was to look for.' 'How is that?' I said. 'Because,' he said, 'it has struck some of us that you are on the look-out for something definite. If you had not been here now, I should have asked for the list of students and gone to find you. I was told that you belong to the group that is to travel to Dornach.'

I was trying at that time to fix up my doctorate work and had come to Rostock because the university there seemed the most likely to accept the theme I had set myself: Iriscopy, diagnosis from the eye. It naturally interested me now to hear that Rudolf Steiner had also worked for his doctor's degree at Rostock University, and in all simplicity I wrote to him that as I was invited to Dornach for the coming Medical Conference, I would make so bold as to consult him about my work, and thereupon I gave an account of my idea of the threefold membering of the eye. Our course was to begin early in January, and we started in advance – it was 1923 – for the Christmas Foundation Meeting at Dornach. We Germans came out of inflation and Depression into the well-ordered conditions of Switzerland, and those who had grown up during the World War – I had been a volunteer – had their first fully conscious experience of a land of peace. On the Dornach hill, however, stood the ruins of the burnt-down Goetheanum, prophetic symbol of the countless ruins which Europe was to experience.

It was swarming with people. One saw an amazing number of interesting faces, the most peculiar individualities. For the first lecture that I was to hear from Rudolf Steiner I found a seat on the stage of the Schreinerei, behind the speaker's desk, in order to be able to observe everything as closely as possible. From here one looked out over the throng who sat and waited. Finally there arose a general movement, faces turned to a doorway... Was it a youth who came striding in? Everyone has his own way of walking, one person bobs up and down, another pushes forward with his head, another has his nose in the air – and here one saw a man calmly advancing who from the distance looked like a youth; one could only say of him that he walked with resting head. He greeted one or other person with a movement of the hand, with a glance of the eyes or a nod, and then he came on to the stage. All I could think of was – What a walk, what a carriage, this man has! That was my first impression of Rudolf Steiner.

Like many homeless souls, I had sampled all sorts of groups, such as the Wandervogel, the Eucken-Kreis, the Lhotzki circle, the Kloster-Beuron, and nowhere had I found a satisfying conjunction of action, thought and speech. Here now was a complete human being. Nevertheless, since many negative experiences had made me cautious and critical, I exercised the skills which I fancied I possessed in order to see through any possible artifices. Up to a point I was familiar with palmistry, physiognomy and graphology. So I sat there and took careful note. I studied the face, tried to see the lines on the hand when Rudolf Steiner raised it... Who is this man? I asked myself. Never before had I seen such lines. It was a full firm hand, the hand of a sculptor, the first finger almost the same length as the middle finger; Jupiter and Saturn, as one was accustomed to say, developed in equal strength.

Then, at an unexpected time, I came to the conversation I had hoped for. Rudolf Steiner stood in the light, I in the darkness. I was struck by his wonderful iris, an iris that shone differently in every light; at the moment it was amber-coloured. Then I had a peculiar experience. I must have observed too closely and without the right respect, and was wordlessly rebuffed. I felt it like a blow that went right through me. It was a repulse and seemed to say: No, not like that. The spoken words, however, were: 'I have received your letter and now that I know you I can say: You can become a university professor – or you can become an anthroposophist.' I was speechless. This was truly no answer to a student's question about his doctorate thesis; yet it was one of those answers which one has to puzzle over for a long time. Moreover, after his unspoken rebuke I had at the same time an overwhelming realisation. I knew spontaneously: I who have felt homeless, this is my home. Here I belong. This home was connected intimately with the personality of Rudolf Steiner. All that is good and fine of which a 24-year-old is at all capable came powerfully to life within me.

During the next three days I heard all the lectures that Rudolf Steiner gave, sitting at one time on the right, at another on the left, or behind, or in front. The figure of the teacher appeared to me immersed in a coloured spirit-atmosphere, and I could not so quickly give up my habit of wanting to test everything. The impression remained unchanged. The people, too, whom I encountered, revealed immediately the fundamental nuance of their soul and spirit. It was an experience that grew too much for me; I could hardly bear it. One day in this mood and for no particular reason I went up to the Schreinerei. There around the corner came Rudolf Steiner. 'Well, are you going to be an anthroposophist?' 'Yes', I replied. He gave me his hand, and with this handclasp all the peculiar experiences of the last few days were taken from me.

During the Christmas Meeting I had taken over the night-watch from one of the watchers (the watch was a precaution prompted by the burning down of the Goetheanum a year before). By night and sometimes also by day I now walked round the grounds. Once I had to take duty between midnight and 3 a.m. From my post I could see the Villa Hansi, where Dr Steiner lived, and was aware of the light burning in his room. As I was relieved at 3 o'clock it went out; but when for some reason or other I went over to my quarters in the Sonnenhof an hour later, I saw that it was already burning again. So he had slept for only one hour.

When the conference was over, the course for young doctors began in the early days of the New Year. And now all the questions and longings that I had carried within me found their answer. Until then I had not seen my way in the world. To be sure, I had got through my first medical examination quite well, but through my study of medicine had not the human being become more than ever a mere pieced-together, mosaic picture? The idea of the archetype of man was lacking, and since I had not found this, the real human relevance of my studies was also lacking. Now, for the first time, I gained a picture of man and so, too, of the universe. Until then I had been a stranger on the earth, even though I had often been in the mood for all sorts of frivolous nonsense. Sometimes I could take myself by the ear and ask: Man, how do you come to be here? Are you really you? Now, for the first time, I felt myself truly incarnated and awake; at last I had found the wholeness of universe, earth, man. I was a blind man whose bandage had been removed, who looked round and rejoiced: 'Oh, how beautiful it is in the world. Spirit and nature are one.' All at once I became happier and healthier.

A second course for young doctors was promised for Easter, 1924. Heinrich Hardt and I were in the middle of the state examinations, between two sessions, but we could not resist travelling from Rostock to Dornach for at least a few days. Coming from the north, where there was still hardly a hint of spring, we plunged into the superabundantly blooming garden-world of Dornach. We walked through white cherry-tree clouds along the Bretterweg to the Glashaus, where the windows for the first Goetheanum had been ground. We could not stay till the end of the course; the date of the examination was unalterable. I was overcome by the feeling that if I could take leave of Rudolf Steiner personally, I should be able to do everything. It was difficult to get near him, so that in the end I had to push rather forcibly through rows of colleagues, but it was successful; I could say adieu and thank him. The same afternoon we got back to Rostock and the examinations began in the evening.

This time in Dornach, amidst all the causes for happiness, there had been moments full of unexpected deep anxiety. In my love for my new-found teacher I began to notice everything carefully in a new way, and thus I saw that his bodily forces were lessening. When he came up to the Glashaus, there were no longer the even, winged footsteps; the head no longer sat on a poised body. These moments, however, were quickly supplanted by opposite impressions, and I could hope that I had been deceived.

The state examination was over in May, and after my graduation I began to work as a doctor in a nature-cure clinic at Jena, where my friends Loffler, Strohschein and Pickert were on the point of creating the first Home for Anthroposophical Curative Education at Lauenstein. When Rudolf Steiner came in June to open it, I was able to be there. During a pause between the meetings I presented myself to him as he walked in the garden. I thanked him for the fact that one could cultivate a right nature-sense again, notice whether one were walking on flint or chalk, how the flora reacted to this or that, what animal life was present... And how one could now arrive at results; if one puzzled over a problem in the evening, the answers would come in the morning. 'Yes, Magerstädt,' he said kindly, and smiling a little in jest, 'The Lord gives to His own in sleep.' Then he became serious. 'In the night, thoughts are accepted, or not. If they are right, it is possible to come to results; one finds remedies and so on.'

A pupil of the home came up with a little Kodak camera in his hand and asked Dr Steiner if he might photograph him. This was agreed, and in the silence I was already looking forward to the snapshot (of which, unfortunately, nothing came out). Rudolf Steiner invited the boy to take a second snap, but for this he would have had to fetch another film from the house, and now the child's will was negative – he no longer wanted to do it. Dr Steiner pointed out how this incident already provided a certain diagnosis – namely, that the child was failing to bring his interest down into the metabolic-limb system, because his etheric and physical bodies struggled against it. In the Curative Education Course he would return to the case of this child in detail; I had decided, however, on the spur of the moment to take advantage of the precious time and remained at his side. We walked slowly out of the garden and passed a lime-tree that had a large protuberance in the wood. Rudolf

Steiner pointed to the tree, which, as he said, was not developing vertically, but horizontally, away from the direction of growth. He would like to have this excrescence, he said, if someone would cut it off for him, so that experiments could be made with it in the Dornach laboratory. When I asked in what way, he replied that the wood would be reduced to charcoal and then worked on further.

I was anxious to take up one of his remarks during the midday meal. He had mentioned how all the men who had brought about movements of some importance in Jena – Schiller, Goethe, Fichte, Haeckel – had come from outside, and my local patriotism as a Thüringian thus came off badly. Even if the Thüringians, I said, had set going no great events, yet they were very strongly connected with nature and had a special relation to the art of healing. 'Yes,' he responded, 'the link with nature and the relation to healing are there; it was not without cause that Goethe laid his Brocken scene in the Thüringian landscape – he could as well have chosen the Inselberg for it. A connection with the elemental spirits can be found all over Thüringia.'

We were walking now on a road high above the valley of the Saale. A lovely blue early-summer sky spanned the day, and I could see how profoundly Rudolf Steiner's senses were open to all the beauty around. Might I still put a few questions? I enquired, and he assented with fatherly kindness. 'Here is the wild rose,'? I said. 'The nature-cure people say they use the inner part for stone in the kidney.' 'Yes, that is quite true, but look at the red rind of the rose-hip. it has been reddened by cosmic astrality. Make a decoction of this rind...' He explained in what way the fluid should be used in order to be 'a wonderful remedy' for kidney complaints. Then he stooped down and from the wayside took a leaf from the rosette of *Plantago major*, the broad-leaved plantain. He divided the ribs and took out a tiny piece about the size of a square centimetre. 'If you put 10 or 12 such bits on the salad when it is made, you have a good blood-purifying remedy for the children of Lauenstein.' 'Then what is it that is active in the broad-leaved plantain?' I asked, and to my astonishment I was told, 'Manganese.'

After that we spoke about aesculin and the horse-chestnut, and now I felt I could ask if there were anything in the alchemical methods of the Rosicrucians, the way they made remedies? Personally, I did not like alcohol in the homoeopathic potencies. I had the impression that remedies became too strongly mummified. He went into this question with great warmth: 'Undoubtedly this is quite an important matter. One must make a plant extract at a temperature of 37° [98.6° F]. The 37 degrees is a cosmic heat-entity. If you make an extraction of portions of a plant – leaves, flowers or whatever you like – for one to three days at 37 degrees, you get 'a very good remedy.' (Later on various remedies were developed on the lines of this indication.) 'Here is cow-wheat,' I said, 'with its two complementary colours – the corona yellow and the flower itself violet: how is such a thing possible?' Rudolf Steiner answered: 'That I cannot tell you at the moment.' This was an example of the way in which Rudolf Steiner investigated such things; if I could have been with him again the next day, the answer might well have been given.

All anxiety about the beloved teacher had vanished that day; my worries at Easter seemed to have been unjustified. Although he kept to a strict diet, he was fresh and apparently quite unburdened. And when we came again to Dornach in September, that month in which he gave over 70 lectures, and I was able to attend the Drama Course as well as the one on Pastoral Medicine, there was nothing unusual to be noticed. The question seemed much rather to be: How can *we* endure all that is offered us? In unfathomable fulness the Spirit streamed forth. Every domain which Rudolf Steiner touched became as fresh as dew. Every aspect was completely new: there was no repetition, either in the formulating or in the train of thought. An overflowing spring poured out its blessings for us. We drank, and did not guess that we were seeing our Teacher for the last time in his earthly body.

The Beginnings of Eurythmy

Lory Maier-Smits

D URING THE WINTER MONTHS of 1903 my mother heard Dr Rudolf Steiner speak for the first time in Dusseldorf. It was a public lecture given in the largest concert hall of the town. My mother, already a member of the Theosophical Society, was so strongly impressed by the personality of the speaker, by the style and content of the lecture, that she approached Rudolf Steiner with the request that he would come regularly and give lectures in Dusseldorf. So it came about that he was a guest and spoke in our house once or twice a year from 1904 onwards.

I was 11 years old when I saw him for the first time. To my sorrow, he addressed me from the first as *Sie* [which means 'you'; in Germany it is customary to say *Du* – thou – to younger children] because 'that is what one does in Austria'; I greatly envied my younger sisters whom he often played with and took on his knee. To make up for this, however, I was allowed as early as 1907 to come and listen to a lecture in the room, after he had apparently observed that my listening at the door was not merely a sign of curiosity and love of sensation. I still remember clearly that he spoke about the Rose Cross, and about the two black beams lying in the same directions of space as the human and animal spine, about the red roses, the chaste and passionless blood of the plant; about man, who, because of his desire-enfilled blood is, at it were, crucified on these black beams, and has the possibility and the duty to work in such a way as to transform and purify his blood (compare the description of the Rose Cross mediation in *Occult Science: An Outline*). In November 1911, my father died quite unexpectedly, and two weeks later my mother travelled to Berlin to see Rudolf Steiner after he had expressed his sympathy in a telegram – 'My thoughts are with you' – at a time when he could not have received the news either by telegram or by letter.

She had to wait awhile in his Berlin flat in the Motzstrasse, and while doing so entered into conversation with an acquaintance who told her that her daughter was very happy and successful as a teacher of the Mensendieck system of gymnastics; this reminded my mother of my wish to study some method of dancing or gymnastics. During her ensuing talk with Rudolf Steiner, he asked her suddenly and apparently on the spur of the moment: 'What is your daughter Lory going to do?' My mother told him of my wishes and also of the conversation she had just had.

'Yes,' said Dr Steiner, 'one can naturally be a good theosophist and also practise Mensendieck gymnastics, but the two things have nothing to do with one another. One could, however. build up something of the kind on a theosophical foundation, and I am very willing to show your daughter how this could be done.' He had already made a similar suggestion to somebody else, but had met with no response.

My mother asked whether one could not, by means of rhythmic movements which stimulate and strengthen the etheric forces, call forth healthy and healing processes in the human being? This question was to be confirmed some months later, in the indications given for the very first exercises. 'Something stimulating – hygienic – pedagogical – good for – against'. Such remarks were frequently written beside the drawings and explanations concerned. In that very first conversation Dr Steiner said that this new art of movement would in the first place have to do with the spoken word, not with music. Thereupon the first exercise was given: 'Tell your daughter that she should step alliterations; she should take a strong, somewhat stamping step on the alliterated consonants and then make some 'pleasing' kind of arm movement where this consonant is absent. While doing this she should think that alliterations really appeared only in the north – hence in lands where it is very windy. She should picture an old bard and imagine him striding along on the seashore, a lyre under his arm. Each step is a deed, is a battle and a victory over the storm. And then he strikes the strings and makes his song one with the song of the storm.'

In the late autumn my mother returned from Berlin with this gift, but we certainly had no notion that it was to be the introduction of a new art. And now began the weeks of most beautiful, most earnest expectation, a real Advent time. In January, 1912, my mother took me with her to Cassel, where Rudolf Steiner was giving lectures, and one day he had time for us also. He looked at me very kindly, smiling a little. 'Yes, your little daughter must now learn a great deal; afterwards she must forget it all again.'

He then drew up the following plan of study. I was to learn to know the human body with its bones, joints, muscles and ligaments; he recommended for this work an *Anatomical Atlas for Sculptors*. Secondly, I was to look as much as possible at Greek sculpture, but really only look at it, never try to imitate the actual postures or gestures. I was also to read as much as I could about the Greek dance. He recommended a book by Agrippa von Nettesheim: in this book I would find drawings in which the human form was portrayed in various geometrical positions. I was to practise jumping quickly from one of the postures to another, and in so doing pay particular attention to the parallel or contrary movements of arms and legs; on the other hand, I was to take no notice of the planetary and zodiacal signs shown in the drawings. As a wonderful octave to these apparently 'to be forgotten' things, he gave as the last exercise in the important Eurythmy Course of 1924: *Ich denke die Rede...*, 'I think Speech...' Except for a slight change in the order of the movements, geometrical figures appear again here, but now full of content. How significant and suited to modern consciousness are these postures with their short accompanying sentences.

Then came speech exercises. I was to form sentences containing only one vowel, speak them, and while doing so, observe closely what was taking place in my larynx, and this I should then – dance! As an example, he wrote and spoke the following:

Barbara sass stracks am Abhang

He drew the line over the sentence, at the same time repeating it once more, strongly accentuating each syllable and bringing out the *a* (English ah) with special modulation. *Bar* is a sudden upward movement, a short *a*; *ba – ra – sass* are three long sounds, the third being especially extended, all three are stretched out on a level; *stracks* is again a sudden movement, but this time downwards; *am Abhang* consists of three wave-like movements.

I should like here to interpolate a remark which can perhaps throw light on Rudolf Steiner's procedure in pedagogical matters. He once gave us a very beautiful explanation of the word *unterrichten* (to teach). *Unter-richten* means: something is directed, is brought into a right direction, is guided rightly – but below the surface. Children in school are guided; the professor in a university expounds or lectures. Now I was guided like a child. The child was given a task; she had to practise, practise over and over again (this preparatory work lasted a good six months), and at the same time, under the surface, faculties were awakened that did not come fully to consciousness for a long while, but gradually became part of one's flesh and blood, if I may so express it. That this 'above or below, this stretching or curving', arose through the interplay between vowel and consonant, was something that had to be actually experienced and done, not only known. It was certainly better done as long as the head could not interfere, and one had only to ask one's heart again and again: 'Now what do you really feel here?' This 'asking one's heart', and letting all one's knowledge and understanding rise up out of its depths, was regarded by Rudolf Steiner as a fundamental basis for any artistic eurythmy work: 'You must learn to let your heart rise up into your head.' This means making a movement over and over again and always listening inwardly, for these movements can tell the practising eurythmist ever more and more, can reveal even deeper secrets. Mere head knowledge is of no use here: first the heart must intuitively sense and know; then it can and should rise up into the head also, and there become fully conscious.

Later he said on one occasion: 'You are doing this quite rightly, but that is not enough; you must know exactly how you are doing it, you must be able to explain it to your pupils also.' That was in the spring of 1913, when he came to Dusseldorf and we were able to show him what we had learned in the meantime. Then, with regard to one particular exercise, he said suddenly to those who were looking on: 'Lory walks quite rightly; she walks just like a tight-rope dancer, or like a savage in the primeval forest.' It was then that I was called upon to make it clear to myself how I walked in order to explain it to my pupils. It took much time and trouble before this 'had risen up into the head' and could be clearly formulated as the threefold walking familiar today to every eurythmy student.

This apparently instinctive way of walking correctly must, however, have been just one result of his *Unter-richtens* (guidance below the surface). Rudolf Steiner had once shown me two pictures: one represented an Egyptian statue with the strange earth-bound posture of the legs, the other a Greek statue with its characteristic standing posture. At the same time he drew my attention to the difference between these two leg-positions. 'Speaking from the purely human standpoint, the legs and feet would have to bear man's weight equally, as is shown in the Egyptian and early Greek sculptures. And if no other impulse had taken hold of the human being, he would have had to remain always on the same spot, like a plant. However, another impulse enters into him and now he tries to revolt against being earth-bound. One foot begins this revolution and resists the earth, wants to get away from it, withdraws from its force of attraction, and in so doing transfers the whole weight on to the other foot. In this connection, therefore, the essential thing in Greek sculpture is not the standing leg, but, on the contrary, the other leg, which has freed itself from the fetters of the earth.' And he added laughingly: 'You see, no progress is really possible – even in space – without Lucifer.'

That was one thing. Besides this, in addition to the speech exercises, other tasks were given: 'And then you must learn to write with your feet. By doing this one acquires a very delicate feeling in the feet and learns to make intimate, differentiated foot movements.' I had of course done both these things; I had often tried to experience and inwardly to become aware of the contrast between the Egyptian leg-and-foot position and the 'standing-leg' of the Greeks. I had also practised writing with my feet a great deal, and so the correct way of walking – 'like a tight-rope dancer' – was to some extent already the fruit of these efforts – that is to say, the result of his guidance.

Rudolf Steiner had never given indications for eurythmic walking, had never even stressed the necessity of trying to discover how to do it. But it seems to me that he had done everything to prepare for it, so that this walking was called forth, apparently 'instinctively'. And a clear indication that our later formulation was the right one is that in the last lecture-course, given in July, 1924 (*Eurythmy as Visible Speech*), it was used word for word.

I devoted the following year, from January till July 1912, to this preparatory work. I read about the Greek dance, but I soon discovered that the real object of my research was not to be found. Dr Steiner had spoken about Mystery Dances. But only one scanty allusion by Lucianus pointed in this direction: 'And then there were also Mystery Dances, but about these it is not permitted to speak, for that would mean introducing Mystery Dancing among the people and the consequence would be death.' It had also occurred to the philologist Kirchhoff that one could find no information in Greek literature about this art of dancing, although there were frequent references to it. He was of the opinion that the Greeks made no use of such information because they could read the movements from the text. Everything that he reconstructed with regard to rhythms and steps was fully recognised by Rudolf Steiner and incorporated in the work for the development of foot movements, but completed by corresponding movements for the arms and hands.

I tried further, with the aid of diagrams in the *Anatomical Atlas for Artists*, to study one joint after another, with all the muscles and ligaments, and to experiment with all this in my own body, in order to achieve a more conscious relationship to the physical body and its possibilities of movement. From the next task, the looking at Greek works of art, there arose a completely different experience, especially when I was able to look at the actual works themselves, not only at their pictorial representations. In the face of this divine beauty – repose, yet within this repose flowing movement – I felt my own bodily organisation in a new and different way. I had a dawning sense of being at home in my own body, in a way that was justifiable, indeed god-willed. It was even possible to shut one's eyes and still feel how one's breathing was different, how the blood flowed and pulsated in a different way. One felt like a plant which had been growing in dusty, parched earth, and had begun to droop and fade without water in the heat, but was now watered and permeated with new life right into the smallest leaves and fibres. Was it a delicate, as yet unrecognised perception of one's own etheric body in face of these works of art from the time of the most beautiful, harmonious, penetrating grasp of the physical body? We are Greeks no longer; our physical body has become harder and heavier, our etheric body is firmly imprisoned within it and is no longer perceptible. Nothing of essential value would be gained by however faithful an imitation of the gestures and movements of Greek works of art. We moderns must train ourselves to experience our etheric body as the first supersensible member of our being, at home in the last, the lowest heaven: we must find the way again into the higher heaven out of which it has descended. The way to this re-ascent was shown to us. One of the keys was given by Rudolf Steiner with the 10 or 12 drawings done by his own hand, which he entrusted to a 19-year-old girl. They were the foundation of a completely new art, an art which can awaken the very strongest impulses and quicken healthy, harmonious forces, having their source in the supersensible structure of the human being.

July came, and in July the rehearsals began for the Munich Festival Plays. [Yearly conferences 1907-13 were held by the then Theosophical, later Anthroposophical, Society, with courses of lectures and performances of dramas by Eduard Schuré and Rudolf Steiner.] I was allowed to be present during these weeks and was given instruction myself. When my mother and I arrived, work had already begun on Rudolf Steiner's new, third Mystery Play, *The Guardian of the Threshold*. Something completely new, taking all participants by surprise, was included in one of the scenes: beings were to appear on the stage and these beings were 'to dance'. Just as I entered the hall, a big gymnasium which had been taken for the rehearsals, these dances were being practised. Luciferic and Ahrimanic beings were represented, who, according to Rudolf Steiner's stage directions, carried out dance-like movements corresponding to the thought-forms, to the words of Lucifer and Ahriman. The movements and forms cannot be elucidated within the framework of this essay; nevertheless, it was the first eurythmy which was shown, although nobody knew that this new art would develop out of it.

I waited from day to day until Dr Steiner should send for me and the lessons begin. At last I met him one day as he was coming out of a door. Perhaps I looked at him questioningly and expectantly; in any case he laid his hand on my shoulder and said, 'Yes, little one, the wisdom of the whole world is involved – I cannot tell you yet. I cannot spare the time that I need during these weeks. Would it be possible for you to come to me in September when I am in Basle? Then I shall have time.' However, the day before our departure from Munich, my mother and I had a surprise. We were sent for by Rudolf Steiner, and during our conversation that evening he gave the first concrete indications about three vowels. He said approximately the following: 'Stand quite upright and try to feel like a pillar from the balls of the feet up into the head; this pillar, this upright position you must learn to experience as *I*' [English E]. I believe he was not satisfied with what I tried to do, for he called, while I was still doing my best: 'The weight rests on the balls of the feet, not on the heels.' Now it went better, more or less. I stood in the given position and felt all at once how, starting from the balls of the feet, something streamed upwards, as it were, into the vertical. I experienced it in front of my body as though it were carrying breast and heart up into the forehead, the latter seeming as though it must become warm and begin to shine.

'Now change the position of this pillar so that the head is further back than the feet, and then you have the posture which you must learn to feel as *A* [English ah].' This was a completely different experience. The weight is transferred to the heels the pillar rises upwards as though outside the body and yet maintaining its upright position. It takes hold of and penetrates the vertebral column so that one now has a definite experience of the bony system and therewith a certain sensation of weight, of being bound to the earth. To make up for this, however, the breast and heart are, as it were, opened to all influences. The whole world and the whole heavens send their rays into me. And all these rays meet in the heart. In comparison with what is experienced in connection with the first position, there is now a slight sense of pain, of being affected by something one is open to, and also at the mercy of the outer world.

'And now comes the third position: for this, bring the top of the head of the pillar in front of the spot where the feet are standing; you will learn to feel this as *O* [English oh].' Again there was a considerable difference between this and the first two sounds, when practice taught me to experience it. Out of the *A* [ah], out of this feeling of being plunged down into the physical body, until one experiences the spine, the ribs; until one becomes actually aware that the arms are really ribs which have made themselves free and are not just appendages – out of this *A* one passes through the *I*, which is the experience of gravity being overcome in the vertical, to the *O*. There then arises in a delicate and yet convincing way the feeling that the sentient soul, released from the constraint of the body, can experience itself outside, in the 'otherness' to which this slightly inclining gesture draws it near. Through this exercise the astral body, the third member of the human organisation – the instrument of eurythmy – is called into activity, and a first delicate consciousness is thereby awakened of how the sentient soul can unite itself in a threefold way with its own body and with the outer world.

There was about a fortnight between the weeks devoted to the Munich Drama Festival and the course of lectures given in Basle on the Gospel of St. Mark. A kindly providence, one might almost say an artistic intervention of destiny, made it possible for me to put this time to good use by absorbing the most varied impressions of nature in the mountains, by the Bavarian lakes, on Lake Constance and by visiting the Rhine waterfall. Added to this, changing weather conditions contributed to ever new, and in part strongly contrasting, moods and humours which took possession of my young heart, made doubly sensitive by the weeks spent in Munich: moods of astonishment, of wonder, of reverence, and also a somewhat anxious feeling of being overwhelmed. And so, on the 14th September, we arrived in Basle.

On the very first evening, after the lecture, Rudolf Steiner made an appointment for us the next morning at Bottmingen, a country suburb. Our daily journey thither led us through gay autumn flowers and rustling trees along the side of a stream until we reached the little house where Rudolf Steiner was living during his stay in Basle. He received us in a tiny little room on the ground floor. There were a couple of chairs in this room, and a small sofa on which Rudolf Steiner always sat. Only a very little space was left. On our first two visits we were with him alone; on the third day we were joined by Marie von Sivers – later Frau Marie Steiner – and Dr Steiner said with a smile: 'Yes, now Fraulein von Sivers is also interested in our affair. She has asked me how I could possibly show all the steps in this little room.'

On the first Monday afternoon – it was the 16th of September, 1912 – after a short, affectionate greeting, Rudolf Steiner entered immediately into the primal, most fundamental basis of eurythmy – the vowels. 'You must learn to acquire a fine, differentiated feeling for the individual sounds. And for this you must learn to let your heart rise up into your head. First, the heart must speak and later the head... Learn to feel *A* [ah] as a defence. Learn to feel *O* as a loving embrace, *U* as a tending upwards, shown by big arm movements when in serious vein, but in lighter mood by a spring.' Dr Steiner gave not only all the vowels, but also the modified vowels and diphthongs during this first lesson at Bottmingen; and in addition he gave a slight indication as to how one should work. First one should try to make each single sound into an experience; then one should combine two sounds, for instance *I* and *O*; then three sounds, *I, O, U* [oo]; and then, taking this order of sounds, let one pass over into the other, 'forming the movements almost at the same time'. 'You will see how beautiful this is and how a differentiated experience is expressed by this means.' There was such a ring of expectant joy in his voice – so much expectant joy that the unforgettable sound was always a help, supporting one when later on difficulties arose in the work, or when times of painful flatness came along.

At the end of the first afternoon Dr Steiner spoke about three consonants. He had impressed upon me that one must feel, and live through and with, the vowels in their tendencies towards movement – stretching, seizing, bending, crossing, striving. The soul does indeed live in all this activity and expresses itself in ever-varying ways. 'The whole realm of the soul is portrayed, as far as the feeling life is concerned, in the vowels.' Over against this weaving life of pure soul were now placed three specific consonants; with these, something belonging to the outer world is made use of, for we 'have something in our hand'. One's whole attention, all one's adaptability, must now be focussed on this 'something', this object. The realm of the vowels was blotted out, that realm in which the soul expresses what it experiences as strange and hence astonishing; what it experiences as purest consciousness of self in the upright posture; what it experiences as loving inclination towards an object of admiration and wonder; what it experiences when, cold and forsaken, it turns to a Higher and a Greater. With the consonants, something taken from the outer world was given into man's keeping, and one must adapt oneself to it, to its nature and character; one must give oneself over to a completely different element, imitating, copying, reforming what is outside oneself in the outer world. Warmth of feeling and a sense of truth must be developed when expressing the vowels; with the consonants one must become skilful, clever, quick-witted.

It would be impossible to relate in detail all that happened during those September days, for this would offer a perspective of such richness that even today it has not by any means been explored in all its possibilities and consequences. This first part of eurythmy is now called 'Dionysian Eurythmy'. In the case of most of the group or round dances, the indications originally given used to place the figure of Dionysus in the centre of the circle, and for two round dances, in particular, Dr Steiner gave the following explanation: 'Had one passed by a temple dedicated to Dionysus shortly before the outbreak of war, one would have heard the characteristic cry with which Dionysus inspired the warriors in a definite, cultic dance. For us, this is the 'Energy Dance', which gives strength for working in common with others. After the battle the second cry could have been heard, the purpose of which was to calm and bring peace once more to the souls excited by warfare.' Dr Steiner called this second dance the 'Peace-Dance'. Nearly all such dances had to be carried out in the anapaestic rhythm [two short, unstressed syllables followed by a long, stressed syllable]. Dr Steiner showed me himself how the call of Dionysus should be given, for both the Energy Dance and the Peace Dance, by making use of the three Dionysian sounds. *I*, *E* [ay], *U* [oo]. At the same time he tapped the anapaest pointedly with a pencil, so pointedly that the top of the case sprang off. He put it on again and began afresh; a second and third time it sprang off – but ever since then I knew: it must be an anapaest. In this way I had also received the answer to the question about the Mystery Dances of the Greeks, not to be found in books.

Then came forms for the personal pronouns – for I, thou, he and their plurals. It is really most delightful, every now and again, to look over lyrical poems and see how many of them can be expressed in a completely satisfying way when one takes this particular point of view into consideration. As a further step, poems should be studied with a view to discovering whether they express the thinking, feeling or willing soul, and the forms should be designed accordingly. Thinking demands straight lines; willing, rounded forms; and feeling, a combination of both. Each calls for a quite different spatial experience, a different way of filling and feeling space. And so we had the possibility, even then, of experiencing what Rudolf Steiner was later to work out more in detail in one of his lectures – that thinking takes place in the first dimension, feeling in the second, and willing in the third. Thus, in the very first beginnings, there was the possibility already of verifying the truth of what Rudolf Steiner said in his introductory words on the occasion of the founding of this new art: 'This new art of movement is intended to be the means whereby things which demand a too intensive attention from the onlooker, or are so deep that their full significance cannot be expressed in words, may be imparted to the understanding of the onlooker in this new way.'

On the last of these days in Bottmingen, Dr Steiner gave me two special pieces of advice. The first was pedagogical, the only advice of this kind that he ever gave me. He said more or less in these words: 'Now when you have learned all this and go out into the world to bring it to other people, and you are confronted with a pupil who makes, let us say, six mistakes, do me the favour of telling him only of the seventh. You were present recently at the rehearsals in Munich and you will have seen that I actually say or correct very little, and yet people do everything as I would have it in the end.' The second piece of advice was the following: 'When you go into the world and teach people, you must let them pay, and pay well, for their lessons. This new art of movement has been taken by *force majeure* from Ahriman, and he must have its equivalent.' I do not wish to pass over these words in silence, because I believe they are of importance to many, not only to eurythmists. Experience shows that when somebody lacking a sense of responsibility has lightheartedly made a 'gift' of eurythmy to others, it has never proved to be fruitful in the right sense of the word.

And then in September, 1912, at the last lesson in Bottmingen, the new art received its name. When Rudolf Steiner said somewhat meditatively and thoughtfully, 'Now we must find a name for this affair of ours,' Fräulein von Sivers said quite spontaneously and naturally, 'Eurythmy', and to this name Dr Steiner agreed wholeheartedly and immediately. If mothers ought to know the names of the children who come down to them, then Marie Steiner-von Sivers was, in this connection also 'the mother' of eurythmy. The days passed all too quickly; we returned home and the work began.

At the end of April, 1913, when Dr Steiner came again to give lectures in Dusseldorf, he visited us also, and soon after lunch we assembled in a large room decorated with fresh young birch boughs, and showed him what we had learned up to that time: Erna Wolfram, Anne-Marie Donath, my younger sisters and I. The six others wore pale green dresses, a 'Dionysian green'; I myself wore white. For the rod exercise, the first we had worked out in different rhythms, we used wooden rods bound with copper wire. In Bottmingen, Dr Steiner had given us this advice: 'If it is difficult to obtain copper rods, let us use wooden ones, bound with copper wire. But it must be copper, for that imparts an inner certainty to the movements; one will move rightly by instinct, one will handle things purposefully – for instance, one will go to a bookshelf and at once pick out the right book.'

We began with alliterations, and metrically rhythmic exercises. In both cases Rudolf Steiner required a very marked acceleration, and with one dactyl [a long stressed syllable followed by two short, unstressed syllables] – it was the chorus from *Pandora* – he took the book from my mother's hand – she had been reciting – and spoke himself. I believe I have never heard anybody else speak so quickly, and yet with such control and such clear accentuation. At first we showed the rhythm with our arms and legs, then, as it became quicker and quicker, it was no longer possible to make a 'beautiful and exact' dactyl: one was nothing but a dactyl, there was absolutely nothing else, one was caught up in an actual happening, in a living reality. It was a powerful experience, and I re-experienced it with the same intensity when Rudolf Steiner called for a similar acceleration of tempo in the later 'Curative Eurythmy Course'. Many of the exercises given there should be carried out 'quickly, quicker, still quicker', and only rarely is one expressly told: 'This exercise should not be taken so quickly, and between in there must always be pauses.' The acceleration of tempo is actually a means whereby one's own clever head is to some extent put out of action, and in its place the actual power of the sound can make itself felt. Naturally, well-considered, careful preparatory work must precede any such acceleration.

We then proceeded to show other rod exercises, and especially one with which we had taken considerable pains because its purpose was to correct bad habits of posture, and it was therefore very necessary for us all. As soon as we had finished, Rudolf Steiner took a rod himself and showed us various ways of holding and catching it, with movements which he said, 'may also prove to be very health-giving and efficacious'. He showed great pleasure in all this, attempted the most difficult catches with the rod – which often fell to the ground – and the rest of us were all very busy imitating him, picking up the rod and trying again, letting it fall and picking it up. We were extremely happy and full of zest; and when we showed our prepared work, taking one exercise after the other, in the same order as earlier in Bottmingen, he was glad and pleased too, and he took a very kind and positive attitude towards our efforts. He pointed out little unimportant things to those who were looking on. 'Just see how charmingly little Thea runs backwards!' Or when I drew eights and spirals on the floor with chalk for my pupils, 'It really is something to be able to do that so dexterously.'

For one form we had been able to find no suitable text – it was the form for the pronoun 'he' – but this proved fortunate for us. 'I see, what you need are the words. I will compose them for you.' After a few moments' silence and reflection, he called us three 'big ones'. We had to stand in a small circle, our faces turned to the centre, and he then spoke, in a resonant, powerful voice, the first poem composed especially for eurythmy, at the same time directing our movements in space:

He who illuminates the clouds,	*Der Wolkendurchleuchter,*
May he illuminate.	*Er durchleuchte.*
May he irradiate,	*Er durchsonne,*
May he inspire,	*Er durchglühe,*
And fill with warmth and light,	*Er durchwärme,*
Even me.	*Auch mich.*

We repeated it several times, and I believe all of us, onlookers and performers, had the same experience – now true eurythmy is born; in its sacramental and forming power it has become alive. He then gave us new tasks, and, turning over the leaves of an anthology of lyrical poems, chose after some search a little poem by Richard Dehmel, *Hieroglyphe*, which begins with three very interesting rhymed couplets. This brought our 'lesson' to an end. Dr Steiner, who was accompanied by Fräulein Waller and Frau Helene Roehling, then took his leave, for he had to give a lecture in Dusseldorf the same evening. I do not relate what follows for any personal reason, but simply to describe his greatness of heart, his kindness and never-failing support. He took my hand in both his own and... thanked me. When, disconcerted and completely taken aback, I stammered, 'But, Herr Doktor, it is we who must thank you', he again took my hand and repeated: 'No, I thank you.' And yet again, before he got into the car, there was a pressure of the hand and 'I thank you'. In this way, with all his simple greatness and sustaining warmth, he gave us an example of the virtue of gratitude, so largely lost today.

During the whole of May 1914, several of us, Flossy von Sonklar (later Frau Leinhas), Elizabeth Dollfuss (later Frau Baumann), Ada Smits and I were in London. I gave lessons every day, and moreover I gave them in English. To make this possible, Mr Collison had tried, together with me, to translate what was most necessary into English. This was not achieved without conflict, for when I had translated something, he said it was not English, and when he translated, I said it was not eurythmy.

The outbreak of war interrupted the eurythmy classes, owing to difficulties of travel. In the summer of 1915, however, I was able to get a passport and go to Switzerland. Just at that time Rudolf Steiner gave the so-called second part of eurythmy, the Apollinian, in a course in which Frau Kisseljeff, Erna Wolfram, and Elizabeth Dollfuss took part. For many exercises, Dr Steiner needed larger groups, and other Dornach eurythmists joined in these.

In this course a new second world of eurythmy was revealed: to the creative fiery-radiant Dionysus, arising out of one's own soul, there came now Apollo with his formative forces, drawn from a more objective spirituality. The movements in space of this Apollonian eurythmy were based on the grammatical character of the single words, and even the representation of dramatic situations followed strict and clear-cut laws. With all this we had a programme of work which needed several years to be fully assimilated and developed. It lay in my personal destiny that I was not able to take part in the further development of eurythmy in Dornach for about two years. During this time Dr Steiner began to give individual forms for poems. These forms described by him as 'Standard Forms', were forms which, when worked out, brought to expression the individual characteristics of a poem.

At the beginning of the last year of the war, 1918, Rudolf Steiner gave some lectures in Nuremberg in which I, too, was able to participate. During these days a quite small eurythmy demonstration was arranged for a private circle of intimate friends. It had to be small, for Frau Marie Steiner-von Sivers and I bore the whole brunt of it. Added to this, Frau Marie Steiner had a bad cold, and was so hoarse after the rehearsal that she feared she would not be able to recite in the afternoon. Rudolf Steiner promised to read for her should this be necessary. But it was not necessary. She managed the whole programme, and her voice became ever freer and better. 'You see, one must always try, then somehow things go all right,' said Dr Steiner to her afterwards.

After a few words about my performance, he gave me a vivid account of the eurythmy in Dornach, which I had not seen for a long time, as I had been prevented by war conditions from travelling. 'Yes, Eurythmy has really taken a big step forward in the last weeks. At last we have succeeded in putting a humorous poem on the stage; the *Gebratene Flunder* (the 'Roasted Flounder') by Peter Schlemil, from *Simplicissimus*. The roasted flounder itself appears, as well as the burning oil lamp, the yellow silk family sofa and the rocking chair. In the end the lamp is knocked over and there is a terrible to-do. But, you see, this really means considerable progress in eurythmy, and we shall work out many things along these lines. I should like always to have a humorous last part in our programmes.'

How important humour and satire were to him, I experienced some years later in Dornach. I was doing one of Nietzsche's most beautiful poems, *Liebeserklarung* ('Declaration of Love'). It is addressed to the albatross, whose lofty flight is described with wonder and longing. The poem ends with these words: 'O winged albatross, my ceaseless impulses drive me up towards the heights – I think of thee; then my tears flow – yes, I love thee.' Rudolf Steiner saw it in the rehearsal and was pleased; I was to do it at the next performance in the Goetheanum (the building was already open). 'Only,' he said, 'there is one thing you have not noticed.' He pointed to the epilogue, in small print: 'With which, however, the poet fell into a ditch.' 'Now, I have drawn a coda (*Nach-takt*) for you. Leave everything just as you have done it, but then, when you have held the last posture for a moment, plunge quite suddenly into this silent *Nach-takt*.'

Now for what followed: the last posture at the end of the poem was one which bore heart, soul and all the forces of the will upwards to 'star and eternity'. Then came the coda, an angular, straight-lined form with abrupt changes of direction, and in order to illustrate the position, a little figure was drawn at the side: the upper part of the body had to be bent forwards almost in a right-angle , and the arms drawn backwards on a level with the head. The entire form of the *Nach-takt* was to be danced in this posture. I practised most diligently, but nevertheless at the dress rehearsal I was overtaken by mischance, and; just when I should have been leaving by running backwards on the last line of the form, sat down suddenly in the middle of the stage. This pleased Dr Steiner so much that from then on I had to practise this sitting down, and had even to remain seated until the curtain fell. We then went on tour with the programme, and I sat in the middle of the stage in Stuttgart, Dresden, Leipzig, Halle and finally in Berlin. In Berlin this drew spontaneous applause; it was only there that the audience immediately grasped the humour of the situation.

One person alone could naturally practise sitting down suddenly, but how about two? We were doing *Seance* from Goethe's *Parabolisch*. In this humorous poem the letters of the alphabet make their appearance; the vowels, clad in scarlet, take the seats of honour; the consonants, walking with stiff steps, make a more modest entry and have their places allotted to them by President A. It was just at this point of the poem that it happened. Ilse von Baravalle and I were the consonants S and L, and we had to cross the stage with quite stiff legs making an S form, one from left to right, the other from right to left. All went well in the rehearsals, but at the performance our legs became entangled – and right and left... our places were suddenly allotted to us! A roar of applause. Naturally, we both jumped up again and went on.

Behind the stage – our *Séance* was one of the last numbers – our 'interlude ' gave rise to eager chatter and laughter. Rudolf Steiner joined us and laughed as heartily as the rest. 'We can never do it again,' he said, 'for the audience will naturally expect you to repeat your performance and you will not be able to do it. The way you both fell – it was an absolute hit; and it came at the one right moment! The way you sprang up again, and went on, and everything absolutely together. Such symmetry. It was simply magnificent. But we can never do it again.' And indeed from that time the *Séance* was cut from the programme. In conclusion – in order that my contribution to this collection may have some slight correspondence to a eurythmy programme, which should end with a humorous piece – I should like to describe just one more humorous number. One day Frau Marie Steiner brought us a form which Rudolf Steiner had just drawn for the *Hystrix*, a poem from the *Galgenlieder* by Christian Morgenstern. She asked me if I would like to study it. Not only were the forms very interesting, but very exact, and strange directions were written by the side of them. 'The whole thing is to be danced with the feet turned inwards, and the legs must often be crossed one over the other, making an *E* [ay]. Besides this, the upper part of the body should be waggled from left to right and from right to left. The head should often be turned round and round like a top.'

I was naturally thrilled and set to work with great delight, but my pleasure very soon vanished and gave place to a positively dreadful, terrifying experience. Even by carrying out the first two indications – feet turned inwards and legs crossed in an *E* one had the feeling that the arms had become long, heavy and unfree. The upright human posture was lost. And when, added to this, there came the waggling of the upper part of the body, and the top-like turning of the head, the human form was completely broken up, blotted out – nay, changed into its opposite. It was really an animal that stood there. I felt changed, even in the very form of my face; I no longer had a mouth; the lower jaw was pushed forward and transformed into the muzzle of an animal ... at any moment, I might foam at the mouth. The change I felt in my face was particularly horrible, and I looked once more through the directions given with the forms. What did I find? The very first direction referred to the costume and began as follows: 'With a pale blue veil thrown over the head...' So Rudolf Steiner had foreseen that it would be necessary to throw a protective veil over this somewhat too crass metamorphosis. It would really not have been possible without this veil. But the veil was there, and something else was there besides. The waggling to and fro of the upper part of the body and the top-like turning of the head were to stop with the last verse and during the whole of the final silent form, so that from the outset, indications were given for a diminishing of the 'non-human' element and a return to a certain measure of equilibrium. The longer I worked at this task, the clearer it became to me, that in the long run it could be mastered only with humour.

Rudolf Steiner recommended humour to us as a most necessary equipment for every artist. Once, in answer to a question from a woman painter, he defined it as the 'controlling power of the soul' (*beherrschende Seelenkraft*). On a higher level it was given artistic form in that being whom Rudolf Steiner himself called 'Cosmic Humour', and for whom – in order to achieve 'balance' – he found a place in the grouping of the figures in that great work of art which he carved in wood and called the Representative of Humanity.

Prelude to Eurythmy in England

Vera Compton-Burnett

IT WAS IN SEPTEMBER, 1920, that I first saw Rudolf Steiner and came into personal contact with him. My sister, a friend with whom we had worked in the Theosophical Society, and I had come to Dornach together and were present at the opening of the First Goetheanum. It was a time of uncertainty and strain for all three of us, and one day, when we were standing in the vestibule of the building after a lecture, a somewhat forlorn and bewildered trio, a voice from behind us said: 'Have a moment's patience and I will come to you.' It was Rudolf Steiner. He came; he listened intently to our questions, and his way of answering them removed all doubt; removed too the pain caused by certain experiences we had met with on this first visit.

In 1922 Rudolf Steiner came to England three times, and it was again as a trio that we attended his lectures in Stratford-on-Avon and in Oxford. In the autumn of that year my friend was taken ill and had to undergo an operation. I wrote to Dr Steiner, who was then in Holland, telling him of this and saying how much I hoped that he would be able to visit her. I remember very early one November morning standing with my sister and others on a draughty platform of Liverpool Street Station, waiting for Dr Steiner's train to come in. The moment he got out of the train he glanced up and down the platform, came straight up to me and said: 'How is Miss – ? Come and fetch me this afternoon at two o'clock and we will go to her.'

The three of us went to Dornach again for the Christmas Conference 1922-23 and experienced together the burning of the Goetheanum. This short account of personal recollections is not the place to describe an event of such tragic moment, nor could words easily be found to portray the figure of Rudolf Steiner as he watched those smouldering ruins.

I did not return to London, but remained in Dornach to study eurythmy. It was usually on Monday that Frau Marie Steiner decided on the programme to be given the following Sunday. Dr Steiner would generally be present for part of the time, and would often bring with him the eurythmy forms for any new poems that were to be studied. Sometimes one had the good fortune to see him draw the form for a musical composition while this was being played.

I remember one occasion when he drew a form for a little Bach musette and gave it to a eurythmist who was anxious to learn it. About three weeks later she told him that there was too much form for the music and she could not manage it. 'So? Well, let me hear it again.' The musette was played again; he drew the form again, and it was the same form. 'You see,' said Dr Steiner, 'There is nothing to be done about it, that is the form' – and he returned it to the astonished eurythmist, who finally mastered its difficulties and performed it successfully.

There came a day when I was given a solo, and at the dress rehearsal I was uncertain how to arrange my eurythmy veil. Everybody else seemed perfectly competent; only I was at a loss. Suddenly I heard Rudolf Steiner's voice: 'I must pin the veil for your first solo,' and this he proceeded to do with infinite kindness, to my relief and joy.

The year 1923 was a significant one for the development of the Anthroposophical Society in England. Two summer schools were arranged. At Ilkley, Rudolf Steiner gave a course of lectures on education, and these, together with those he gave at Oxford and Torquay, proved to be the foundation of all the educational work in England. At Penmaenmawr, at the request of Mr D N Dunlop, the organiser of the conference, he spoke on 'Evolution of the World and of Humanity'. Eurythmy played an important part at Penmaenmawr, and it was mainly in preparing the arrangements for these eurythmy performances that I had the opportunity of going to see Dr Steiner in his studio at Dornach. This led to other visits. I was the only English student at that time and was inevitably somewhat lonely. I often met Dr Steiner on the hill on the way from the studio to his house. Nearly always he would stop for a kindly word, and there were occasions when he would say: 'After the workman's lecture tomorrow I have time. Wait for me.' I would wait and go with him to his studio, where the great statue of the Christ carved in wood made an overwhelming impression. Those minutes were few, but they were precious and never to be forgotten.

In December, 1923, the time came for me to return to London. I had worked extremely hard, but felt sorely inadequate to the task of teaching even the elements of eurythmy. Frau Marie Steiner, naturally enough, took the same view. I made my farewells behind the scenes after a eurythmy performance. Marie Steiner, always very outspoken in her sincerity, said that it was really impossible for anyone to teach eurythmy after so short a period of training. Rudolf Steiner said, 'No, it is necessary for London that she goes now, but she will come back to us again and again'; and taking my hand in his, he said, '*Aufwiedersehen, aufwiedersehen, Sie werden es schön machen*' ('Goodbye, goodbye, you will do well'). The warm tone of his voice, the encouraging words, the pressure of his hand, these things I took with me to England, determined 'to do well'.

I saw Rudolf Steiner next in the summer of 1924 in Torquay, when he gave the course of lectures on 'True and False Paths of Spiritual Investigation'. I saw him personally in London also. He showed great interest in the English eurythmy, asked how things were going, seemed satisfied with the beginning that had been made, but then, after a moment's silence, said with great earnestness, 'You know, there should very soon be work in London for at least four eurythmists.' That was the last time. I never saw him again.

These recollections and impressions, although lightly sketched, do not deal with little things. In a few words I have tried to show Rudolf Steiner as I knew him, as I remember him. Such memories do not grow dim with passing years, but continue to shed their light upon the whole of life.

New Directions in Agriculture

Ehrenfried E Pfeiffer

IN 1922-23 ERNST STEGEMANN and a group of other farmers went to ask Rudolf Steiner's advice about the increasing degeneration they had noticed in seed-strains and in many cultivated plants. What can be done to check this decline and to improve the quality of seed and nutrition? That was their question.

They brought to his attention such salient facts as the following: crops of alfalfa used commonly to be grown in the same field for as many as 30 years on end. The 30 years dwindled to nine, then to seven. Then the day came when it was considered quite an achievement to keep this crop growing in the same spot for even four or five years. Farmers used to be able to seed new crops year after year from their own rye, wheat, oats and barley. Now they were finding that they had to resort to new strains of seed every few years. New strains were being produced in bewildering profusion, only to disappear from the scene again in short order. A second group went to Dr Steiner in concern at the increase in animal diseases, the problems of sterility and the widespread foot-and-mouth disease being high on the list. Among those in this group were the veterinarian Dr Joseph Werr, the physician Dr Eugen Kolisko, and members of the staff of the newly established Weleda, the pharmaceutical manufacturing enterprise. Count Carl von Keyserlingk brought problems from still another quarter. Then Dr Wachsmuth and the present writer went to Dr Steiner and put questions dealing particularly with the etheric nature of plants, and with formative forces in general. In reply to a question about plant diseases, Dr Steiner told the writer that plants themselves could never be diseased in a primary sense, 'since they are the products of a healthy etheric world.' They suffer rather from diseased conditions in their environment, especially in the soil; the causes of so-called plant diseases should be sought there. Ernst Stegemann was given special indications as to the point of view from which a farmer could approach his task, and was shown some first steps in the breeding of new plant types as a first impetus towards the subsequent establishment of the biological-dynamic (biodynamic) movement.

In 1923 Rudolf Steiner described for the first time how to make the biodynamic compost preparations, simply giving the recipe without any sort of explanation – just 'do this and then that'. Dr Wachsmuth and I then proceeded to make the first batch of Preparation 500. This was then buried in the garden of the Sonnenhof in Arlesheim, Switzerland. The momentous day came in the early summer of 1924 when this first lot of 500 was dug up again in the presence of Dr Steiner, Dr Wegman, Dr Wachsmuth, a few other co-workers and myself. It was a sunny afternoon. We began digging at the spot where memory, aided by a few landmarks, prompted us to search. We dug on and on. The reader will understand that a good deal more sweating was done over the waste of Dr Steiner's time than over the strenuousness of the labour. Finally he became impatient and turned to leave for a five o'clock appointment at his studio. The spade grated on the first of the buried cowhorns in the very nick of time.

Dr Steiner turned back, called for a pail of water, and proceeded to show us how to apportion the horn's contents to the water, and the correct way of stirring it. As the author's walking-stick was the only stirring implement at hand, it was pressed into service. Rudolf Steiner was particularly concerned with demonstrating the energetic stirring, the forming of a funnel or crater, and the rapid changing of direction to make a whirlpool. Nothing was said about the possibility of stirring with the hand or with a birch-whisk. Brief directions followed as to how the preparation was to be sprayed when the stirring was finished. Dr Steiner then indicated with a motion of his hand over the garden how large an area the available spray would cover. Such was the momentous occasion marking the birth-hour of a worldwide agricultural movement.

What impressed me at the time, and still gives one much to think about, was how these step-by-step developments illustrate Dr Steiner's practical way of working. He never proceeded from preconceived abstract dogma, but always dealt with the concrete given facts of the situation. There was such germinal potency in his indications that a few sentences or a short paragraph often sufficed to create the foundation for a farmer's or scientist's whole life-work; the Agricultural Course is full of such instances. A study of his indications can therefore scarcely be thorough enough. One does not have to try to puzzle them out, but can simply follow them to the letter.   Dr Steiner once said, with an understanding smile, in another, very grave situation, that there were two types of people engaged in anthroposophical work: the older ones, who understood everything, but did nothing with it, and the younger ones, who understood only partially or not at all, but immediately put suggestions into practice. We obviously trod the younger path in the agricultural movement, which did all its learning in the hard school of experience. Only now does the total picture of the new impulse given by Rudolf Steiner to agriculture stand clearly before us, even though we still have far to go to exhaust all its possibilities. Accomplishments to date are merely the first step. Every day brings new experience and opens new perspectives.

Shortly before 1924, Count Keyserlingk set to work in real earnest to persuade Dr Steiner to give an agricultural course. As Dr Steiner was already overwhelmed with work, tours and lectures, he put off his decision from week to week. The undaunted Count then despatched his nephew to Dornach, with orders to camp on Dr Steiner's doorstep and refuse to leave without a definite commitment for the course. This was finally given.

The Agricultural Course was held from 7 to 16 June, 1924, in the hospitable home of Count and Countess Keyserlingk at Koberwitz near Breslau. It was followed by further consultations and lectures in Breslau, among them the famous 'Address to Youth'. I myself had to forgo attendance at the course, as Dr Steiner had asked me to stay at home to help take care of someone who was seriously ill. 'I'll write and tell you what goes on at the course,' Dr Steiner said by way of solace. He never did get round to writing, no doubt because of the heavy demands on him; this was understood and regretfully accepted. On his return to Dornach, however, there was an opportunity for discussing the general situation. When I asked him whether the new methods should be started on an experimental basis, he replied: 'The most important thing is to make the benefits of our agricultural preparations available to the largest possible areas over the entire earth, so that the earth may be healed and the nutritive quality of its produce improved in every respect. That should be our first objective. The experiments can come later.' He obviously thought that the proposed methods should be applied at once. This can be understood against the background of a conversation I had with Dr Steiner en route from Stuttgart to Dornach shortly before the agricultural course was given. He had been speaking of the need for a deepening of esoteric life, and in this connection mentioned certain faults typically found in spiritual movements. I then asked, 'How can it happen that the spiritual impulse, and especially the inner schooling, for which you are constantly providing stimulus and guidance, bear so little fruit? Why do the people concerned give so little evidence of spiritual experience, in spite of all their efforts? Why, worst of all, is the will for action, for the carrying out of these spiritual impulses, so weak?' I was particularly anxious to get an answer to the question as to how one could build a bridge to active participation and the carrying out of spiritual intentions without being pulled off the right path by personal ambition, illusions and petty jealousies; for these were the negative qualities Rudolf Steiner had named as the main inner hindrances. Then came the thought-provoking and surprising answer: 'This is a problem of nutrition. Nutrition as it is today does not supply the strength necessary for manifesting the spirit in physical life. A bridge can no longer be built from thinking to will and action. Food plants no longer contain the forces people need for this.'

A nutritional problem which, if solved, would enable the spirit to become manifest and realise itself in human beings. With this as a background, one can understand why Dr Steiner said that 'The benefits of the biodynamic compost preparations should be made available as quickly as possible to the largest possible areas of the entire earth, for the earth's healing.'

This puts the Koberwitz agricultural course in proper perspective as an introduction to understanding spiritual, cosmic forces and making them effective again in the plant world.

In discussing ways and means of propagating the methods, Dr Steiner said also that the good effects of the preparations and of the whole method itself were 'for everybody, for all farmers' – in other words, not intended to be the special privilege of a small, select group. This needs to be the more emphasised in view of the fact that admission to the course was limited to farmers, gardeners and scientists who had both practical experience and a spiritual-scientific, anthroposophical background. The latter is essential to understanding and evaluating what Rudolf Steiner set forth, but the biodynamic method can be applied by any farmer. It is important to point this out, for later on many people came to believe that only anthroposophists can practice the biodynamic method. On the other hand, it is certainly true that a grasp of biodynamic practices gradually opens up a wholly new perspective on the world, and that the practitioner acquires and applies a kind of judgment in dealing with biological – i.e. living – processes and facts which is different from that of a more materialistic, chemical-using farmer; the former follows nature's dynamic play of forces with a greater degree of interest and awareness. But it is also true that there is a considerable difference between mere application of the method and creative participation in the work. From the first, actual practice has been closely bound up with the work of the spiritual centre of the movement, the Natural Science Section of the Goetheanum at Dornach. This was to be the source, the creative, fructifying spiritual element; while the practical workers brought back their results and their questions.

The name, Biodynamic Agricultural Method, did not originate with Dr Steiner, but with the experimental circle concerned with the practical application of the new direction of thought. In the Agricultural Course, which was attended by some 60 persons, Rudolf Steiner set forth the basic new way of thinking about the relationship of earth and soil to the formative forces of the etheric, astral and ego activity of nature. He pointed out particularly how the health of soil, plants and animals depends upon bringing nature into connection again with the cosmic creative, shaping forces. The practical method he gave for treating soil, manure and compost, and especially for making the biodynamic compost preparations, was intended above all to serve the purpose of reanimating the natural forces which in nature and in modern agriculture were on the wane. 'This must be achieved in actual practice,' Rudolf Steiner told me. He showed how much it meant to him to have the School of Spiritual Science going hand in hand with real-life practicality when he spoke on another occasion of wanting to have teachers at the school alternate a few years of teaching (three years was the period mentioned) with a subsequent period of three years spent in work outside, so that by this alternation they would never get out of touch with the conditions and challenges of real life.

The circle of those who had been inspired by the Agricultural Course and were now working both practically and scientifically at this task kept on growing; one thinks at once of Guenther Wachsmuth, Count Keyserlingk, Ernst Stegemann, Erhard Bartsch, Franz Dreidax, Immanuel Vogele, M K Schwarz, Nikolaus Remer, Franz Rulni, Ernst Jakobi, Otto Eckstein, Hans Heinze, and of many others who came into the movement with the passing of time, including Dr Werr, the first veterinarian. The biodynamic movement developed out of the co-operation of practical workers with the Natural Science Section of the Goetheanum. Before long it had spread to Austria, Switzerland, Italy, England, France, the north-European countries and the United States. Today no part of the world is without active collaborators in this enterprise.

The biodynamic school of thought and a chemically-minded agricultural thinking confronted one another from opposite points of the compass at the time the Agricultural Course was held. The latter school is based essentially on the views of Justus von Liebig. It attributes the fact that plants take up substances from the soil solely to the so-called 'nutrient-need' of the plant. The one-sided chemical fertiliser theory that thinks of plant needs in terms of nitrogen-phosphates-potassium-calcium, originated in this view, and the theory still dominates orthodox scientific agricultural thinking today. But it does Liebig an injustice. He himself expressed doubt as to whether the 'N-P-K' theory should be applied to all soils. Deficiency symptoms were more apparent in soils poor in humus than in those amply supplied with it. The following quotation makes one suspect that Liebig was by no means the hardened materialist that his followers make him out to be. He wrote: 'Inorganic forces breed only inorganic substances. Through a higher force at work in living bodies, of which inorganic forces are merely the servants, substances come into being which are endowed with vital qualities, and totally different from the crystal.' And further: 'The cosmic conditions necessary for the existence of plants are the warmth and light of the sun.' Rudolf Steiner gave the key to these 'higher forces at work in living bodies and to these cosmic conditions.' He solved Liebig's problem by refusing to stop short at the purely material aspects of plant-life. He went on, with characteristic spiritual courage and a complete lack of bias, to take the next step.

And now an interesting situation developed. Devotees of the purely materialistic school of thought, who once felt impelled to reject the progressive thinking advanced by Rudolf Steiner, have been forced by facts brought to light during research into soil-biology to go at least one step further. Facts recognised as early as 1924–34 in biodynamic circles – the significance of soil-life, the earth as a living organism, the role played by humus, the necessity of maintaining humus under all circumstances and of building it up where it is lacking – all this has become common knowledge. Recognition of biological, organic laws has now been added to the earlier realisation of the undeniable dependence of plants upon soil nutrient substances. It is not too much to say that the biological aspect of the biodynamic method is now generally accepted; the goal has perhaps even been overshot. But, important as are the biological factors governing plant interrelationships, soil structure, biological pest control, and the progress made in understanding the importance of humus, the whole question of energy-sources and formative forces – in other words, cosmic aspects of plant-life – remains unanswered. The biological way of thinking has been adopted, but with a materialistic bias, whereas an understanding of the dynamic side, made possible by Rudolf Steiner's pioneering indications, is still largely absent. Since 1924, numerous scientific publications that might be regarded as a first groping in this direction have appeared. We refer to studies of growth-regulating factors, the so-called growth-inducers, enzymes, hormones, vitamins, trace elements and bio-catalysts. But this groping remains in the material realm. Science has progressed to the point where material effects produced by dilutions as high as 1:1 million, or even 1:100 million, no longer belong to the realm of the fantastic and incredible. They do not meet with the unbelieving smile that greeted rules for applying the biodynamic compost preparations, for these – with dilutions ranging from 1:10 to 1:100 million – are quite conceivable at the present stage of scientific thinking. Exploration of the process of photosynthesis – i.e. of the building of substance in the cells of living plants – has opened up problems of the influence of energy (of the sun, of light, of warmth and of the moon) in other words, problems of the transformation of cosmic sources of energy into chemical-material conditions and energies.

In this connection we quote from the book *Principles of Agriculture*, written in 1952 by W R Williams, Member of the Academy of Sciences, USSR: 'The task of agriculture is to transform kinetic solar energy, the energy of light, into the potential energy stored in human food. The light of the sun is the basic raw material of agricultural industry.' And further: 'Light and warmth are the essential conditions for plant life, and consequently also for agriculture. Light is the raw material from which agricultural products are made, and warmth is the force which drives the machinery – the green plant. The provision of both raw material and energy must be maintained. The dynamic energy of the sun's rays is transformed by green plants into potential energy in the material form of organic matter. Thus our first concrete task is the continuous creation of organic matter, storing up the potential energy of human life.' And still further: 'We can divide the four fundamental factors into two groups, according to their source: light and heat are cosmic factors, water and plant food terrestrial factors. The former group originates in interplanetary space...'

Or again: 'The cosmic factors – light and heat – act directly on the plant, whereas the terrestrial factors act only through an intermediary (substance).'

We see that the author of this work rates knowledge of the interworking of cosmic and terrestrial factors as the first objective of agricultural science, while ranking organic substance (humus) second on the list of objectives of agricultural production. This is what was published in 1952. In 1924 Rudolf Steiner pointed out the necessity of consciously restoring cosmic forces to growth processes by both direct and indirect means, thereby freeing the present conception of plant nature from a material, purely terrestrial isolation; only through such restoration would it be possible to re-energise those healthful and constructive forces capable of halting degeneration. He had said to me, 'Spiritual scientific knowledge must have found its way into practical life by the middle of the century if untold damage to the health of man and nature is to be avoided.'

Our research work began with the attempt to find reagents to the etheric forces and to discover ways of demonstrating their existence. Suggestions were given which could only later be brought to realisation in the writer's crystallisation method. Then it was our intention to proceed to expose the weak points in the materialistic conception and to refute its findings by means of its own experimental methods. This meant applying exact analytical methods in experimentation with physical substances, and even developing them to a finer point. We proposed to work quantitatively as well as qualitatively. During my own years at the university, for example, it was my regular practice to lay my proposed course of studies for the new term before Rudolf Steiner for guidance in the choice of subjects. On one occasion he urged me to take simultaneously three main subjects, chemistry, physics and botany, each requiring six hours a day. To the objection that there were not hours enough in the day for this, he replied simply, 'Oh, you'll manage it somehow'.

Again and again, he steered things in the direction of practical activity and laboratory work, away from the merely theoretical.

Suggestions of this kind were constantly in my mind during the decades of work which arose from them. They led me not only to work in laboratories, but also to apply the fundamentals of this new outlook to the management of agricultural projects both in a biodynamic and in an economic sense. Dr Steiner had insisted on my taking courses and attending lectures in political economy as well as in science, saying, 'One must work in a businesslike, profit-making way, or it won't come off'. Economics, commercial history, industrial science, even mass-psychology and other such subjects were proposed for study, and when the courses were completed Dr Steiner always wanted a report on them. On these occasions he not only showed astounding proficiency in the various special fields, but – what was more surprising – he seemed quite familiar with the methods and characteristics of the various professors. He would say, for example, 'Professor X is an extremely brilliant man, with wide-ranging ideas, but he is weak in detailed knowledge. Professor Z is a silver-tongued orator of real elegance. You needn't believe everything he says, but you must get a thorough grasp of his method of presentation.'

From these and many other suggestions it was clear what had to be done to promote the biodynamic method. There was the big group of practising farmers, whose task it was to carry out the method in their farming enterprises, to discover the most favourable use of the preparations, to determine which crop rotations build up rather than deplete humus, to develop the best methods of plant and animal breeding. It took years to translate the basic ideas into actual practice. All this had to be tried out in the hard school of experience, until the complete picture of a teachable and learnable method, which any farmer could profitably use, was finally evolved. Problems of soil treatment, crop rotation, manure and compost handling, time-considerations in the proper care and breeding of cattle, fruit-tree management and many other matters could be worked out only in practice through the years.

Then there was the problem of coming to grips with agricultural science. Laboratories and field experiments had to provide facts and observational material. I was now able to profit from the technical and quantitative-chemical education urged upon me by Dr Steiner. This was the sphere in which the shortcomings and weaknesses of the chemical soil-and-nutrient theory showed up most clearly, and where today – after more than 30 years – one can see possibilities of building a bridge between recognition of the existence of cosmic forces and exact science.

The first possibility of breaking through the hardened layer of current orthodox opinion came through discoveries that cluster around the concept of the so-called trace elements. Dr Steiner had pointed out as early as 1924 the existence of these finely dispersed material elements in the atmosphere and elsewhere, and had stressed the importance of their contribution to healthy plant development. But it still remained an open question whether they were absorbed from the soil by roots or from the atmosphere by leaves and other plant organs. In the early '30s, spectrum analysis showed that almost all the trace elements are present in the atmosphere in a proportion of 10^{-6} to 10^{-9}. The fact that trace-elements can be absorbed from the air was established in experiments with *Tillandsia usneodis*. It is now common practice in California and Florida to supply zinc and other trace elements, not via the roots, but by spraying the foliage, since leaves absorb these trace elements even more efficiently.

It was found that one-sided mineral fertilising lowers the trace-element content of soil and plants, and – most significantly – that to supply trace-elements by no means assures their absorption by plants. The presence (or absence) of zinc in a dilution of 1:100 million decides absolutely whether an orange tree will bear healthy fruit. But in the period from 1924–1930 the biodynamic preparations were ridiculed 'because plants cannot possibly be influenced by high dilutions'.

Zinc is singled out for mention here not only because treatment with very high dilutions of this trace element is especially essential for both the health and the yield of many plants, but also because it is an element particularly abundant in mushrooms. A comment by Rudolf Steiner indicates an interesting connection which can be fully understood only in the light of recent research. We read in the Agricultural Course: 'Harmful parasites always consort with growths of the mushroom type... causing certain plant diseases and doing other still worse forms of damage... One should see to it that meadows are infested with fungi. Then one can have the interesting experience of finding that where there is even a small mushroom-infested meadow near a farm, the fungi, owing to their kinship with the bacteria and other parasites, keep them away from the farm. It is often possible, by infesting meadows in this way, to keep off all sorts of pests.'

Organisms of the fungus type include the so-called *fungi imperfecti* and a botanical transition-form, the family of actinomycetes and streptomycetes, from which certain antibiotic drugs are derived. I have found that these organisms play a very special role in humus formation and decay, and that they are abundantly present in the biodynamic manure and compost preparations. The preparations also contain an abundance of many of the most important trace elements such as molybdenum, cobalt, zinc, and others whose importance has been experimentally demonstrated.

Now a peculiar situation was found to exist in regard to soils. Analyses of available plant nutrients showed that the same soil tested quite differently at different seasons. Indeed, tests showed not only seasonal but even daily variations. The same soil sample often disclosed periodic variations greater than those found in tests of soils from adjoining fields, one of which was good, the other poor. Seasonal and daily variations are influenced, however, by the earth's relative position in the planetary system; they are, in other words, of cosmic origin. It has actually been found that the time of day or the season of the year influences the solubility and availability of nutrient substances. Numerous phenomena to be observed in the physiology of plants and animals (e.g. glandular secretions, hormones) are subject to such influences. The concentration of oxalic acid in bryophyllum leaves rises and falls with the time of day with almost clock-like regularity. Although in this and many other test cases the nutrients on which the plants were fed were identical, the increase or decrease in the plant's substantial content varied very markedly in response to varying light-rhythms and cycles. Joachim Schultz, a research worker at the Goetheanum whose life was most unfortunately cut short, had begun to test Dr Steiner's important indication that light activity acts with growth-stimulating effect in the morning and late afternoon hours, while at noon and midnight its influence is growth-inhibiting.

When I inspected Schultz's experiments, I was struck by the fact that plants grown on the same nutrient solution had a wholly different substantial composition according to the light-rhythms operative. This was true of nitrogen, for example. Plants exposed to light during the morning and evening hours grew strongly under the favourable influence of nitrogen activity, whereas if exposed during the noon hours, they declined and showed deficiency symptoms. The way was thus opened for experimental demonstration of the fact that the so-called cosmic activity of light, of warmth, of sun forces especially, but of other light-sources also, prevails over the material processes. These cosmic forces regulate the course of material change. When and in what direction this takes place, and the extent to which the total growth and the form of the plant are influenced, all depend upon the cosmic constellation and the origin of the forces concerned. Recent research in the field of photosynthesis has produced findings which can hardly fail to open the eyes even of materialistic observers to such processes. Here, too, Rudolf Steiner is shown to have been a pioneer who paved the way for a new direction of research. It is impossible in an article of this length to report on all the phenomena that have already been noted, for they would more than fill a book. But it is no longer possible to dismiss the influence of cosmic forces as mere superstition when the physiological and biochemical interrelationships of metabolic functions in soil-life, the rise and fall of sap in the plant, and especially processes in the root-sphere are taken into consideration.

In an earlier view of nature, based partly on old Mystery-tradition and partly on instinctive clairvoyance – a view originating in the times of Aristotle and his pupil Theophrastus, and continuing on to the days of Albertus Magnus and the late medieval 'doctrine of signatures' – it was recognised that relationships exist between certain cosmic constellations and the various plant species. These constellations are creative moments under whose influence species became differentiated and the various plant forms came into being. When one realises that cosmic rhythms have such a significant influence on the physiology of metabolism, of glandular functions, of the rise and fall of sap and of sap pressure (turgor), only a small step remains to be taken by conscious future research to the next realisation, which will achieve an experimental grasp of these creative constellations. Many of Rudolf Steiner's collaborators have already demonstrated the decisive effects of formative forces in such experiments as the capillary tests on filter paper made by L Kolisko, and the plant and crystallisation tests of Pfeiffer, Krüger, Bessenich, Selawry and others.

Rudolf Steiner's suggestions for plant breeding presented a special task. Research in this field was carried out by the author and other fellow-workers (Immanuel Vogele, Erika Riese, Martha Kuenzel and Martin Schmidt), either in collaboration or in independent work. Proceeding from the basic concept of creative cosmic constellations, one can assume that the original creative impetus in every species of sub-type slowly exhausts itself and ebbs away. The formative forces of this original impulse is passed on from plant to plant in hereditary descent by means of certain organs such as chromosomes. One-sided quantity-manuring gradually inhibits the activity of the primary forces, and results in a weakening of the plant. Seed quality degenerates. This was the initial problem laid before Rudolf Steiner, and the biodynamic movement came into being as an answer to it.

The task was to reunite the plant, viewed as a system of forces under the influence of cosmic activities, with nature as a whole. Rudolf Steiner pointed out that many plants which had been 'violated', in the sense of having been estranged from their cosmic origin, were already so far gone in degeneration that by the end of the century their propagation would be unreliable. Wheat and potatoes were among the plant types mentioned, but other such grains as oats, barley and alfalfa belong to the same picture. Ways were sketched whereby new strains with strong seed-forces could be bred from 'unexhausted' relatives of the cultivated plants. This work has begun to have success; the species of wheat have already been developed. Martin Schmidt carried on significant researches, not yet published, to determine the rhythm of seed placement in the ear, and to show in particular the difference between food plants and plants grown from seed. According to Rudolf Steiner, there is a basic difference between the two types, one of which is sown in autumn, nearer to the winter, and the other nearer to the summer. Biochemists will eventually be able to confirm these differences materially in the structure of protein substances, amino-acids, phosphorlipoids, enzyme-systems and so on by means of modern chromatographic methods.

The degeneration of wheat is already an established fact. Even where the soil is good, the protein content has declined; in the case of soft red wheat, protein content has sunk from 13% to 8% in some parts of the United States. Potato growers know how hard it is to produce healthy potatoes free from viruses and insects, not to mention the matter of flavour. Biodynamically grown wheat maintains its high protein level. Promising work in potato breeding was unfortunately interrupted by the last war and other disturbances.

Pests are one of the most interesting and instructive problems, looked at from the biodynamic viewpoint. When the biological balance is upset, degeneration follows; pests and diseases make their appearance. Nature herself liquidates weaklings. Pests are therefore to be regarded as nature's warning that the primary forces have been dissipated and the balance sinned against. According to official estimates, American agriculture pays a yearly bill of many thousands of millions of dollars in crop losses every year for disregarding this warning, and millions more on keeping down insect pests. People are beginning to realise that insect poisons fall short of solving the problem, especially since the destruction of some of the insects succeeds only in producing new, more resistant kinds. It has been established by research (Albrecht of Missouri) that one-sided fertilising disturbs the protein-carbohydrates balance in plant cells, to the detriment of proteins and the layer of wax that coats plant leaves, and makes the plants 'tastier' to insect depredators. It has been a bitter realisation that insect poisons merely 'preserve' a part of moribund nature, but do not halt the general trend towards death. Experienced entomologists, who have witnessed the failure of chemical pest-control and the threats to health associated with it, are beginning to speak out and demand biological controls. But according to the findings of one of the American experimental stations, biological controls are feasible only when no poisons are used and an attempt is made to restore natural balance. In indications given in the agricultural course, Rudolf Steiner showed that health and resistance are functions of biological balance, coupled with cosmic factors. This is further evidence of how far in advance of its time was this spiritual-scientific, Goethean way of thought.

The author is thoroughly conscious of the fact that this exposition touches upon only a small part of the whole range of questions opened up by Rudolf Steiner's new agricultural method. He is also aware that other collaborators would have written quite differently, and about different aspects of the work. These pages should therefore be read in accordance with their intention: as the view from a single window in a house containing many rooms.

Seeking and Finding

Violet Plincke

MANY, MANY YEARS AGO I used to spend my summer holidays in Finland. There I once met a lady who evidently thought my face too serious for a girl of 20. So with a suave smile she said: 'Read Rudolf Steiner and he will make you happy.' The lightning reaction on my part (fortunately silent) was: 'Then I will not even touch a single book by Rudolf Steiner.'

A little later I heard Rudolf Steiner's name again, when somebody told me that Mereshkovsky (whom I had often seen at the meetings of the Religious Philosophical Society in Petersburg) had recently been to Paris, with some of his literary friends, in order to attend Rudolf Steiner's lectures there. A tone of perplexity was in the speaker's words, and I did not ask him why – I was not sufficiently awake to do so.

A few years passed. I was studying philosophy in Frieburg. On a Saturday morning a special seminar was held by our professor, special because it took place not in the university but in the professor's dining-room, and students from all faculties were admitted. So one could see many unfamiliar faces of those who never crossed the threshold of the room where lectures on philosophy were given.

One such unfamiliar student lived in the same part of Freiburg as I did, so we walked home together. Occasionally strange words fell from his lips – for instance, 'Lucifer and Ahriman'. And I thought, 'Surely Ahriman's name should be coupled with Ormuzd – Lucifer belongs somewhere else.'

I did not interrupt him – it all sounded somewhat foreign and strange. But a day came when we happened to talk in my room, and something 'out of the blue' impelled me to say (to my utter suprise): 'You are an educated German – perhaps you could tell me something about Rudolf Steiner.' He sat bolt upright. 'What makes you ask that?' 'I cannot tell.'

The next few minutes' conversation revealed that the student had been a member of the Society for a few years; that he had heard many lectures by Rudolf Steiner, and that his mother and sister were members, too. He continued: 'I am expecting a telegram from my friends in Berne telling me whether Dr Steiner is coming to Berne, or not. If he is, then I shall certainly go. Would you like to go too?' 'No' was my reaction. It all seemed so remote and strange. Three days later I had a postcard from Berne to say that the lectures were in progress.

Christmas was approaching; the students were all leaving Freiburg to spend Christmas with their families; the town became quite empty. Before going to his parents, who lived near Hanover, the student brought me *Knowledge of the Higher Worlds*, *Theosophy*, and *Occult Science: An Outline*. It was in the evening of December 22, 1912. He said he would call again on his return to see how I got on with the books.

That same evening I plunged into *Knowledge of the Higher Worlds*. There was not a moment's hesitation as to which of the books was to be tackled first. From the very first pages onward there was only one dominant feeling: 'At last! I always knew that such a book must exist in the world – and here it is.'

It is impossible to describe how I ate and drank the books, for by the time the student returned in the evening of December 27, I had read *Knowledge of the Higher Worlds*, *Theosophy*, and about two-thirds of *Occult Science: An Outline*. Only when I reached the chapter on the 'Evolution of the World', I thought, 'Why is this written in prose? It should have been written in dithyrambic verse.' The years of search (which had begun quite early) had made me so desperately hungry that I could not do otherwise than read and absorb at this whirlwind pace.

A fortnight after I had opened the first page of *Knowledge of the Higher Worlds*, I announced that I wished to become a member. I was introduced to the local group-leader, who greeted me with the words: 'Are you aware that joining the Society is not like joining a skittles-club (*Kegelklub*)?' I was dumbfounded. 'Does she not see how I want to join, why I want to join?' However, no real objection was made – and my pink card of membership was in my hands within a week or 10 days.

Then, in the middle of February, 1913, Dr Steiner was expected to give two lectures in Tübingen. So we went there and arrived in the old Town Hall while members were leisurely streaming in, stopping to greet one another and talk. The afternoon lecture was for members only, the evening one for the public.

During this gradual gathering of the members I suddenly turned and looked at the platform: a man in a coat with fur collar and snow-boots on his feet was standing and looking through a lorgnette at the people in the hall. 'That is he!' I had seen photograph of him, but his actual presence – what a difference. Something shot through me: 'What comes from this man's lips will always be truth.' That is all.

The subject of the lecture was life after death. He spoke of his recent investigation in connection with the death of a man who had lived in happy and close fellowship with his wife, but after his death suffered sorrowful loneliness because he was unable to reach his wife – nor was she able to reach him. The love of these two human beings had remained in the sphere of the soul and was not rooted in the spirit. The rest of the lecture has lapsed from my memory.

The evening lecture dealt with the same subject, but was adapted for the public. After the afternoon lecture I was introduced to Dr Steiner, and I ventured to ask him when I could come to see him. As four further lectures were to be given in Stuttgart, he told me a date and hour when I could come.

At the appointed time the door opened into that room where Dr Steiner received those who came to seek his guidance and help. The walls were of a rich red hue; on the wall hung an oil painting of a bowl of red roses; the light was subdued. He shook hands and I sat down. Utter stillness. I did not venture to say a word. So silence, utter silence, entered and stayed, on and on. I thought it had lasted for hours. At last, agony took possession of me, and when I could bear no more I said, 'You know why I have come to you'. Then only he began to speak in a quiet, even voice. With endless patience he had waited until I had found the courage to ask. For he had accepted that despairing outcry on my part as a question.

For the autumn term of 1913 I decided to go to Berlin University, in order to be present at all the lectures which Dr Steiner gave to the members, as well as those he gave publicly, in the Architektenhaus. To the members he gave a series of six lectures on 'The Fifth Gospel'. I do not remember the other subjects on which he dwelt.

The public lectures seemed to be not easier, but more difficult, than those for the members. This may seem strange, but it was so. The public lectures were very long, and so vast in substance, that at times it seemed entirely impossible to hold their content. The power of his word was coming out of every fibre of his being, and therefore stretching the capacity of understanding among his hearers to a degree previously unknown to them. Clearly, what he desired to give to his hearers was the immediate experience of the substance he was unfolding in his words. Whether the seed thus received by the open hearts and minds would bear fruit in this life or in a future incarnation – this he left open.

During one of these public lectures it suddenly flashed through me: He speaks, and we do not yet speak... I was startled. What does this mean, that we do not yet speak...? I put it aside; it was beyond my power to fathom it. Later I found a poem by Christian Morgenstern, who had been present at the course of lectures on 'The Spiritual Hierarchies in the Heavenly Bodies and in the Kingdoms of Nature' given by Rudolf Steiner at Helsinki in 1913. In listening to Rudolf Steiner's words, Christian Morgenstern experienced – in a lightning flash – the movements of the planets, the majesty of the Zodiac, the presence of Cherubim and Seraphim, invoked by Rudolf Steiner's words.

It is only after having read Rudolf Steiner's lecture, *Die Wiedergewinnung des Sprachquells durch den Christus-Impuls* (Of Speech and the Archangels, and the Coming of the Christ Impulse), that I have come to realise the actual mystery of Rudolf Steiner's spoken word. Only fragmentary indications of the content of this lecture can be given here. Dr Steiner speaks of three phases in the development of speech. In the first phase, when speech was primarily expressive of the forces of Will, the Archangels, donors and rulers of speech, turned for help in an act of intuition to the Hierarchy immediately above them: Exusiai, Dynamis, Kyriotetes. In the next phase, when speech was to be the bearer of the forces of feeling, the Archangels, turned in an act of inspiration to the Thrones, Cherubim, Seraphim (the languages of Egypt, Babylonia and Chaldea are representatives of this phase, and the last fading elements of it can be traced even in the Greek language). But now it is thought which has to be borne by speech. The Archangels, in having to unfold imagination, have nowhere to turn except to Christ Himself, who has come to dwell in the hearts of men. Through the fact that thought becomes ever more dominant in speech, ever-increasing forces of death enter into it, and only He who has vanquished death can become the living fountain-head of an entirely new power of speech. The secret of Rudolf Steiner's power of speech lay in the fact that it sprang from his being utterly and completely filled with the Christ-impulse. His speech is the embodiment of the goal to which we aspire.

January 1914 saw the last annual general meeting of the Anthroposophical Society before the long war-years. Reports of anthroposophical work in the various centres were given by group-leaders; a lecture on Durer's 'Melancolia' by an older member and a moving display of eurythmy (then in its earliest infancy) filled two afternoons. In the evenings, Rudolf Steiner gave his course of lectures on 'Cosmic and Human Thought'.

It was an unforgettable liberation to listen to those lectures after having lived through years of lectures and work in philosophical seminars, where a rich opportunity was offered to watch the display of brilliant thought, superb historical surveys and agile speculation – but which ultimately left you hungry and longing. Here, at last, thought received its cosmic anchorage, and the constellations of the Zodiac came to be associated with the 12 fundamental philosophical world-conceptions (Rudolf Steiner called them *Weltanschauungsnuancen*), which in their turn could be coloured and modified by the 'moods' of the planets.

He taught us to move from Idealism to Rationalism, Mathematicism, Materialism, Sensualism, Phenomenalism, Realism, Dynamism, Monadism, Spiritualism, Pneumatism and Psychism, and then the circle was closed. And the planetary 'moods' ran from Gnosticism, Logicism, Voluntarism, Empiricism, Mysticism, Transcendentalism, to Occultism. Impartially to experience the validity of these forms of thought with ever-increasing flexibility of mind – this was a lesson brought home on a majestic scale to the listeners.

The cycle of these lectures closed with the words: 'Meditate on the idea,' 'I think my thought', and 'I am a thought, thought by the Hierarchies of the cosmos. My eternal being consists in this, that the thought of the Hierarchies is eternal. And when I have been thought out by a category of the Hierarchies, then I am passed on – even as the thought of man is passed on by the teacher to the pupil – from one category to another, in order that the latter may ponder me in my eternal, true nature. Thus I feel myself within the thought-world of the Cosmos.' The feeling of boundless expansion and, at the same time, the recognition of being closely interlocked with one another, will remain as a memory for ever with those who lived through these lectures.

Many, many are the memories which cannot be recorded here. But, after a leap of 10 years from the lectures on 'Cosmic and Human Thought', there was the Easter Festival at Dornach in 1924, when Rudolf Steiner gave the lectures on the Ephesian Mysteries, and on the Easter Sunday morning we had a eurythmy performance where the humble building of the Schreinerei seemed to be transformed into a temple, for the entire Christmas Foundation Meditation was brought to visible manifestation in the pure movements of the eurythmists. Deep silence filled the hall after the last solemn words of the meditation were uttered. The memory of this celebration is as fresh as ever.

And barely a year later came the end. Now we were knit together in sorrow, stronger and greater than we had known. When we were allowed to enter the Schreinerei in order to let our eyes rest for a last time on the earthly frame of

Rudolf Steiner, then we could suddenly grasp with a clarity unknown before the *sacrifice* in the sign of which his entire life had stood. His every thought and word and deed had been a never-ending outpouring of his being. As long as he was with us, we may have been hardly aware of it. But the sight of his countenance on the death-bed drew away the veil from our eyes, and we can no more forget it.

The inner response to this is to be discovered and held by each individual human being. Rudolf Steiner's strength will sustain us.

Rudolf Steiner as Personal Teacher

Maria Röschl-Lehrs

TO MEET A GREAT PERSONALITY in the relationship of pupil and teacher is a source of strength for life. The invigoration flowing from this source can be used for the fulfilment of tasks brought by life. The details of the instruction received are not of a kind that can be reported directly. What can be given here is only a reviewing of one's memory, and a number of impressions which can help to bring out with some clarity the picture of the teacher's personality. In several of his published books, Rudolf Steiner gave counsel about the inner development of man. This will be spoken of here as his 'teaching'. But he also instructed some people as his pupils individually. This can be called 'personal guidance'. The distinction between teaching and personal guidance should be carefully observed.

The teaching about the inner path which a great individuality gives to his age forms part of the history of human culture. It arises from the facts and conditions of evolution in the period in which it is given, and influences this period in the direction of a further, higher evolution. It is addressed to the many who are willing to seek, and to make efforts, in this realm, and who are prepared to follow such indications. It is given in a form which takes into account the general, healthy average level of inner strength, and which brings about, when rightly followed, an harmonious, positive development of the human being.

Since the teaching is addressed to people in general, it can in our time be published in print. For human beings are now developing to the point where they can begin to experience, both in themselves and in other people, aspects of man's nature which were not previously grasped, and have remained for the most part unknown. The Romantic writers of the beginning of the 19th century spoke in this connection of the 'night sides' of human nature. Several of them gave particular attention to these – for example Justinus Kerner, who as a physician took care of the 'Seeress of Prevorst'. But at that time only scattered phenomena of an unusual and often chaotic, pathological kind were – at least publicly – known. Now an extension of the field of experience for the human soul into the region of the supersensible lies on the general line of development for mankind. We need to understand how such phenomena are related to the condition of man at the present time, and how they can be rightly understood and controlled. Therefore Rudolf Steiner, who had full insight into this realm, published, out of a sense of responsibility, explanations and directions for a healthy inner development. For if these phenomena of the soul's life are not understood, they may be regarded as illnesses, or defined as such even when they are not. Dangerous and unhealthy aberrations into mediumistic or spiritualistic practices may occur, which have nothing to do with a healthy development of the human being in the realm of supersensible experience, as this has been made possible by the teaching of Rudolf Steiner.

Everyone is free to notice and read these books by Rudolf Steiner or to neglect them; to skim through them superficially or to recognise their value; to ridicule them or to make active use of them. This is the sphere of freedom – a freedom which permits neglect, with all its far-reaching consequences. There is also a question of moral responsibility: whether one is willing to recognise the coming into being of the new stage of human development, or believes it one's duty to oppose this for the sake of traditional standards. Looking back over history, one might ask: Why do there continually come into being new directions for the inner training of man? The briefest form of answer would be: because each stage in the evolution of humanity needs a modification of the inner path, owing to the changes in man's psyche and his physiological condition. Different methods were right for oriental man; different methods again for the ancient Greeks, for the medieval Christians, and for people in our time.

The living connection that man exprienced with the divine-spiritual world, as it meets us in the ancient religious and literary documents of mankind, and as it lives particularly in the myths, depended upon early man having a different condition of body and soul. This clairvoyance was gradually lost, and had to be lost. It becomes plain to unprejudiced research that man has purchased his hold upon, and mastery of, the material world, which has meant an immense enlargement of his field of experience through the senses, with a great narrowing of his consciousness in the supersensible. How indeed could a man be active in the modern technical and mechanical fields if he experienced material forces as living beings, as did the men of ancient times?

In this way man has been deprived of his wholeness. The part of his being which could once unite itself in experience with the real supersensible world, and draw from it strength and guidance, had to become silent for a long time. But man is the bearer of a spirit, and cannot, in the long run, work and live in conformity with his real being without the sources of strength that come from the supersensible world which is his origin. The number of those who are aware of this is increasing at the present time, because they feel themselves inwardly broken up by modern civilisation and its demands. And so the cry for the wholeness of man is heard more and more. It is realised that man has become incomplete and through this hast lost power. Many would like to recover this power, and thus to experience their whole nature once more. And so lectures and publications point back to old forms of religion and their methods of training, to oriental books and meditative writings – there is a wide choice. In Rudolf Steiner's book, *Knowledge of the Higher Worlds: How is it Achieved?*, the way into wholeness which is for European and Western man in our time is described. It does not lead to personal power, but to moral purification, to a widening of consciousness into spiritual experience, and to the possibility of fully effective service to others, to humanity. This is the teaching of Rudolf Steiner.

Personal guidance presupposes that the pupil takes the teaching fully into account, and therefore follows its principles, which are of general validity. It acquires its individual character through having as a basis the knowledge gained by the teacher of the pupil's being and destiny. The pupil's individual past, which has formed him as he stands before the teacher, provides the starting-point of his training. And when personal guidance bears fruit, the pupil also recognises sooner or later his teacher's eternal Sign. Full pupillage really begins when this knowledge is attained.

A relationship of this kind between teacher and pupil is just as unique as an individual destiny. And since personal guidance is built, from the side of the teacher, on such a basis, it is not possible to pass on directly the counsels and exercises given by the teacher in such a particular case, as if they were valid also for others. For these instructions are based on preconditions which are not applicable to another person on the special characteristics of the pupil, right into his physiology. They take into account his national origin, and the stage of development he has already reached. There is thus a profound difference between the teaching and personal guidance.

If therefore one is asked to give a picture of Rudolf Steiner as a personal guide, this can be done only in individual outlines, which require for their understanding purely personal preliminaries. But I will select here a particular line, which has a quite general bearing on our present-day culture, and is therefore objectively understandable.

Two regions of experience, connected with one another, stand in the foreground; both occupied my attention from very early childhood. First, and the earlier in time, the child's pondering recognition that some human beings are felt to have significant and desirable qualities, while others arouse opposite feelings. From this gradually developed, in youthful years, the conception of the kernel of a human being. This kernel was very different in particular people – with some, weighty and strong; with others, light and insignificant. Some might be quiet and retiring, and appear outwardly insignificant, but had a worthy kernel. Others appeared colourful and brilliant, but one experienced something quite disappointing as their kernel. Later, this kernel was recognised as the personality, the 'I', of the other.

Similarly, there was from childhood the question of why one should experience at night, in dreams, so much that was beautiful, but so much that was terrifying, too. During the day there were the rich and significant impressions of the surrounding world which the child absorbed attentively in every detail. Fine differences in the processes of blossoming and growth in the trees during spring, below in the garden; the behaviour of the animals in the courtyard close by; exactly observed symptoms of illness in playmates and people of the neighbourhood; all this was intensively absorbed and remained clear in the memory as isolated impressions, about which one neither spun theories nor asked other people. Only later, generally after years, such sequences of memory were linked, often suddenly, into clear knowledge, and provided through the childhood memories, which reached unusually far back, something like a broader basis for understanding waking life.

However, dreaming and sleeping, intervening every night in this other experience, remained a great question. There were dreams in which the figures of fairy stories, and the human beings of the day, reappeared. But there were also dreams which were not dreams, and remained indelible in the memory of the schoolchild, clearly outlined, overwhelmingly moving. About this, too, one asked nobody; it remained a question. Thus at an early age the problem of the different levels of consciousness became a pressing one. How did all this happen? University studies did not give any answer, nor did the culture of my native town, so rich in noble arts. Hence there was nothing for it but to go on observing exactly and studying independently.

In this, Goethe became my friend and leader. A thorough study of his whole life and work did not indeed provide the knowledge of how sleep and dream come to be, but they brought the rewarding and important insight that dreaming was of quite special significance for his creative work. From his youth onwards, his poetry sprang from this condition of consciousness. He himself pointed to the rich world that man cannot yet consciously grasp. The dream-like creative conditions which powerfully, almost violently, took took of him during his youth, he learnt to control and to command by an 'actively contemplative' (*tätig-nachdenkliches*) life. Goethe, therefore, had learnt – as he says himself – to master such phenomena of consciousness: this much my studies showed. They gave to my problem a deepened, significant background. But my questioning and seeking concerning the origin of sleep and dream were not answered in this way, or by studying philosophy and psychology. I found the answer only some years later in the picture of Man given by Rudolf Steiner.

When I then met Rudolf Steiner personally, and he received me into the college of teachers of the first Waldorf School, he asked me to come to him directly, by word of mouth or by letter, with all questions concerning inner development. In this way personal pupillage began. And without my having touched, in any conversation, on the questions which had occupied me from childhood in the way I have recounted, my training began precisely at the point where these questions had their root.

It belongs to the essence of the inner path, as Rudolf Steiner describes it, that in striving for self-knowledge one should face oneself as an observer. This applies also to the individual line of training. From this arose a particular attentiveness to the method of the guidance given to me, to the progress from conversation to conversation, together with a particular feeling for the way in which this guidance was built up. It became evident to me as a living work of art, formed of delicate, steadily increasing clarification and deepening. Every conversation was a step forwards, an enrichment of my inner being. I learnt what delicacy of observation is, and I was endowed with a teaching about life through the discussion of situations and phenomena with which I had to do. A wealth of help, not only for inner endeavour but also for the understanding of the demands of external life, resulted from these conversations. A joyful beauty lived in them, and everything was illuminated by a wise goodness.

This goodness became for my soul the living soil for something which is inborn in man, and yet is so seldom aided in its development by life: I experienced what truth is. Not as logical consistency of facts or thoughts and the like. I felt it shine out in myself as a light illuminating the whole human being. No wish remained in the soul but to become translucent in my whole being for the teacher's gaze. This wish had no personal aim or purpose. I experienced that without this desire to become transparent, I could not have in myself that light which penetrates not only one's own being, but can reveal the surrounding world with its life and its creatures in their own innermost nature. Its rays fell also on the teacher, and in its light his being became ever more transparent.

In this light a confidence in oneself became established, which gave the inner freedom that liberates from the confusion and delusion of conventional opinions. This kind of self-confidence is not based on recognition by others, or on one's own valuation of one's personality, but on the finding of the bridge to those worlds which guide human fate through divine wisdom. It is based on faith in God – something of which one began gradually to realise the true meaning.

A special quality of Rudolf Steiner's guidance was the care with which he left his pupils free. I never felt myself bound by a chain of obligations which would have suppressed my own creative will. He never gave further directions, except when in my own endeavour and seeking I met with a hindrance, could get no further alone, and asked for help. One's own will to endeavour developed in harmonious agreement concerning the goal: the knowledge of the goal, towards which he helped me, and the will to the goal, which answered to it in myself. Thus one experienced Rudolf Steiner as guardian of freedom.

These are indications about the living work of art of his personal guidance; I indeed experienced it immediately as such, but came to recognise its far-reaching significance for one's development and the forming of one's character only at a much maturer age, through further knowledge. Rudolf Steiner was incapable of behaving like a schoolmaster towards another person; rather, he helped the other to bring his own being to full development and blossoming, in an unconditional, objective way, as the sun helps on each particular plant and flower. One felt oneself in the presence of a cosmic power, in the truest sense of the word – one that gave help and aid in a gentle, loving way. Through this, one was rescued from the narrowness of an all-too-personal human attitude, both in the judgment of oneself and in assessing the helpful positivity of the teacher, for this was concerned with what is actually great in the pupil's *higher* being – something that the pupil himself had not yet attained, but had the will to make his goal, seeking to achieve his wholeness.

These characteristics of Rudolf Steiner remain in one's memory as ideals for one's own endeavour and for the relationship of human beings to one another. In spite of the stern clarity of his judgments, the first thing for Rudolf Steiner was to foster another's destiny, to give helpful guidance about the tasks and possibilities which were founded in the other person's innermost being. He did not himself need or use the other person, but led him towards the best that lay within him, or her. Thus I learned to be a pupil in freedom, constantly helped forward by the experience of truth and goodness, conveyed to me not in an overwhelming way, but in beauty.

If during my studies of Goethe I came to know him as a work of art shaped by life, in Rudolf Steiner I experienced an artist in the shaping of life itself. That is how he stands in memory, clarifying and purifying the still unclear, not yet formed substance of the pupil's destiny.

At the Waldorf School

Karin Ruths-Hoffmann

Save us O Lord, Saint George do not forsake
us in our peril, help the dragon to slay
We're a poor folk between the lake
and Danzig in this year of twenty-three

AFTER THE LAPSE OF 33 years I can still hear the voice of our teacher reciting this verse in the scripture lesson. If I remember rightly, the inscription had been found on a centuries-old memorial stone in the very year when inflation was at its peak.

But were the Germans actually such a pitiable folk in the year 1923?

We had flocked to Stuttgart from all directions: there were pupils from Austria and Switzerland, England and Portugal, Denmark and Italy. I am firmly convinced that we are still all at one in realising that at no other time or place could we have experienced the richness of the world in the way that was possible during those years, when old conceptions and certainties were tottering, chasms of distress were yawning ahead, and the breath of the dragon of universal fear was poisoning the hearts and minds of men. The seeds of courage for deeds worthy of man were planted in our souls by the new art of education practised in the Waldorf School. How had it all come about?

In Breslau I had heard Thomastik, the violin-maker from Vienna, give an account of a course of lectures to teachers delivered by Rudolf Steiner at the Goetheanum. A picture was presented of how one-sidedly our modern educational system aims at intellectual knowledge. 'Is it not scandalous that it took a world war to bring home to a man that he ought to learn how to sew on a button for himself?' Thomastik said that in the Waldorf School the boys as well as the girls learn to knit – and I thought longingly of my beloved *Samskola* in Sweden, where the very greatest importance was attached to handicraft (*slöjd*). Rilke had come to know about this school while on a visit to Ellen Key, and had spoken enthusiastically of it in Germany. But here there was something else as well – I realised this from what Thomastik was saying. What could it be?

I myself was then a pupil at the senior girls' school and every day came home tired and bored, laboriously forcing myself to grapple with the homework. In the middle of Thomastik's lecture something whispered inside me: 'Away with it all ...' I went home and told my parents that they had given me the wrong kind of education, that they had forgotten the 'limb-man'. Not one day longer would I attend the school; later on I should be able by some other means to take the matriculation examination. First of all I must go into domestic service.

My father understood and acquiesced in the decision of his 17-year-old daughter, out of whose sight, until then, broom and iron, duster and kitchen-cloth had been kept hidden by three or four servants. As a grammar school boy in Sweden he himself had once thrown his herbarium, with its dried dandelions and grasses, out of the window, and had gone to a shipyard to learn how to forge iron. My mother was tearful, because from the cradle onwards an academic career had been intended for me. But as she had the greatest faith and trust in Friedrich Rittelmeyer, she agreed to my father's proposal that I should go into his household to do domestic work. In the household – 10 in number – of the first leader of the Christian Community, I was now to find the opportunity of making up for the hitherto neglected activity of the 'limb-man' by cleaning vegetables and washing floors. Every Wednesday and Saturday it was also one of my duties to remove the everyday appurtenances from the dining-cum-living room of this large and hospitable family and turn it into a chapel. I did my duty willingly but not really adequately, and enviously admired the writing and painting books which the children of the house, all of different ages, brought home from the Waldorf School in the Kanonenweg. It had been my intention to enquire on the spot whether the Waldorf School could not come to the rescue at any rate of my youngest sister, so that in her case the proper balance between the activities of head, heart and hand might be achieved... I myself at my age would have to rely on self-education. But was I really too old? The rumour came to my ears that one of the girls in the highest class at the Waldorf School was actually engaged to be married, and young Count Keyserlingk was said to be very nearly 20. This gave me courage. I had really no loftier wish than to be one of the throng of boys and girls whose merry voices filled the Kanonenweg every day. I had never seen such happiness on the faces of the pupils at any school known to me in Austria, Germany and Sweden. They looked like a new race of human beings; it was as though one wanted to sing in chorus with them: *With us comes the new age...*

The day and the hour, the colour of the walls in the room, the shimmer of the light during that fateful conversation with a friend which sealed the resolve to apply for admittance to the Waldorf School, are inscribed forever in my soul. On 18th February, 1923, I went confidently up the wide stone staircase to Herr Stockmeyer. 'What do your parents say?' was his first question. 'They do not know about it yet.' 'Then ask them first. We are not really intending to accept new pupils for the highest classes after the unfortunate experiences we have had... But go upstairs to Herr Baumann in the song room.' And so for the first time I went into the room from which later on we could see the colours of the sunsets over Stuttgart, while the choir of the highest classes was singing Baumann's songs: *Wind, thou my friend, long had dark mountains glower'd around me.*

I had already seen Rudolf Steiner on several occasions and had also heard him speak. Before actually setting eyes upon him I had seen his photograph. My father, a Swedish engineer who, like many of his countrymen, had worked for years as a kind of peacemaker between Germans and Slavs in Bohemia and Upper Silesia had returned to Sweden because he felt that the political developments in border regions of this kind precluded that atmosphere of peace in which his children could be educated for true manhood. In my Swedish godfather's library I then saw for the first time not only Leonardo's 'Head of Christ', Michelangelo's 'Creation of the World', and a bust of Goethe on the bookshelf, but also a postcard-size photograph which at once made an indelible impression on me. The man in the photograph was Rudolf Steiner. And so from the first moment onwards he was surrounded in my mind with pictures speaking of the nearness of the Divine and the greatness of the human spirit. Then I had seen him at a eurythmy performance in Breslau when he gave the introductory address, and after the performance, when a respectful crowd surrounded his car before it drove off. He waved and smiled, and my companion, a girl of my own age, said to me: 'Surely goodness itself speaks out of that smile.'

On the previous day, 31st January, 1922, he had appeared for a moment, with his high fur cap on his head, in the central doorway of the Breslau Concert Hall, just before the lecture was due to begin. He looked quietly at the crowded audience waiting in tense expectation, and then disappeared. At that time his name was on everybody's lips. I heard a voice behind me say: 'Everyone who sets store by spiritual things is here today.' In a long black coat, Rudolf Steiner walked quickly to the lecture-desk. It seemed to me that his way of lecturing bore the hallmark of an inviolable probity; there was absolutely nothing suggestive, fanatical or mystical about it, although it was just these elements that might have been expected from him. He was on a three-week lecture tour and this was the 19th evening. He gave me the impression of being overstrained, and to begin with he spoke with eyes closed, as if to ward off the curiosity and insistence of the audience.

Although I was still in my teens, I had already been to schools in three different countries, and in every case what had made the school endurable for me was that there was always one teacher or another whom one could love. However interesting the material, if it was presented by an uncongenial teacher I simply could not assimilate it. What impressed itself upon me this evening was not, primarily, the personality of the speaker, or even the content of his lecture. It was the manner in which he spoke, the tone and the method, the approach to the subject. Because of this completely selfless devotion to his theme, he seemed to me to be the model of what a true teacher should be.

And now, a year later, the moment had arrived when he was to decide whether I could be accepted by the Waldorf School as a pupil in the real sense. The doubt was not so much on account of my age – now 18 – but because it had recently been found necessary to dismiss one or two pupils from the highest class as incorrigibly disturbing elements, and new experiments of the kind were not regarded with favour. Herr Baumann took me behind the curtains and put the request to Dr Steiner. He looked at me for a moment and I saw a memory rise up in him. 'Karin Ruths, the daughter of Karl Ruths? Yes, why not, why not?' I was happy that at this moment when destiny was being sealed, he remembered my father whom, as far as I knew, he had seen two years previously in circumstances more tragic than pleasant. But I must first ask for my father's permission. This I duly received, and his gentle 'Yes' – he did not like being parted for a long time from one of his daughters – resounds across the years and on beyond his death, just as the 'Yes' at the marriage-altar echoes on through the whole of life.

The first day of school was at Eastertide. At the beginning of each school year it was the custom of the teachers at the Free Waldorf School to greet each class individually in the presence of the whole body of pupils assembled in the gymnasium. This time Rudolf Steiner himself – the teacher of the teachers – was present. Together with the others, he went on the platform and addressed the pupils. In Breslau it had been the objectivity of his lecture that had impressed me; now, together with my schoolfellows, I was seized with a heartfelt enthusiasm such as I had never yet experienced. I have forgotten the details of what he said, I remember only that he finished his address with the question: 'Do you love your teachers?' and that I, the newcomer, joined in the 'Yes!', shouted so jubilantly that the walls might have been brought down like the walls of Jericho.

In the very first lesson I knew that one could really love these teachers and also the subjects they had to teach – what they taught and how they taught. Not a single lesson in the following school year – sad to say, there was only one – cast the slightest shadow over this first experience of the character of the school. At that time, when the corridors and classrooms in all other schools were painted grey or brown, leaden yellow or at most white, a rose-coloured glow shone towards one from the stairways and also from the walls of our own classroom.   In the course of this year, Rudolf Steiner's visits to Stuttgart were times of festival. I heard that when the Waldorf School was being spoken of elsewhere, he often referred to it as the 'Free Waldorf School founded by Emil Molt and directed by me' – always mentioning, first, the one who had taken the initiative, and then his own share in it. At one of the monthly assemblies he spoke to us, his pupils, as follows: 'You see, when I come to the Waldorf School I always feel great happiness – and when someone is happy, ideas come to him. And so today a humorous idea came to me...' He then told the story which was included later on in the reading-book compiled by Caroline von Heydebrand, the story of the two children each trying to pick the best bunch of flowers. When they compared their bunches, one of the children had included thistles among the honey-yielding flowers. 'Why thistles?' asked the other. 'So that the donkeys too shall have something to eat.'

But reading a story is not the same as hearing it. It was an unforgettable experience to hear Rudolf Steiner saying *Eseln*, pronouncing it as only Austrians can, and to see the children's eyes, how they hung on his every word – for he had the supreme art of arousing the attention of the youngest and oldest alike. Art seemed the most natural thing in the world. He himself had said that he was happy when he came to visit us, and all the children were jubilant. When he went across the courtyard of the school they clustered around him like the berries on a vine.

An elder girl, who had only recently become a pupil and was taken to him because of her state of health, was asked by him how she liked the school. 'Oh, very much,' she said, 'the only thing I don't like is descriptive geometry.' He was very disappointed, saying that nothing more beautiful than descriptive geometry could possibly be imagined. (One is reminded here of how Rudolf Steiner describes his joy when, as a child, he first came into contact with geometry.) It once happened to me that at the beginning of a mathematics lesson I was called to the blackboard to demonstrate the homework. I knew I could not, and got up hesitatingly from my place. Imagine my fright when the door opened and Dr Steiner, our 'School Inspector', came into the classroom. In an instant I saw myself from top to toe – it was that familiar moment when one wants to sink through the floor. I was conscious of everything, from my clothes to my inmost self, which was now being shown up in all its imperfection and incapacity. Tremblingly I went forward to the blackboard, for there was no drawing back. With his black, broad-rimmed hat still in his hand, Rudolf Steiner sat down in the left-hand corner at the back of the classroom. I made desperate efforts to remember some of the homework and to write and draw on the blackboard. Suddenly the whole tension relaxed; it was as though peace itself had come into the room, and I was completely calm. Out of this calm came the power to do what was required of me. In later years this occurrence has always seemed to me a basic illustration of the effect of Rudolf Steiner's influence: first, agonising self-judgment, painful realisation of one's own shortcomings and incapacities; then, balance of soul, inner tranquillity whence springs the power to attempt the utmost possible.

Pupils who had particular difficulties or irregularities of health were now and again taken to him individually. I remember having heard that he once advised a boy to learn shoemaking. A girl prone to states of depression was to have a blister applied to the pelvic vertebrae every six weeks by Dr Kolisko, the school doctor. Asked about the reason for this, Dr Kolisko explained to her: 'You see, a person who easily gets depressed walks about with a bent head and bowed back. A blister like this stimulates the forces for holding oneself upright.'

In my family there were several cases of a disease generally regarded as hereditary. As the time was approaching when we should have to decide in what profession we wanted to pass on the impulses received in the Waldorf School, this became a vital question for me. Would not a tendency to such a disease prove a burden rather than a help to the Movement? The teacher to whom I went for advice sent me to Rudolf Steiner. The conversation with him took place in the teachers' room at the Waldorf School. Dr Steiner received me standing up, scrutinizingly, seriously. My smile of greeting was not returned. This worked like a shock – in smiling one goes out of oneself, smiling has a uniting effect. I felt thrown back upon myself, upon my own person. He wanted to see my handwriting. I ran back to the classroom, happy that just today I happened to have my tidiest exercise-book there. Dr Steiner put it aside, almost with irritation: '*This* writing is not really characteristic of you, it is one you have acquired.' In fact it was not my usual writing; I had been making strenuous efforts at the time.

'What ought I to do?' I asked him, after having spoken of my plans and apprehensions.

'You ought not to give a single thought to heredity,' he replied with emphasis. 'I am not afraid of it, I am only reckoning with it.'

'You should not reckon with it either,' he rejoined with equal emphasis. 'What you need is great variety' – he made a sweeping gesture. 'Become a Waldorf schoolteacher. When you are standing in front of a class, there you have the variety you need.' Now he was smiling, and I went away as if the wings of Mercury were on my feet.

Why was it that everything Rudolf Steiner said carried such weight? There is a pleasing story which seems to me to illustrate this. It was told us by Dr Walter Johannes Stein, our history teacher, during a lesson on current affairs. Shortly after the First World War, he had taken the *Appeal to the German People and to the Civilized World* to certain leading men in Austria, including Hermann Bahr, the writer. 'From Steiner Rudi?' asked Bahr, even before he had read it. 'Whatever comes from him I will sign.' And when he had read it, he said: 'I would have signed that even if it had not come from Steiner Rudi.' One felt that objective truth itself spoke through this personal allusion.

The end of the final term was drawing near. As the Waldorf School was not yet five years old, nobody in our class had been able to go through it from the start, and all of us would have preferred to be beginning now, rather than leaving. Then one day in the late afternoon, when, reluctantly as always, we were obliged to tear ourselves away from our classroom, an idea came to one of us – I think it was Valdo Bossi, the Italian boy. 'Could not all of us together ask to have a talk with Dr Steiner before we have to leave here?' This talk was promised to us.

The sun was shining into the teachers' room and they all sat around us along the walls, while we were told to take our places at the conference table, at the head of which, with Frau Dr Wegman beside him, sat Rudolf Steiner. There he was – a leader of mankind, the most universal spirit of our age, of whole epochs – and he took us, a few boys and girls leaving school, so seriously that he listened to each individually. But to begin with he addressed us all together. He said that when life brought us face to face with crucial decisions, we should feel the spirit of the Waldorf School behind us, whispering the right resolutions into our ears. 'The relationship with your schoolfellows will be of the very greatest significance for you; think back to it again and again.'

We were then asked to say what we wanted to be in life. He said he could well imagine that many of us would like to be Waldorf schoolteachers – but naturally not all at this particular school, because it was to be hoped that the teachers we loved would not so soon be dead. (He pointed to them sitting along the walls.)

The 'best' scholar among us, our most capable mathematician at any rate, actually spoke of his readiness to become a teacher. But he was advised to train for a commercial career. 'Go to England and America – see how things are done there – and then come back and do them here as they ought to be done.' Another wanted to be an architect. For him Rudolf Steiner proposed a technical training; he should try to carry right into technology the artistic element he was seeking. Two of us who wanted to go in directly for teaching were advised to study physics, chemistry, philosophy and psychology. To a classmate who was thinking about becoming a kindergarten teacher, Dr Steiner said that the one and only thing that mattered there was that the children should love her – a kindergarten teacher might sometimes be quite stupid intellectually. Looking back afterwards, it seems to me that while entering into our youthful problems in the most loving way, Rudolf Steiner wanted at the same time to keep us from losing our heads, in order first and foremost, to prevent spiritual arrogance. The following may be a still better illustration of this.

The eldest of us, who was already engaged to be married, had originally wanted to study medicine, but we were all so thoroughly convinced of the entirely new impulse in Waldorf education that to enter the traditional life of a university seemed to us a retrograde step. 'After the Waldorf School I simply could not endure an ordinary medical training – it would kill me,' the girl said with emphasis. 'But why?' rejoined Rudolf Steiner, pointing in a friendly way to Frau Dr Wegman at his side. 'She has stood up to it very well.' He continued: 'In your position' – meaning that of a girl shortly to be married – 'it would be a good thing to learn curative eurythmy, because that is not a full-time profession.' (This was before the days when it became one.)

Then he turned to us who were racking our brains over our 'lofty spiritual tasks' for the future. 'Above all, dear girls, the most dreadful thing for the Waldorf School would be if it produced a lot of inveterate old maids – it is to be hoped that you too want to marry.'

Almost with indignation I cried out: 'But, Herr Doctor, marriage is not a profession!'

'In what sense not a profession? It is a generally recognised one.'

'But men marry and have a profession as well.'

'Yes, but I was speaking of this quite special case.'

To a girl whose desire was to become a nursing sister, he said: 'That is a profession which demands great sacrifice. The patients in the Arlesheim Clinic sometimes do not get better at once because an interesting lecture which the nurses want to hear is being given up at the Goetheanum... A good nurse must have something about her that does the patient good the moment she comes through the door.'

A classmate who wanted to devote herself to artistic work was advised to go to Dornach. It was also mentioned at this point that the Goetheanum could not yet take the place of a 'high school' – in the sense in which the Waldorf School now took the place of an ordinary school. But in this conversation it was clear to me that Dr Steiner regarded the inauguration of a 'high school' in the real sense as desirable. When he then made the suggestion that we should come again to Stuttgart in the autumn in order to exchange the first experiences in our careers, it seemed to me that the present gathering was like a veritably new beginning. I thought I understood Dr Steiner to mean that we should come back once a year, in our holidays, for an extension course under the guidance of our former teachers.

In September 1924 we had the second and last conference with Rudolf Steiner. He listened attentively to what we had to say – I remember especially that he seemed to be delighted when a pupil spoke about his work in a factory, describing how entirely the character of a department where woodwork was going on differed from another where iron was being manipulated. He went into this point and then began to talk to us about the Threefold Social Order. 'The idea of the Threefold Social Order is not dead,' he said, 'only at present it has not been understood. And I hope that understanding of it will grow from the circle of Waldorf School pupils.' That is more or less what I remember.

When another of us spoke of his wish to go to South America, in order to work out certain scientific matters on the spot, he was told: Whatever is being studied, whether it be plants or minerals, one should try not to rely on collections in museums or in some artificial setting, but to explore them in their actual locality and natural environment.

We were also invited to the Youth Course on education which was planned for November, but could not be given. On 28th September Rudolf Steiner gave his last address, and the future autumn gatherings of former Waldorf pupils, which we owe to his incentive, were destined to take place without him.

During the first days of April 1925, a few of us met in the Schreinerei at Dornach. Without any previous arrangement we encountered one another outside the studio where the earthly sheath of our teacher was lying. We were allowed to go in. The breath of life in death stirred through the stillness of the room where the greatest spirit of our epoch lay at the foot of the work wrought by his own hands – the statue of the Representative of Humanity.

When we left the Waldorf School he had given us words of guidance for our lives. We listened to them standing up and afterwards received them from him in writing. When we were together for the last time he enjoined us to medidate on them assiduously – we should soon become aware of their effect. The words thus given to us confirmed and set their seal upon the fact that our training during youth was under spiritual leadership, and that what our hearts had been able to receive must be mirrored along our paths of life and preserved in the depths of remembrance.

The Birth of Curative Education

Albrecht Strohschein

FTER THE FIRST WORLD WAR, as a student in Jena, I got to know some of the workers at a large Children's Home. They wanted to hear about anthroposophy and they came along one after another, until finally there were eight. One day I was invited by those in charge of the home to go and see them, and was asked if what these young people brought forward at conferences was anthroposophical. (It was in connection with the education of handicapped children.) Since these workers could not be called educationally experienced or anthroposophically trained, I felt I must give them some support. I was successful in this, for first Siegfried Pickert and then Franz Loffler became teachers in the home. They were not appreciably older than the others, but they had been connected with anthroposophy for a longer time.

Now the great Christmas Foundation Meeting in Dornach was at hand; our seven or eight wanted to go, and we set about finding the journey-money. Germany had just changed from the paper-billions to the Rentenmark, and we were all as poor as beggars. Pickert and Loffler were now working with backward children, and it grieved them that their endeavours to gain knowledge of Man and the universe had to be made apart from the practice of their profession. On the other hand, in their daily life with the handicapped children they were constantly confronted with decisions which they had to reach merely on the basis of feeling, and not from any penetrating pedagogical knowledge. That was the cleft which my friends were experiencing.

I myself, through an inner experience at the the age of 15, had been led early to seek for the knowledge of what life actually is. It became clear to me that Rudolf Steiner was the initiate of this mystery when, before I was 20, I returned from the First World War and a friend read to me, in the space of a few days, *Occult Science: An Outline*.

It appeared that in connection with the Christmas Foundation Meeting, Rudolf Steiner was to give a Medical Course, and I thought this might perhaps offer a possibility for my friends. But since about 800 people had gathered in Dornach for the Christmas meeting, how was a young man to approach Rudolf Steiner, whose burden of work was so obvious?

On one of the first days – we had had our lunch in the canteen – I was walking up the hill from the Glashaus to the Schreinerei, lost in thought, and as I looked up, there before me was Dr Steiner coming down alone. I raised my hat and would have respectfully made a wide circuit, but he held out his hand and asked, 'How are you?' This question from him, the great Initiate, could not be merely conventional, and so I took courage, began immediately to give an account of the

167

work at Jena, and asked if it were possible for my friends Pickert and Loffler to attend the Medical Course. I had turned back with Dr Steiner; we had gone down the hill and now stood before the Glashaus. 'That is something I must think about,' said Rudolf Steiner. 'I must speak with Frau Dr Wegman who is arranging the course. Come to me again.'

From this time onwards Pickert and Loffler urged me every evening after the lecture to go and get the answer. All I could learn, however, was, 'I have not yet found the time, come again.' After I had asked several times in vain, and when my friends were no less insistent the next evening, I got angry, flung at them some downright rude words, turned on my heel – it was in the anteroom of the Schreinerei – and found myself facing Dr Steiner. He had appeared at a side-door, and now he beckoned me. 'Very well, you can come, you three.' 'Herr Doktor, I asked only for my two friends,' I faltered in the surprise of the moment. 'Yes, come, you three,' he calmly replied, whereupon I felt obliged to say that I should then be the third and that I was not studying medicine, but psychology. 'Yes, come,' said Rudolf Steiner conclusively.

At a meeting ten years later, Dr Wegman took occasion to relate this episode. 'I have three young people,' Dr Steiner had said to her; 'They will take part in the Medical Course. They are, it is true, not students of medicine, but they will take part.' His words appear to have been spoken with such decision that it simply did not occur to her to ask what it was about these three. The incident seems to me to be an example of how Rudolf Steiner knew exactly the moment when impulses in the soul were ripe, and how he then accepted them and gave them form and order.

So now we actually attended the Medical Course, sitting unassumingly in the back row behind the young doctors. After the last lecture Dr Steiner walked down the rows and said to us, 'Come to me in the studio early tomorrow at 10.' There was astonishment, puzzling and guessing among us as to why we had been summoned; we realised, however, what was necessary and therefore got our questions in order. When we arrived at the studio at the appointed hour, Rudolf Steiner was sitting in his armchair quietly waiting, and he let us ask and say all that we had to say. Then came the answers to everything we had asked and, far beyond that, to much that we carried unexpressed in our souls. He spoke so impressively of how these 'abnormal' children cannot incarnate completely with their ego and astral body, and for this reason are already concerned with shaping a future earthly life, that we could only listen and take it in with all our senses. The impression was so great that later none of us could give a connected account of all he had said. I know that when at the end I asked what such a difficult earthly life really meant for the souls of the so-called pathological or feeble-minded children, Rudolf Steiner waited a little while and then quietly replied: 'When in my investigations I look back, starting from the genius of today, I always find that a genius has gone through at least one such feeble-minded incarnation.' Siegfried Pickert remembered that Dr Steiner had said, 'When I visit the class for mentally backward children at the Stuttgart Waldorf School, I say to myself: "Here one is working for the next earth-life, quite apart from what is accomplished now, which however can be a very great deal".' Finally he shook hands with each of us, said goodbye and added, 'Perhaps it will be possible sometime for me to give advice on the spot.' Those simple words meant for all three of us a searching question: What was intended? Were we to invite him to come to Jena to that children's home? Would he give lectures there? It seemed to me that he would never go there; that the friends must start something on their own – but they, on their part, protested that they were too young and inexperienced.

So the other two returned to their work and I to the university. But whenever I met someone on my way there, I asked him whether he knew of a large house in Jena that was available. Finally the anthroposophical doctor, Ilse Knauer, came with the promising news that a large empty house up on the hill at Lauenstein was to let. Now the creation of the Rentenmark had made not me alone, but most of our older friends, as poor as church-mice. Nevertheless, Ilse Knauer and I went at once to see the house. The woman-owner named a shameless price; I offered half. That was at midday. In the afternoon I sent my landlady's son to my two friends to ask them to come to see me that evening as soon as they were free. Our discussion culminated in the question, 'Are you willing or not willing?' And they at once said 'Yes.'

The next day I borrowed 20 Marks and took the train to Stuttgart, as I knew that Dr Steiner was there for the Easter Conference. When I got to the Gustav-Siegle-Haus, a friend told me that I ought to take my stand at the stage-entrance; Dr Steiner was expected immediately. There was much unrest in Germany at that time, and after threatening incidents in Munich we had begun to guard the entrance and exit doors. Nothing pleased me better, and in fact Dr Steiner came almost at once. I asked him if I might have a talk with him. He replied that this would be difficult; I had better come to the Waldorf School one morning and try to catch him in one of the intervals. 'One morning' – but my soul was on fire. I was convinced that we must act immediately. I could not help it – I began to talk at once. We went behind the stage in the Siegle-Haus, and standing at the window I told Dr Steiner about the chance of obtaining a house. He listened to it all quietly; then he said, 'If you can get the accommodation, we shall certainly find the form of co-operation.' But there still remained the ton-weight of our economic situation! 'Yes, Herr Doktor, but we have no money at all' I confessed, adding 'I will try to find some.' At this, Rudolf Steiner looked me up and down and said with an emphasis that quite unmistakably applied to the money-question, but only in this one case and particular connection: 'You need not take that into consideration.'

I sent in my name at noon to Emil Molt, the benevolent director of the Waldorf-Astoria cigarette factory. He had founded the Waldorf School and so I thought he would view this new foundation with understanding. But when he had heard all about it, he exclaimed, horrified, 'I beg you, let us start nothing new. We have cares enough already with the Waldorf School.' The disappointment of the moment made me lose control of what I said, and it is thanks solely to the greatness of Herr Molt that he overlooked it and later expressly showed me friendship. 'Herr Molt,' I said 'I have not come to seek advice; I asked you for money,' and got up to take my leave. 'Wait a moment,' he said, 'I will give you 1000 Marks.' 'As a loan?' I asked, still extremely cool. 'Non-returnable,' he replied.

That was the first money for the budding curative education. In the afternoon a few more thousands were acquired, and the proposal of an agreement for a lease went to my friends by express letter. Two days later came a telegram: 'Please return. Make agreement.' The agreement was made, and by pooling resources we had the rent for several months. We did the most necessary repairs at Lauenstein ourselves, and now my purchase of 30 old army beds at an auction two years previously, with the idea of starting a students' hostel, turned out to be money well spent. We sent for the beds – they filled a wagon as they could not be folded up – painted them, and bought the cheapest mattresses to be had. We begged the rest of the essential pieces of furniture, and received touching help from elderly friends.

In May of the same year, 1924, we were able to move in and receive the first children. I had kept on my student room in the town, and while Pickert and Löffler carried out the organising work at Lauenstein, I undertook the necessary journeys for additional furniture and money, above all the journeys to Dornach or Stuttgart to see Dr Steiner, whose advice we continually needed. Thus, among other things, we felt we must get out a prospectus, and we thought we could simply take over our predecessor's description of the home at Lauenstein, a doctor who had wanted to found a 'Home for Pathological and Epileptic Children'. 'No,' objected Dr Steiner, 'it must be clear from the title what is being done there.' I looked at him inquiringly, and he said: 'Curative and Educational Institute for Children in need of Care of the Soul'(*seelenpflegebedüftig*, expressed in English homes as 'children in need of special care').

I still looked at him inquiringly, not fully understanding the new expression, but I took out my notebook and he dictated to me word for word: 'Care of the Soul, large letters; in need of, small letters' and added, 'We must choose a name that does not stamp the children immediately.' Now I slowly realised for the first time that 'care of the soul' was something belonging to all education, which everyone might be called upon to practise; there was therefore nothing in it to separate our children from others. And with this, our future centres of curative education had received their name.

During one of these visits to the Dornach studio, Rudolf Steiner said of his own accord, 'I will come to you,' and, after we had talked it over, 'but there is no need for anyone to know. I will give a course for you.' His visit to Lauenstein began towards 12 o'clock in the evening of the 17 of June, 1924. Dr Steiner came to Jena in the express train from Breslau, where he had given the Agriculture Course; we three met him on the platform. Following his instruction that 'no one need know about it', we had told none of the numerous Jena members of his arrival, however bad we felt about it. His instruction obviously meant that on this visit he wished to speak only with those who were connected with our work.   Very few people got out; he arrived with two members of the Dornach Vorstand, Dr Elizabeth Vreede and Dr Wachsmuth, walked slowly along the platform and was the first through the barrier. He held out his ticket to the collector – but the man looked at this traveller with such astonishment that he made no attempt to take the ticket. I stood directly behind and saw the fascination. Dr Steiner waited a moment, handed him the ticket, and went on. We drove by taxi to the old Bear Hotel, 'Zum Bären', where Luther had lived, and in passing through the hall Rudolf Steiner looked at the oil paintings on the walls. When the reception clerk asked for registration in the visitors' book, he took his fountain pen and entered: 'Dr Rudolf Steiner, writer; Dr Guenther Wachsmuth, travelling companion; Dr Elizabeth Vreede.' At 8 o'clock the next morning I went to fetch him; he was already sitting at breakfast with Dr Vreede and Dr Wachsmuth. He said he had a fine room and did I know who had stayed there? Alas, I had to say 'No,' although I had looked at the room and had been assured it was the best in the hotel. I had missed the little silver plate fastened to the head of the bed saying that Bismarck had slept there on such and such a date. I felt ashamed and took the lesson to heart, although it had been no more than a simple allusion. A few minutes later Rudolf Steiner stood up, being always very punctual, and as the four of us got into the taxi, he asked to go first to the post-office, as he wished to send a telegram. I got out with him, hurried to the counter, took the proper form and stood, pen in hand, ready for him to dictate, but was told that he would write it himself. We then drove on to Lauenstein.

Our friends and fellow-workers were already standing at the door, together with our first five children and a few others who had also to be presented. We then led Dr Steiner through the whole house, and as we came to the cellar stairs a woman pressed past us in the narrow space. I was immediately asked about her. I replied that she was a cleaning-woman, and received for answer 'You must see that you remain in contact with her.' (The remarkable thing in the destiny of this woman were two children aged 13 and six years, both albinos of a peculiar kind. In the gleam of their delicate light hair they looked like two fairy-tale princesses. They were to be presented to Rudolf Steiner, a fact we had not yet mentioned to him.)

We stood a little while in the courtyard, looked at the building from outside and then at the picture of the landscape in the light of summer. This landscape is so beautiful that even the Jena guidebook notes: 'One should not miss seeing a sunrise up at Lauenstein.' Rudolf Steiner at this moment bent towards me and asked quietly, 'Tell me, how have you actually done this?' I scarcely made reply – I myself did not know exactly how it had been done.

Soon after the arrival we wanted to get to work, and therefore led the guests into the reception room, where, since we had to be very economical, the chairs that stood round the table were cheap ones. For the day's festival we had hired a comfortable armchair and had had it brought up from the town with no other thought than that Dr Steiner would use it. We had not reckoned, however, with his exemplary courtesy. He offered it at once to Dr Vreede, the leader of the Mathematical-Astronomical Section at the Goetheanum, and after she in her energetic way had declared, 'Herr Doktor, the armchair is for you,' he invited the next lady. She accepted; he sat down on one of the simple chairs and we had had our lesson.

Werner Pache, who had come as a fellow-worker soon after Lauenstein had been taken over, now brought in the children one after the other. He remained for the discussions and could record the most important things in shorthand, which was of great importance to us. The first boy, a quite feeble-minded and very restless child, first ran round the table and then went up to Dr Steiner and leant confidently against him. He became for the moment quite quiet and friendly, so that his true fine nature broke through. Rudolf Steiner interested himself in his sense-perceptions, and it was established that he could see very little at a distance. When we remarked on the boy's bad teeth, Rudolf Steiner said that the finger-nails, too, were weak and soft. 'Has nothing struck you about the mother?' he asked. We knew neither father nor mother, having been in touch with the parents only through correspondence. 'It is really an individual destiny, it has not much to do with the family,' he explained. 'It is a remarkable karmic case. The astral body is over-mature. Something is working in from the former incarnation. He spent only a short time between death and a new birth, so that he still has something of the astral body of the previous incarnation. He still has remarkable dreams at night; this will be shown by his saying strange things in broken sentences on waking up. He might see snakes writhing out – if he has already seen ordinary snakes. It is a bad astral body, located mainly here at the back of the head' (Rudolf Steiner laid his hand with intense interest on the stiff black hair). He went on 'One could deal with that by administering the opposite astrality; it could be done with the help of seaweed. Seaweeds draw in the astral forces of the surrounding air; mushrooms still more. But there is no need to start at once with the strongest. Parasitic plants draw in astrality strongly. Through seaweed injections, healthy astrality is drawn in, the opposite of what is in the body. There is bad astrality there.' He then gave the therapy, consisting of a seaweed preparation and belladonna, together with the exact potencies.

The case of the second child gave us experience of Rudolf Steiner's educational attitude. This was a pupil who had gone normally through elementary school, but had moral difficulties, told lies, swaggered boastfully and was inclined to steal. As the boy was brought in and introduced, he went forward and said, with self-assurance and emphasis, 'Good morning, Herr Doktor.' Now one had an immediate feeling that the way Dr Steiner handled this boy was both educative and healing. For instance, he asked, 'Can you do sums and write?' 'Yes, naturally,' came the arrogant reply. 'What is your father's name?' 'Karl.' 'Then please write down: "I am from Berlin, my father is named Karl".'

Dr Steiner explained to us that there was a great weakness of the ego which caused the moral failings. Even today I doubt if any of us would have come to this diagnosis from the boy's outward self-assertion. Once, for instance, he had come downstairs wearing the shoes belonging to one of our fellow-workers. And as the latter took him to task the boy retorted, with self-confident ease: 'You're not thinking, perhaps, that these are your shoes?' For his educational therapy we were told, among other things, that he ought to mend the shoes of everybody in the house, in order to improve his relation to social life. Then, however, indications were given for medical treatment. We were astonished: moral delinquencies to be treated medically? Yes, certainly; the sugar formation in the blood must be regulated; one must work on the warmth organisation, since it is there that human soul-qualities unfold.

When all the children had been considered, we fellow-workers received a word of advice. Dr Steiner pointed out that at least one of us ought to have a teacher's certificate – he foresaw coming necessities. Now all three, Pickert, Löffler and I, had been active for a certain time in educational work, yet none of us in the course of his studies had thought of taking the teachers' certificate. In fact, we had none of us meant to go in for curative education. Löffler had originally been a Hungarian officer. Destiny had connected us with the problems of mentally backward children and we had simply sought for anthroposophical light in a sphere where we saw others helpless. The advice relating to the teachers' certificate was followed, and it very soon transpired how necessary this was if our organisation was to get concessions.

At about the same time perplexed parents had brought pathological children individually to Rudolf Steiner at Dornach, and in her energetic way of tackling things Dr Wegman had taken a small house for them, 'Die Hölle'. The first backward children had appeared at the Stuttgart Waldorf School, and Rudolf Steiner had entrusted them to the Austrian teacher, Dr Karl Schubert. It was evident that the hour for putting curative education on a new basis had struck before we were even clear about our own aims in life, and before the general public guessed that these children for whom Rudolf Steiner found the phrase *seelenpflegebedürftig* were to become an ever more pressing problem over the whole civilised earth.

It was time for the midday meal. I sat next to Dr Steiner and said grace, and he joined in the Amen with his warm deep voice. It seemed like a benediction, a gracious protection for this table, at which ate together the messenger of the spirit to our age, pathological children, members of the Dornach Vorstand and we novices of curative education. Conversation began, and we found that Dr Steiner knew Jena better than we did: he drew our attention to the phenomenon of the tower in which one can see the stars in daytime. But he also related jests and amusing stories, among them the accident that had just happened at Koberwitz. He had written something at night, having already retired, and a spot of ink had fallen on the pillow. Countess Keyserlingk, the hostess, however, was fortunately not at all conventional, and when he had apologised the next morning she said joyfully that this pillow would be preserved. Dr Wachsmuth leant forward: it was to be hoped that this ink-blot would not be treated like the one at the Wartburg, which was attributed to Luther and was stained again from time to time for the benefit of visitors.

Walking through the garden, Dr Steiner told us that every child must learn to know all the trees and flowers growing there, and we were by now able to grasp that this was not only a matter of awakening an interest in natural science. Knowledge of the surrounding world is decisively important for the life after death. From an exact knowledge of the surrounding world one can form a knowledge of the inner world for the next life.

It was gradually coming to be evening, although the sun still stood high in its summer course. Dr Steiner had to think of continuing his journey. He said he would much like to stop a short time in Weimar. Hearing this wish, I suggested ordering a car to drive him the 20-odd kilometres. Instead of replying, he called to Dr Wachsmuth, 'Wachsmuth, can we afford a taxi to Weimar? Have we enough money left?' We were relieved when the question was answered in the affirmative, for what Dr Steiner accomplished in those weeks passed all imagination. We felt dimly, though none of us younger ones realised it consciously, that one day all this might be too much for the strength of an earthly body.

The 18th of June was at an end. If we celebrate this date in many Children's Homes as the Foundation Day of our curative education work, it is also because this one day which we were able to spend with Rudolf Steiner became for us in every sense a prototype for the whole future life with the children. If we were told later that a special tone prevailed in our Homes, it was the tone that he had given; it was our endeavour to acquire it and carry it on. It became clear to me during this visit that from then on I must not merely arrange external affairs in this field, but must myself take an active part in the coming work of curative education.

Two days later we four travelled to Dornach for the Curative Education Course. We had to wait a few days, however, for Rudolf Steiner had found an immense amount of work awaiting his return. He had said that this course would be confined to those who were directly concerned. From Stuttgart came Dr Schubert and Dr Kolisko, the curative educationalist and the doctor of the Waldorf School; from the teachers, Dr Ernst Lehrs; from the priesthood of the Christian Community, Licentiate Emil Bock, while Frau Lili Kolisko, founder of the Goetheanum Research Institute at Stuttgart, came for a few days. Together with the members of the Dornach Vorstand, the doctors of the Arlesham clinic – among whom was Dr Julia Bort, who later devoted herself entirely to curative education work – we were altogether about 20 persons. Rudolf Steiner wished that no stenographer should be called in, but if one of us could write shorthand, he had nothing against the lectures being taken down. Three of those present did their best to produce a transcript.

We sat with great expectations in the hall of the Schreinerei; only the front rows of chairs were occupied, and Rudolf Steiner spoke from a desk down below to this unusually small audience. What exists as lecture-notes can never convey the impression. How he developed the incarnation process, normal or irregular, manifesting in various diseases; how he presented the children who were in Dornach for treatment, read out the history of their maladies, and then, starting from the notes of the doctors, illuminated the various symptoms with reference to karma; or how he occasionally expounded certain educational measures, such as the release from insistent ideas – these were impressions that cannot be reproduced. 'A complete catechism for incipient curative educationalists is contained in these 12 lectures,' was said later by Dr Karl Konig, who came to us after the death of Rudolf Steiner.

Another friend pointed out that undoubtedly Rudolf Steiner gave the Curative Education Course with such pleasure and satisfaction, and entered so warmly into the spirit of the young people who wanted to be active in this field, because he himself after his university studies had been occupied as a private teacher in this very field. Dr Steiner once said that this work had at that time offered him the sole possibility of a livelihood and saved him from one-sidedness. He wrote in his autobiography of how destiny had assigned a special task to him in the pedagogical field.

As tutor in a family where there were four boys, he had to take three of them through to elementary level and then coach them for a secondary school; the fourth boy, who was about ten years old, was entrusted entirely to his care. This was the family's problem child; he was considered to be so abnormal that it was doubtful if he could be educated. 'His thinking was slow and dull. Even the slightest mental exertion produced headache, lowering of vitality, pallor and a state of mind that caused anxiety. After I had come to know the child, I formed the opinion that the sort of education required by such a bodily and mental organism must be one that would awaken the sleeping faculties... I had to find access to a soul which was, as it were, in a sleeping state and must gradually be enabled to gain mastery over the bodily manifestations. In a certain sense one had first to draw the soul into the body. I was thoroughly convinced that the boy actually had great mental capacities, though they were then hidden... This educational task became for me a source from which I myself learnt very much. Through the method of teaching which I had to employ there was laid open to my view the association between the element of soul and spirit in man and the bodily element. In this way I went through my own real course of study in physiology and psychology. I became aware that education and instruction must become an art that has its foundation in a real knowledge of man.'

We know that this pupil of Rudolf Steiner was led on to the Lower Sixth, that he was then so advanced as to need no further special guidance, that he passed the university entrance examination, took his medical degree, and fell as a doctor in the First World War. Thus in his own first task in life Rudolf Steiner set before us the model of what curative education can and will accomplish. He himself provided this living example of the ideal goal of future curative education. In the Curative Education Course, three and a half decades later, concrete instructions for reaching this goal were given. Our expectations were fulfilled beyond measure.

New and beneficent knowledge was imparted to us; immense enthusiasm for the work was instilled into our souls, and the fact that after only a few years a number of new Homes could arise was due entirely to all that Rudolf Steiner bestowed on us.   Nevertheless, these days of the course were at the same time our parting from him. When we celebrated the first anniversary of the founding of Lauenstein, he was no longer on earth. But work in anthroposophical curative education has since developed in very many countries from the seeds sown at that time.

The Last Years

Guenther Wachsmuth

THE SEEDS OF FAR-REACHING EVENTS were sown with the setting up of the research laboratory at the Goetheanum in Dornach in the summer of 1921. The arising of such institutions from the impulses of the anthroposophical movement never came about because, on external grounds, it was decided to found an institution in order to carry out certain tasks or experiments, or for any other external reason. It resulted directly from the meetings of persons who, in the course of life, were led by destiny, and by their own free decision, to work for Spiritual Science in a particular field. I may be permitted to say that this research laboratory in Dornach arose at that time through my contact and friendship with Ehrenfried Pfeiffer. Brought together in a united work by destiny and by freedom, in the same place and with the same interests and objectives, it was inevitable that we were soon searching for premises where we could carry out experiments to test and bring to realisation what was in our thoughts.

To think of those days calls up amusing memories, for the laboratory started in a primitive cellar which had just one advantage – gas and running water – but in other respects reminded one of the formless void of Genesis. Rudolf Steiner had agreed to our request to use this space in the basement of the Glashaus, where on the first floor the glass for the windows of the Goetheanum was engraved, and there we made the most primitive preparations for a laboratory by borrowing a few tables and chairs and procuring some indispensable glass vessels, retorts, Bunsen burners, and so on. Our research was aimed at obtaining insight into rhythm and the life-forces, and I remember very clearly a large Torricelli barometer as one of the first instruments. It was so cumbersome that it soon proved unusable for measuring air pressure, but its vacuum and its quicksilver were very handy for other experiments.

In order to give some idea of the boundless problems confronting this elementary groping, let me relate how Ehrenfried Pfeiffer and I, with a thirst for knowledge and some primitive work behind us, went to Dr Steiner and asked him how the life force, the formative forces – in short what he called the life ether – could be won from nature or in some way introduced into an experiment. I do not know whether he took our very high-flung question quite seriously or with a good percentage of kindly amusement, but, after all, the questions of beginners invariably reach out first for the stars and then, afterwards, for something more attainable. At all events he replied that this was quite a simple matter: all we had to do, for example, was to get a fly into a vacuum. Armed with this indication for an experiment, which in the joy and excitement of prospective achievement we understood more or less correctly, we clattered down to our cellar. Catching a fly and putting it into a vacuum was soon done, but then for both of us the crucial question arose – 'What next?' Perhaps we really had the life force there within the vacuum; but what we lacked was the possibility of establishing this fact, of testing or confirming, assessing or putting it into practical application.

This trifling first experiment, in itself perhaps to be taken humorously, nevertheless influenced us decisively, for we now realised that our prime need was for a re-agent, a test, something to indicate whether, where and how these forces are present, grow stronger or weaker, and the like. In the framework of this chapter it is not possible to describe the many labyrinthine ways we were obliged to take at the beginning in order to reach the goal, or to mention the countless other, even more concrete indications and stimuli given us untiringly by Rudolf Steiner during the following years, or to record the successes and failures, the lines of thought and experiments involved in the further development of this work. Nevertheless it can be affirmed today that at many decisive points the aim was achieved, as is shown by numerous publications and their success in many different countries. Here I will mention particularly the fields of application which became apparent to us as time went on. We realised above all that two basic foundations must be established for further research work: first, a systematised knowledge of the teaching concerning the etheric formative forces, and then a practical testing of experimental arrangements which, by producing reactions to the phenomena of life and the underlying action of the formative forces, could make the workings of these forces evident, their rhythms and form-building functions perceptible, and even reflect their normal and abnormal, healthy and unhealthy, components. After a discussion with Rudolf Steiner at that time, I began to attempt a systematic exposition of the teaching of the formative forces, on the basis of his indications, by drafting the book, *The Etheric Formative Forces in the Cosmos, Earth and Man: A Way of Research into the Living*. This went forward under Rudolf Steiner's kindly guidance.

1922: Through the founding of the biological research laboratory, active investigation and experimentation had been going on since 1921 in connection with the etheric formative forces, plant cultivation, and the study of the delicate reactions that can occur between living organisms and substances in solution and in course of crystallising. Rudolf Steiner participated in all this work with constant advice and help, encouraging, correcting, indicating directions to be followed. Together with fellow-workers, I had also arranged a discussion evening on questions of natural science as an extension of the practical work. A small circle of us met every week in the old 'Baubureau', as the room was called, usually in the presence of Rudolf Steiner himself, who helped us by answering our questions. We sat in a semicircle round a blackboard on the wall, presented our problems, difficulties, experiences and ideas, and in these free and spontaneous conversations received from him corrections and impulses for our further work.

In this primitive little wooden room, many important results of spiritual investigation were communicated by Dr Steiner during our lively discussions. The principles of a science of formative forces, systematic experiments in the domains of chemistry, physics, geology and botany, and also general problems of cosmogony – all these subjects were discussed and clarified. To give a concrete example, on one occasion we came to speak of the very first manifestation of forms of movement in the cosmos, and in this connection I asked Rudolf Steiner how the original lemniscate-movement [as that which forms a figure 8], so often referred to by him, was to be explained. Thereupon he spoke in a most graphic way about the primal beginnings of the cosmos, the 'Saturn condition', and described how the first movement in the cosmos arose from the rotatory balancing of huge bodies of coldness and heat, how the whole cosmic system then began to move around yet another axis and how the lemniscate movement developed through the combination of such movements of the cosmic system, both inwardly and around different axes. These expositions were accompanied by lively gestures of the hands or sketches on the blackboard, and helped us to gain gradually deeper insight into the fundamental laws of cosmic evolution.

Those Tuesday evenings, with their vigorous and fertile conversations, remain unforgettable, and have been rich endowments for our paths of life and for practical activities in the laboratory and in agriculture. In spite of his overwhelming burden of work, Rudolf Steiner devoted a great deal of time to me; with every readiness to help he indicated literature for preliminary study, made suggestions about the ordering and grouping of the material, and gave me courage, energy and substance for the writing of my projected book. When fear of being swamped by the sheer abundance of the material, and by one's own inadequacy to master and arrange it properly, had made one now and then despondent, a few words from Rudolf Steiner in conversation could restore one's vigour, power of concentration and self-confidence for months, and give a right direction to the work.

In connection with the laboratory founded by Ehrenfried Pfeiffer and myself, even while the work was in its first modest and germinal beginning, Rudolf Steiner had recommended investigation and experimentation in the field of biological phenomena, of the life-processes and their rhythms, particularly also in that of plant cultivation. Hence we now went to ask him how these indications and experiments could be turned to practical use in agriculture, and it was then, for the first time, that he gave us the impulse to obtain preparations from the animal and plant kingdoms. These preparations were to be exposed to the rhythms of the cosmic and earthly forces in summer and winter, in such a way that their life-promoting energies would be concentrated and enhanced, and then, in a state of extremely fine dilution – but having a powerful dynamic effect – could be applied beneficially in practical agriculture.

Measures of this kind have since been tested so extensively and with such unmistakable success that a few details only need be mentioned here. I still have a vivid memory of how staggered we were when Rudolf Steiner advised us to procure cow-horns, fill them with certain substances, bury them somewhere nearby and leave them to winter under the soil. After our first astonishment had subsided, we naturally began to ask many practical questions – for example, whether when the horns to be buried had been filled, they should be covered at the top with linen, wax or something of the kind, how long the wintering period should be, how deeply the horns should be buried, and so forth. Rudolf Steiner immediately gave definite answers to all these questions, describing what was to be done and what avoided. With regard to the latter, I remember asking whether the animal and plant preparations should have certain metallic supplements added to them, whereupon Rudolf Steiner gave a highly instructive talk about the harmfulness of certain chemical products used in modern methods of manuring and the elimination of pests. In answer, for example, to a question about the use of quicksilver, he said that its injurious influences would affect not only immediate nourishment but also subsequent generations, and must therefore be avoided under all circumstances.

At that time I was also able to lay before Rudolf Steiner certain problems in the spheres of physics and technology with which we were intensely occupied, trying to find new solutions. It was the time when radio had just developed out of wireless telegraphy, and radio instruments (which had formerly been used for special purposes only and were still very primitive in comparison with those of today) were beginning to find their way into private homes, thereby exercising a far-reaching influence on everyday life. I had in my house one such primitive apparatus with interchangeable gadgets – young people of today will hardly be able to picture anything of the kind – and when I asked Rudolf Steiner whether I might make one for him, he raised no objection. But we spared his studio from this infliction. The problem now occupying our minds was that here was an apparatus for the transmission of speech, of the word – man's highest and noblest expression – which depends on electricity and magnetism; that is, on forces and mechanical devices utterly alien to the delicate life-processes operating in human speech. In a conversation which Dr von Dechend and I had with Rudolf Steiner on this subject, we asked him whether it would not be possible to find a more delicate form of reaction to the spiritual and physical formative forces contained in speech, and after brief reflection he said: 'You must work with the sensitive flame.'

In this and in later conversations he gave us deep insight into the unique position occupied by the element of warmth in the sphere of transition between the psychical and physical process in nature. He spoke of the delicate interweaving of inner, psycho-spiritual processes with the warmth-processes in the human body, the relation between consciousness and temperature in the life processes, and the formative action of the speech-organs on the air outbreathed and warmed through by man when he speaks. He then recalled the discovery of Tyndall, who had observed the delicate changes caused in open gas flames by noises, musical notes and words in the same room, and he advised us to concentrate our thought and research in this direction. An extensive series of experiments in the physical laboratory, which had been set up in addition to the laboratory for biological research in Dornach, arose from these indications given by Rudolf Steiner, and in the hands of Paul Eugen Schiller they led to valuable results. So, as in the realm of the life-forces, the new knowledge opened up by Rudolf Steiner has made fruitful the work of a wide circle of students in the study also of substance and energy, and in the domain of physics and technology. Rudolf Steiner had promised to give me a sketch of his own for the title-page of my book, *The Etheric Formative Forces*. This had been somewhat delayed owing to the mass of other work, and I did not venture to ask about it once more. Then one night on a railway journey – these journeys were often made by night because of the scanty time available – there suddenly came a knock on the door of my sleeper just as I was dropping off. Rudolf Steiner looked through the door and handed me a sheet of paper on which was the finished sketch in colours for my title-page. In spite of all the strain upon him, he had found time to complete it, even while travelling by night. This token of remembrance has since accompanied the book through all its destinies, and in the following months Rudolf Steiner was also kind enough to read through the contents, discuss them thoroughly with me, amending and expanding them. With such guidance and help, the writing of a book was a joy.

1923: The long railway journeys with Rudolf Steiner were for us the most treasured times of personal contact with this great individual, who could go out to meet every single person with such understanding, cordiality and open-heartedness. The return journey from Vienna to Dornach on October 4th, 1923, with its atmosphere of gaiety, still lives vividly in my memory. It was my 30th birthday, and Rudolf Steiner had arranged to give a little party for me during the long journey in the sleeping-car of the Arlberg Express. On such occasions one had direct personal experience of his inexhaustible kindliness and warmth of heart. We sat for hours round a little table in the narrow carriage, and in the course of lively conversation he soon began to recount amusing reminiscences of his own life; and then he went on to answer some deep questions concerning esoteric life, of the kind that confront the individual and the community today and to expound their far-reaching connections.

This strange little group in the Arlberg Express, composed of such different kinds of people, must in some way have attracted the attention of the other travellers – Rudolf Steiner's striking figure in his black overcoat, and the rest of us with our often exuberant and worldly behaviour, alternating between merriment and long, earnest conversations. Next morning, before the train arrived at Basle, one of our friends heard a fellow-traveller ask the sleeping-car attendant whatever kind of people these could be. The attendant thought for a moment and replied: '*C'est une famille religieuse.*'

Rudolf Steiner's lectures and words were always adapted to the given situation, to the character of the audience, of the country and its people, to the spiritual quality of the environment. In one country he would speak more from the philosophical aspect, in another he would often take history and mythology as his starting-point, and so forth; in England he liked to go straight into the world of facts, into the factual realities of occult, supersensible phenomena. Indeed, we were all astonished at the International Summer School organised by the initiative of

D N Dunlop at Penmaenmawr in Wales, when in his lectures (which were attended by many people unfamiliar with anthroposophy, as well as by members) he dealt not only with concrete phenomena of supersensible experience, but also with the fallacies and aberrations of many endeavours in the sphere of occultism. With the most concentrated and seemingly relentless directness he led his listeners into the realm of spiritual investigation, its results, its dangers and the mastering of them, the errors, temptations and victories, the battle-arena of spiritual strivings at the present time.

After the morning lectures [published in English as *The Evolution of the World and of Humanity in the Past, Present and Future*] there were opportunities to go off in larger or smaller groups or alone, up the high, rocky hillsides to the dolmens of ancient Druid centres, whose history and decline, significance and influence, had been brought near to us in the lectures. It was an unforgettable experience when Rudolf Steiner asked me one day to go alone with him to the high plateau on the crags above Penmaenmawr in order to see the Druid circle. In spite of his 62 years, he climbed rapidly and nimbly. In keeping with the spiritual atmosphere of the locality, our conversation centred on the Druidic Mysteries and their counterpole in Europe, the Mithras cult, which came up against the northern Mysteries from the south. During this walk I was able to tell him about the unusual experience I had a few years earlier, when I had discovered an old Mithraic centre by the Danube. While climbing steadily and without tiring, Rudolf Steiner explained to me the great antithesis of the Druidic and Mithraic cults, the Mysteries of northern and southern Europe, how the spiritual stream going out from the north, from Ireland, met the stream from the south in Middle Europe – the Mystery-centres in the region of the Danube being evidence of this – and how both these Mysteries then met their fate in the Christianity which was then arising.

When we reached the crags high above Penmaenmawr, there lay before us the lonely expanse of the plateau, framed by rocky peaks, with massive stones of the Druid circle in the middle of it. It was a moment in life still vividly remembered, a strange, unique picture, when Rudolf Steiner walked into the middle of the Druid circle in the isolation of this high plateau. He told me to take a sight over the towering stones at the peaks of the mountains surrounding the plateau, and with retrospective vision as intense as if everything were happening at the very moment, he described how once upon a time the Druid priests, by thus studying the constellations passing across the horizon during the course of the year, experienced the spiritual cosmos, the Beings working actively within it, and their decrees for men. He related how the priests arranged the sacred festivals and rites of the year in accordance with these cosmic rhythms, and issued their injunctions to the people; how the happenings of the yearly seasons had to be mirrored spiritually in cult and ritual, and physically in the practice of agriculture. He spoke of the experience of sunlight and shadow in the innermost stone chamber of the ancient holy centres, and of how the visions and impulses received there by the priests spread far over the earth. When we left the Druid circle and the silent plateau to return to

Penmaenmawr at the foot of the mountain, it came to me as an inner conviction that in this place something real, something that transcended time, had taken place through the fact that a seer such as Rudolf Steiner had been here, was able to read the spirit-happenings of the past at this place, and to communicate what he had seen to men who in our day desire to tread the path of spiritual training for the tasks of the future.

The sacrifice demanded of Rudolf Steiner by the work and travelling in connection with the new constitution of the Anthroposophical Society in all the countries comes vividly to remembrance when, looking back, one realises what a devastating strain upon his physical health he bore during these years in order to prepare the way for the decisions to be taken and to help people to shoulder spiritual and earthly responsibilities. In the year 1923 during the many journeys in Europe, he still had the strength for the indescribable pressure imposed by all the external arrangements and procedures, the lectures, conferences, discussions, and so forth. Those of us who accompanied him, who were with him every day, often had cause to fear that the excessive strain of this year would show itself in early symptoms of impaired health. In the following year the strength for all these activities had to be drawn from the bodily reserves, and the unexampled energy of one who was now 63 years of age had to be wrested from actual physical illness. Yet even then he continued these lecture-tours – indeed, there were not fewer, but more of them. During those journeys of 1923, with his untiring joy in initiative, his open-heartedness and the unceasing work both by day and night, he set before us all the example of a man who, while bearing the heaviest burdens himself, lightens those of others.

It would be an entirely misleading picture to imagine that at this time, when Rudolf Steiner was inaugurating all the new development out of the esoteric core of the movement, he would have tolerated in his environment any note of solemn importance in outer behaviour. How cheerful, open and happy he was on those unforgettable night journeys, at meals and during evening conversations in the hotels of the great cities of Europe. When, for instance, in November 1923, we were sitting together one evening in the stately hotel, 'Oude Doelen' at The Hague, he told us many delightful and amusing anecdotes from his eventful life, and how heartily he could laugh when we gave unadorned accounts of our crazy battle with the water supplies in our rooms the previous night. I still remember a gentleman who followed him steadily during a walk at that time with an expression of funereal profundity, and how Rudolf Steiner suddenly turned and said with a friendly smile: 'What a face to go about with all the time!' He wanted to have around him happy, free, gay human beings, who were serious at the proper moment but also cheerful and life-loving, and he often quoted with amusement the words of an Italian member, Princess d'Antuni, who in her original way of talking spoke indignantly of people who always go about with 'a face reaching down to the stomach'. These things are mentioned only in order to give some little examples of the balance of seriousness and merriment that was always present in the environment of this great man.

Although there were never enough hours in the day for meeting the innumerable demands upon him, Rudolf Steiner had an extraordinary capacity for getting through an enormous amount of work with speed and concentration. When I took him his letters in the morning, he had generally already received a number of visitors or was writing an article, or he was carving at the great wooden statue which had been set there in his studio, or he was modelling, or painting, or writing, or he was engaged in discussion. Yet in the midst of these other tasks he was at once ready to concentrate on his correspondence; he went straight into it and gave his comments and instructions quickly and clearly. For anyone who had had previous opportunities of making reports to the chief of a big organisation, it was a particular joy to experience his method of working – the uniquely harmonious way in which he combined a grasp of great matters with care for the smallest details, and a kindly human understanding with unambiguous precision in giving directions for the work.

Many people who have studied the life of Goethe have perhaps found it strange that this prince of poets should have troubled himself, as a Minister, with the minutiae of administration, including mining, river control, road-building, uniforms for recruits, and various even more specialised matters affecting his department. In Rudolf Steiner this interest in every person and every detail could be observed in fullest measure. He devoted himself equally to spiritual principles and to the most specialised questions that came up in the daily round. He created the model for the new Goetheanum, and at the same time concerned himself with the design of the crockery for the Dornach canteen. At one moment he would give someone the most far-ranging advice for spiritual work, and then, when the caller was leaving, would warn him not to go out in the hot sun without a hat. He looked on every human being as a whole to such an extent that nothing about the person, inward or outward, great or small, right down to external traits of behaviour, escaped his interest. This gift for noticing everything, because it was never used pedantically, but always with generosity, kindness and a readiness to help, strongly stimulated everyone around him to look at the things of everyday life with wide-awake, affectionate attentiveness.

1924: After the founding of the agricultural movement at the home of Count and Countess Keyserlingk at Koberwitz in June, 1924, Rudolf Steiner went to Jena on the way back. He had again asked me to accompany him, and I still remember vividly how during the journey from Breslau to Jena, after a period of silent reflection about the Koberwitz conference, he said suddenly, with joyful emphasis, 'Now we have got this important work started, too.' Seldom had I seen him so happily moved after the completion of a task. Several times again during the journey he spoke with pleasure about that gathering.

On the following day, June 18, we visited the home for children in need of special care which had just been opened on the slopes of the Lauenstein, near Jena; here Dr Steiner gave some of the first directives for the work which has become widely known as Curative Education [see the chapter by Albrecht Strohschein,

'The Birth of Curative Education']. From Jena we went to Weimar, and there Rudolf Steiner went round in search of all the places that were so rich in memories from the decisive Weimar period of his life. He showed me the house where he had lived, stopped before another building and gazed for a long time in silence at the windows of the first floor. Then he said that someone whom he greatly respected had lived there, and he spoke with evident inner emotion of his experiences and vicissitudes during that time. He took me also to the café where he had so often had stimulating discussions with artists and Goethe enthusiasts. He paused here and there before a house or at a street-crossing and told me wonderful anecdotes about striking personalities of the '80s and '90s. During this day in Weimar I felt in him a mood of fulfilment, sustained by the work of the preceding days, and also of retrospect, conjured up by the Weimar atmosphere. Exactly 35 years had passed since he had come here from Vienna to examine the Goethe Archives – a visit which led to the fateful seven gears of his work at Weimar on Goethe's scientific writings. The experiences and stages of those years came back to him most vividly while we walked through the familiar places, after 35 years of his earthly work had been accomplished.

Something else happened during this visit to Weimar which may be mentioned here, for it bears on his relation not only to Goethe but also to the works of Schiller. While walking through the town he stopped suddenly in front of a hoarding and pointed to a notice announcing the performance of a play by Schiller in the Weimar Theatre on that very day. Since a little while before I had foolishly made a not very enthusiastic remark about some of Schiller's dramas, he now said, 'We must really see this'. It happened to be a not very distinguished performance for the Weimar girls' boarding school, and so in the theatre – I believe we were the only men present – there came about the curious picture of the striking figure of Rudolf Steiner in a black suit in the midst of a sea of young girls in white, who in accordance with educational custom were being made acquainted with Schiller's work. In spite of the somewhat inferior quality of the production, he leant over several times and said to me encouragingly, 'There are really many excellent passages in this.' Two years before, on his advice, I had read Deinhardt's *Contributions towards the Appreciation of Schiller's 'Letters on the Aesthetic Education of Man'*; now, through this visit to the theatre, he gave me the impulse to come to terms again with Schiller's writings as a whole, in spite of having had my taste for them ruined at school. This was a characteristic example of the way in which Rudolf Steiner kindly but effectively corrected inadequate and one-sided judgments on the part of his pupils.

After this moving and eventful visit to Weimar, we went on to Stuttgart. Late in the evening, directly after our arrival, Rudolf Steiner had a session with the teachers at the Waldorf School. As his companion, I had to take part, and this night session has remained vivid in my memory, for after all the strenuous activities of recent weeks – conferences, journeys, continual discussions, visits to towns and institutions – I was naturally rather weary, and yet in Rudolf Steiner there was no sign of weariness, although he had gone through incomparably more than I had, and he was in his 63rd year. I had to do my utmost to keep my eyes open, but he, in spite of the illness already seriously affecting him, showed such wakefulness and energy that no one could have guessed at his past exertions. He conducted the session with the most vital intensity and concentration. As on so many previous occasions, questions with regard to the curriculum, the spiritual and practical foundations of the school, were thoroughly discussed, and he not only gave advice and help in cases of special difficulty brought up by the teachers but also fundamental suggestions for the further development of the pedagogical work.

Often during this period it happened that when the night session was over, after many hours, he would call immediately for the car, and in the same night we covered the 150 miles from Stuttgart to Dornach. Dr Steiner had the capacity to relax and fall asleep for a short time while travelling in the car, although the roads then were far from good. When we reached Dornach in the grey of dawn, he was able immediately to go to work, beginning the strenuous round of the day, as full of tasks as the days at Dornach always were. Yet on the same evening he appeared on the platform of the Schreinerei, gave a report on his latest journey to the impatiently expectant gathering, and then launched immediately into the first of a series of lectures arranged for the coming weeks.

Often during these years the car trips from Stuttgart to Dornach would take place in the following way. He would ask me to have the car ready, perhaps, at noon. But when the time came, the stream of callers waiting for interviews at the house in the Landhausstrasse where he stayed was still growing. He would then come out with a friendly smile and say: 'We will leave after coffee,' and disappear again. This would be repeated again and again – at 5 o'clock, 7 o'clock, 9 o'clock in the evening; and only when the night was well advanced would he actually get into the car and start the journey to Dornach.

Ricarda Huch, in her book, *The Meaning of the Holy Scriptures*, speaks of the fate of the great spiritual leaders in the history of humanity: 'Everyone who is called is a sacrifice which feeds the flame; but, while he is being consumed, he illuminates and warms the wide world.' This was the destiny and the deed also of Rudolf Steiner in the 20th century.

The sacrificial flame consumed him during the months that remained until his return into the spiritual world. His sufferings kept his physical body tied to a sick-bed from September 1924, until his death on March 30, 1925. And even throughout this time of suffering the sacrificial flame gave light and warmth.

Where his workroom was, there Rudolf Steiner stayed during the months when he could no longer go out among people. He never returned to his house, but remained until his death in his studio on the Dornach hill, in the simple, lofty room where he had worked for decades and had given counsel and help to many thousands. His bed was at the foot of the Christ statue on which he had been carving as long as he could. Now it had to be quieter in this workroom. He could speak directly with only a few persons, his voice became weaker, his hearing a tax on his physical forces. The countenance had become thinner. Because of his suffering, the form of the noble head was even more plastically evident. His eyes spoke of pain, but they were kinder and more brilliant than ever. His lofty spiritual powers created in the stillness and concentration those gifts which from now until the end were bestowed on human beings through the written word.

Upon entering the studio during these weeks and months, one generally found Rudolf Steiner resting half-erect on his bed, reading or writing. He continued to work without interruption. Almost every day during this time he asked me to bring him his correspondence at the usual hour of 11 o'clock; he had the letters read to him, dictated answers and instructions, or gave directions for replies to all parts of the world. For the stream of questions and of requests for advice from all quarters never ended. If, in order to protect him, I showed him as little as possible, his questions drew into the discussion what had been withheld, for even in this time of apparent external separation he shared most intensely in the life of the society, of the friends, of his students. Every week Albert Steffen received for the weekly journal, *Das Goetheanum*, an instalment of his autobiography, *The Course of My Life*, painstakingly written in bed with his own hand. During conversations in the studio there came to light constantly new glimpses into the nature of significant individualities, into the tasks of mankind, and into contemporary events. Many things connected with the work, and especially the personal care and treatment of Rudolf Steiner, lay in the hands of Dr Ita Wegman, in whose advice and friendly assistance he had the utmost confidence.

During these months Rudolf Steiner addressed himself week by week to the whole body of his students in a letter called *To the Members*, published in the news-sheet. Here he was leading them more deeply and fully into the inner essence of the new age of Michael. These weekly letters were a concentrated epitome of what he had been bringing home to the consciousness of modern man during the long years of his activity as spiritual teacher; and at the same time they gave practical help and guidance for making further progress with courage and independence along these paths. Each letter ended with a concise *Leading Thought*, making it possible for the student to unite himself through concentration and meditation with the spiritual substance of the knowledge given, and thus gradually to make it ever more his own.

Besides this creative work, carried on day by day from his sick-bed, Rudolf Steiner continued as always to do an extraordinary amount of reading, keeping himself continuously abreast of new publications in science, art, history, and all other fields of work. Since he could no longer visit the bookshops and the dealers in antiquarian rarities, I was given the difficult job of regularly selecting and buying books which might be of interest to him. This was an exacting but richly rewarding task, for it was really hard to guess what he already knew, what might or might not interest him, what he would consider important or unimportant. Every few days, accordingly, I visited the bookshops in Basle, and often in other towns, looking for books which might be what he would care to read. And then, whenever

I came to his bedside with a great pile of books, it was always a time of suspense as he thoughtfully took one book after another, looked at the title and the name of the author, turned a few pages, and made his choice. The books that he wished to keep and read he stacked on the right side of the bed, and the others on the left. I was proud, naturally, when most of the books lay finally on the right; but I had to go at once in search of others if the heap on the left was the larger. It was very instructive to notice what he considered interesting or important in the flood of new publications in world literature; often, too, he characterised author and theme in a few words, and placed them in general perspective. How he managed to study the huge pile of books lying on the right side of the bed, in the midst of all his other work, and in spite of his illness, was a mystery, but chance remarks on the next occasion when I brought him books showed that in the meanwhile he had made himself thoroughly acquainted with the contents of their predecessors.

As an indication of his heartfelt concern for the persons about him, it may be mentioned here that he did not forget during his illness to co-operate by means of letters to friends in bringing about a worthy celebration of the 40th birthday of Albert Steffen on December 10, 1924. On the day before this event he wrote for the notice-board in the Schreinerei some words which marked his feelings:

'To our friends at the Goetheanum: On Wednesday, 10th December, friends wish to assemble at the Goetheanum to do honour to Albert Steffen on his 40th birthday. I cannot be present in person, but I shall be altogether present in spirit; for my heart is filled with admiring recognition of Steffen's life-work, and with warmest spiritual joy that we can call him our own.'

In December 1924, a work of construction had to be made secure for the future: the building of the second Goetheanum. Already the scaffolding, the foundation, and the walls of the great edifice, following the model made by Rudolf Steiner, were rising on Dornach hill; and repeatedly he called on those working with him in this spiritual movement to become fully conscious of the significance of the Goetheanum and to labour energetically for its realisation. Thus, in a letter dated December 30, he wrote the following words as a reminder of the need for steadfastness:

'For a year I carried about with me in my head the idea for the new Goetheanum. The transformation of this idea out of the medium of wood, used for the first Goetheanum, into the artistically unyielding medium of concrete was not easy. Then, at the beginning of this year, I began to work on shaping the model... For many years, in my anthroposophical writings and lectures, I have emphasised that anthroposophy is not only a theoretical conception of the world, but from its nature gives rise to a special style of art. And, since that is so, a building for anthroposophy must grow out of anthroposophy itself... I beg you to believe that this results from an iron necessity.'

This creative fulfilment of what was known to be right and necessary according to spiritual laws – to produce out of anthroposophy itself the building where science, art and religion were to come together in a new unity based upon the

Spirit – had from the beginning indwelt his creative purpose. He had called upon human beings in the spirit of Michael, the Time Spirit, to be true to this task, to carry further the work which he had placed in the stream of evolution by establishing it in space and time. He now again summoned all those responsible to be consciously active in this spirit, so as to assure for him a working place in the future.

1925: As he drew his last breath, he himself closed his eyes; but this filled the room with the experience, not of an end, but of a sublime spiritual action. The forward-striding figure of the Christ statue, pointing into the expanses of the universe, which he had created and at whose feet he now lay, spoke for the eyes of those left behind on the earth of what was here taking place for the spirit of a great human being who had dedicated his life to the annunciation of the Christ. Even in dying, Rudolf Steiner bestowed upon humanity the supreme gift of consolation: the certitude that death is a waking entry into worlds of spiritual life and deed.

What Rudolf Steiner gave to humanity in this earthly life was not only a teaching that can be accepted or rejected; not only a work that can be developed or destroyed. Teachings and works have always been subject to the destiny prepared for them by their contemporaries. Rudolf Steiner achieved in the course of his life the deed of receiving out of spiritual worlds, and incorporating in the earthly sphere, the spiritual Being, Anthroposophia. Such a Spirit Being, now dwelling in the earthly sphere, cannot be overcome by opposing powers through the fact that one or other of its forms of expression on earth is destroyed; it does not forfeit its existence because a blind decade will not look at it; it does not die even though a part of earthly humanity is not ready to accept it, or betrays or destroys its place of work and its dwelling. For it is of a supersensible nature, and so constantly rebuilds for itself constantly its earthly body.

The Last Months

Juliet Compton-Burnett

IT WAS IN THE AUTUMN OF 1922, after the educational conference at Oxford, that the eurythmy work in London began to be carried on in a consecutive way. Rudolf Steiner took the deepest interest in this beginning, and he always gave a specially warm welcome to any of the English teachers who returned to Dornach to continue training. We tried to arrange the work in such a way that one or the other of us could always be in Dornach, and great was my joy when it fell to me to return just in time for the lectures on 'Eurythmy as Visible Speech'.

This was in July, 1924. The first Goetheanum still lay in ruins and all the work had to be carried on in the first Schreinerei, the wooden building which had been used before the Goetheanum was completed. Owing to a eurythmy performance in London, I had to arrive a day late for the course, and, as I had been absent from Dornach for some months, I waited at the door leading behind the stage to speak to Marie Steiner as she went in. Going up to greet her as she approached, I was dumbfounded when she said, between severity and anxiety, 'You should not go into the lectures; people who do not follow the whole course add to Dr Steiner's burden.' Standing there in utter perplexity, I heard the familiar footstep. Dr Steiner passed by and was about to follow Frau Dr Steiner, when he suddenly turned. He came towards me and said abruptly, 'What is the matter?' Explaining my difficultly, I repeated Marie Steiner's words. Then came the warm handshake and the kindly smile: 'Go in – and do not worry.' So began the unforgettable experience.

In these last months of Rudolf Steiner's life, everything about him seemed to be intensified. The impression was not only of immeasurable goodness and greatness; it was as if the spiritual world revealed itself through his physical presence. It was in this atmosphere that the lectures unfolded their mighty content. Decades of study and practice now lie behind us. They have only served to prove the inexhaustible nature of what was then given.

The lectures, given to a specialised audience, had of course a character of their own, as so much depended upon demonstration. Rudolf Steiner corrected and made suggestions, showing himself here as the kindly teacher. But this was not all. Anticipation had run high, but who could have foreseen the reality? Cosmic horizons widened, and the eurythmists were carried on the wings of his spirit into undreamed-of realms, and were strengthened in their resolves when he spoke of his love for this new art which he had given to the world.

At this time Rudolf Steiner was often present at the rehearsals, and I recollect two incidents which I should like to set down because they are examples both of the strictness and pliancy of his approach. A certain eurythmist was showing a poem by Albert Steffen. As she finished, Dr Steiner got up and said, 'That will not do'; and he went on to say that for this poem he had already given a form and this being so, no other form should be used. 'For any poem there is only one true form' – his voice, stern and earnest, remains in my memory. What might have appeared a slight matter was once and for all given its full significance.

On the other occasion Marie Steiner was preparing a programme. A cello solo was to follow a solo poem. She turned to Rudolf Steiner, saying, 'But for both these solos only white is worn.' 'Well,' was the reply, 'for the cello piece let us take red and blue.'

The last weeks were passing. We prepared for the journey to England. The Torquay conference and the superhuman activities of the weeks which followed were experienced by many English people.

Michaelmas approached. That Rudolf Steiner's health gave cause for concern we knew; lack of strength could indeed sometimes be observed. Yet when, on that Friday, we went up to the Schreinerei for the members' lecture, nobody in my neighbourhood appeared to connect the long delay in opening the doors with possible illness. But the lecture was not given, nor was the lecture on the following day. Unexpressed anxiety filled our hearts.

When it became known, on Michaelmas day, that Rudolf Steiner would give his lecture, a load seemed lifted. Thus we assembled for the last time. Already, before he entered the hall, there was a sense of foreboding. The approaching footstep was altered, as though forced and heavy. The voice, too, was changed. It was loud and strained, as though strength had to be mustered. But strength did not last for the full hour, and Rudolf Steiner left the hall.

As we dispersed, we spoke of the content of the lecture, of the treasure we had received. Neither then, nor in the ensuing months, did I hear anyone voice the fear that Rudolf Steiner would not recover. Yet, looking back, I believe that those to whom this final experience had been granted knew, in their innermost hearts: This was the last time.

Rudolf Steiner in Holland

F W Zeylmans van Emmichoven

ALTHOUGH I had already heard the name of Rudolf Steiner once or twice, it took a chain of events to bring me into closer contact with him and with anthroposophy. This came about in the following way.

From my school days onwards I was always deeply interested in modern painting; while still at a Grammar School I often conducted my classmates through art galleries and was an ardent champion of Cézanne, van Gogh and Gauguin. It was the colours themselves that interested me primarily, and the new message that was trying to express itself through them. In 1916 this led to my making the acquaintance of the painter Jacoba van Heemskerck who together with Franz Marc, Kokoschka and Kandinsky, among others, belonged to the Expressionist movement; and in the great exhibition at The Hague I got to know not only her paintings but also her friend Maria Tak van Poortvliet, who later on had all her estates in Walcheren and North Brabant cultivated according to the biodynamic principles of agriculture indicated by Rudolf steiner.

These two ladies gave me a number of books on anthroposophy, every one of which I read. At that time the general view I held was that in the course of the centuries a few personalities of real significance have appeared in the world. The Buddha and other outstanding figures may be reckoned among them, and now, certainly, Rudolf Steiner as well – that is what I thought to myself. All of them are there to reveal aspects of the 'eternal truth'. But it was far from my mind to think that I should ever have anything to do with one of these personalities in particular.

In the years 1917 and 1918, while still a medical student, I was a frequent guest of the two friends on Walcheren, and we had many discussions about modern painting, above all about the new use of colours apart from objects. What effect do colours make upon the human soul ? We carried out tests with schoolchildren and I investigated how the pulse reacted to different colour-impressions, and other things of the same kind.

When the First World War was over, summer visitors came to Walcheren from Germany, among them acquaintances of Jacoba van Heemskerck: Professor Spalteholtz, the author of a well-known text-book on anatomy, and his wife. Spalteholtz was of opinion that the most favourable conditions for colour-experiments of this kind would be found in Leipzig, in Professor Wundt's laboratories. So in June 1920 I went to Leipzig. In the mornings I worked in Professor Flechsig's neurological clinic and in the afternoons carried out tests in the Wundt Laboratory. When I had time I was always able to go to the musical evenings held in the house of the Spalteholtz family in the Mozartstrasse, at which many members of the Thomaner Choir (of the Church of St Thomas, Leipzig) were often present.

Marie Tak had asked me to convey greetings from her to the leader of the anthroposophical group in Leipzig, and this I duly did. When I told this lady that I was in Leipzig for the purpose of making colour-tests, she enquired whether I would care to attend the course on the theory of colours then being given by Willy Stokar, a young Swiss who was studying in Leipzig. I went to his course, but thought that everything he put forward was fundamentally unsound, and, sad to relate, I made things so difficult for him that one day he said to me in despair that if I went on like this I should ruin the whole course. He was quite right. So I went to the university library, borrowed the volumes of Goethe's writings on natural science and began with Rudolf Steiner's introduction. It was as though rays of light suddenly fell in showers from the sky, penetrating right through me, when I read Rudolf Steiner's sentence: 'It follows that "the world", which confronts our senses, is a sum-total of percepts in continual metamorphosis, without any material substratum.' This single sentence left me spellbound. It gripped me so deeply that as I walked every day from the Brockhausstrasse through the park, watching the colours displayed by nature, it was constantly before me; a whole world arose from colour as though from a living being.

From the autumn onwards I had many valuable talks with Willy Stokar. And when I heard that a course of lectures on medicine had been given by Rudolf Steiner – until then I had no idea that anything of the kind took place – and that Professor Romer, who held the Chair of Dental Surgery in Leipzig, and a few other members of the Anthroposophical Society, were proposing to study this course, I went to the leader of the group and told her that I wished to join the society. 'Why?' she asked. 'Because I should like to participate in this work.' 'That is quite out of the question. What do you know about the subject?' 'Very little, but that is just why I want to study it.' The lady said she would think it over because after all, as, she said, I was a respectable person; I was to return the following week. When I came as arranged, she had the dressmaker in the house and opened the door a very little way. 'Who is there?' she asked. 'Zeylmans.' 'What do you want?' 'I want to become a member.' 'I have nothing against it,' she replied... so I became a member through the chink of a door.

In December 1920, I went to Dornach. My relation to anthroposophy had meanwhile become such that I had an intense desire to meet Rudolf Steiner. This was the decisive event. It came about in the following way.

On December 17, in the evening, I was sitting in the Schreinerei with my fiancîe, who was studying eurythmy in Dornach. Happy at being together again, we were waiting for Rudolf Steiner's lecture. Outside it was bitterly cold; Dornach lay covered in snow. Suddenly the blue curtain by the side of the stage lifted, and Rudolf Steiner went to the lecture-desk. At that moment I had the direct experience of recognition. The impression was so strong that a whole series of pictures simultaneously arose before me, pointing indeterminately to earlier situations – as if I were seeing him as my teacher through ages of time. It was the most memorable experience I have ever had in all my life. For some time I sat as though carried away and did not realise until later that his lecture had already begun. It was the first of the three lectures subsequently published under the title: *The Bridge between the Spirituality of the Cosmos and Physical Man*. These lectures were mentioned by Rudolf Steiner himself later on when some young doctors asked him what he would recommend for preparatory study.

When I came to myself again and saw Rudolf Steiner standing at the lecture-desk, I had the strange feeling that for the first time I was looking at a Man! It is not at all easy to describe this impression. I had met many well-known and famous people, among them scholars and noted artists, and had always moved in circles where a great deal was going on – it had by no means been a humdrum existence. But now I realised: this is what Man is meant to be. I began to question myself: What is the explanation for this? You have encountered many human beings – what is it that is so significant here? I said to myself first of all that it was his whole bearing, the bearing of one who is like a tree that grows freely between earth and sky. This impression was connected not only with his straight, erect figure, but above all with the poise of the head – it seemed to hover between heaven and earth. The second feeling was profoundly moving: from this beautiful, powerful voice came forth words which lived on even after they had been spoken. And thirdly, there were the thoughts. I was obliged to confess to myself that I could not always understand them, but I realised that they were not there merely to be understood intellectually, but they had another, quite different significance as well. Listening to professors, what always mattered was whether one understood everything they said. What mattered here was not whether I actually understood – it was something different. Today I could speak of 'ideas', of seed-bearing impulses and the like, but at that time I could not. I knew only that different impulses were at work here.

When the lecture was over, my fiancée said that she would now introduce me to Rudolf Steiner, for he liked this to be done; he wanted to meet young people. I had not thought of anything of the kind, but if it was the custom – well and good. I went to the front with her and was introduced. Rudolf Steiner said: 'I have been expecting you here for a long time.' I thought he meant that I had already been in Dornach for a long time. 'But, Herr Doktor, I arrived only late this afternoon.' He smiled merrily: 'That is not at all what I mean.' Having now been introduced, I was anxious to ask certain questions arising from my colour-experiments in Leipzig, and I asked if I might be allowed to have a talk with him sometime. 'Please come to my studio to-morrow at 3 o'clock,' he said.

The next day I came punctually to the anteroom of the studio, where a lady was carving wood. She asked me in a not very cordial way what I wanted. 'I have an appointment with Dr Steiner.' 'Herr Doktor is not receiving visitors today.' 'But please, he told me to come.' 'No, he is seeing nobody today.' This was really going too far. 'Will you please be good enough to tell him that I am here.' Before there was time for another refusal, the door opened and a Dutch lady came out, saying: 'Come in, Herr Doktor is expecting you.' So I went into the studio where Dr Steiner was sitting by a fiercely burning stove. An empty chair was standing as close to the stove as his. Luckily, I too like warmth and so felt comfortable.

The questions I put were on the following subject. In the course of my experiments I had discovered that the so-called active or warm colours stimulate the will-nature in the human being, whereas the passive, or cold colours cause a psychological retardation. When I encouraged the subjects of the tests to speak, asking them what they experienced, it was actually the case that after looking at active colours, they used expressions deriving from the sphere of will or passion: after impressions of the blue-violet side of the spectrum, they spoke more in terms of thought, contemplation or mysticism. Green lay midway, producing neutral qualities of feeling, with mere nuances of like or dislike. In the case of the peach-blossom colour [*purpur*, which Goethe termed pure red since it was free from both the blue tinge of mauve and the yellow tinge of the ordinary end of the spectrum; 'purple' in English would be misleading] lying at the other pole of the spectrum, also at a zero point, the effect was a kind of synthetic enhancement, all the qualities from the right and the left merging together. Green was a zero point because here the feelings were in equilibrium; peach-blossom colour also a zero point because intense will-activity balances out the qualities of thought and contemplation when these are enhanced to the utmost. I had discovered this by experiments, but a great deal was still obscure to me; above all, I had a number of questions relating to the peach-blossom colour.

'Have you really discovered all this?' Dr Steiner said with a smile. 'Yes, Herr Doktor, that is what resulted from the tests.' 'Then you have been lucky. You should really not have discovered it at all, considering the way in which you experiment. For you see' – he took writing-pad and pencil – 'it is like this. The spectrum with the seven colours is only one part of the whole spectrum, the part that is visible in the solar spectrum. To understand the whole spectrum one must draw a circle, and then here are the seven colours of the solar spectrum and on the other side the five peach-blossom colours. You ought really to have taken your start from these 12.' Then he said: 'One sees these seven colours because there the astral body swims, as it were, in the colours. But the peach-blossom colour is so subtle and ethereal that it hardly appears at all in external nature; there the "I" is living in the etheric; peach-blossom is actually the colour of the etheric.'

He explained all this quite quietly, tore off the sheet and put it on my knee. He had drawn a rough circle and had indicated the seven colours by letters on the one side, and on the other side the peach-blossom colours.

I sat there as if spellbound. It was almost impossible to believe that anyone could speak in this way about colours, for here were the answers to all the questions which I could not formulate properly, but which had lived within me subconsciously for the last six months. Suddenly, quite spontaneously, Dr Steiner said: 'You are a doctor, aren't you? What the doctors nowadays do not know but really ought to understand, is the law of reversal (*Umstülpung*).' He made the movement of pulling off a glove which turns it inside out, so that what was formerly inside, directed towards a centre, is now outside, directed towards the periphery. 'Only when that principle is understood can the human organs be understood in their relation to the universe. This applies especially to the spinal cord and the brain... Goethe surmised it but did not fully understand it.'

He gave certain other examples of organ-metamorphoses, and I stood up to go, noticing only at this moment that I had been sitting the whole time with my back to the Christ statue. According to the standards of art previously acquired, I did not really think the statue beautiful, but for all that it gripped me, and he saw what I was feeling. 'Yes, that is how the eyes of my spirit saw the Christ in Palestine,' he said. I stood still for a time while he waited in silence. Then he continued: 'But it is very difficult to show everything that would really be necessary.' He pointed to the robe. 'If it could be truly portrayed it should be nothing but flowing love.' He took up the chisel and hammer lying there. 'I have had to find a technique of my own, like this ... one must always take care that the left hand keeps turning, while the hammer is held by the right hand.' He gave a few knocks with the hammer while I stood there speechless, and then we said goodbye. Only later on did it dawn upon me that he was trying to convey to me certain laws of the etheric forces and movements with which a doctor ought to be conversant.

During this conversation I had felt aware, to my surprise, of the greatest inner freedom I have ever known in the presence of a human being. Just picture it: one was in the presence of Rudolf Steiner, the great Initiate, who could see through and through one – and one would have expected to feel great embarrassment. To my astonishment it was exactly the opposite. I felt freer than ever before, as though caught up into another world where only essentials count, where what is usually considered essential lapses into insignificance. This gave a wonderful feeling of happiness and freedom. The fact that because we were sitting side by side and not facing one another, he was not looking at me all the time, strengthened the feeling of freedom. He was mostly looking in front of him and only turned quite suddenly at crucial moments it was then that the whole sunlike power of the eyes was revealed. There were moments when without giving the slightest impression of inattentiveness, he was not listening while I was trying to speak about something or other, but was obviously listening to something else in my soul.

At Easter, 1921, when I went to Dornach again, the Goetheanum with blossoms all around it revealed to me more clearly than three months earlier that its forms had been shaped according to the laws of plant-life, the laws of the living; it seemed to me to be a living being with which from then onwards I felt united, and I tried to understand how such a great building could produce such an organic, living effect. When I had set eyes on it the first time, I had merely felt aware of some very unusual effect without being able to define it; now it was an actual experience. The meaning of the forms in their metamorphoses dawned upon me; I understood why pillars – which no longer fulfil any real purpose in modern architecture – were standing here, and I felt them as the ego-force within these metamorphosing forms. The light streaming through the coloured glass windows harmonised in a most wonderful way with nature in spring.

It was also very impressive to hear Rudolf Steiner speaking in the great auditorium of the Goetheanum. This was the first time I had heard him here, for at Christmas he had spoken in the Schreinerei, the temporary wooden structure where work in connection with the Goetheanum was carried out. It was as if his voice could resound to the full only in the great auditorium. His words remained there, and lived on. In one of the lectures – he had spoken of it in the second medical course which was being given during the same period, but this time it was in the presence of a public audience – he showed how natural science must develop into Spiritual Science, and that to practise magic in any form whatsoever was not permissible. In parenthesis he cried: 'Oh, but it would be possible!' He stood there seeming suddenly to have grown gigantic, like a magician, with arms outstretched. It was a deeply moving moment, because one realised what strict, undeviating principles he had prescribed for the course his life was to take.

This second course for doctors, like the first, was built up entirely on the basis of questions. It was given in the Glashaus, and one or two people came to the first lecture a few minutes late. After a remark by Rudolf Steiner on the virtue of punctuality, nobody failed to arrive exactly on time. The contents of the lectures entailed hard struggle. Would one ever be capable of correlating what was said with the knowledge and habits of thoughts acquired from seven or eight years of medical studies? On the other hand, every sentence strengthened the feeling that a door was opening into a hitherto unknown world.

At that time I also had conversations with Rudolf Steiner about patients, partly from my own practice, for in the meantime I had taken a post as medical superintendent in a department of a mental hospital near Rotterdam. My questions were inspired by the hope that from now onwards one would be able to cure every sufferer. But in discussing specific cases, Rudolf Steiner explained to me that the trouble might originate in destiny and that nothing could really be achieved; nevertheless in every case I was given advice about medicaments. This astonished me, for the attitude that one tries to cure in spite of the fact that nothing can really be achieved is unknown in orthodox medicine.

In November 1921, Rudolf Steiner made a long tour through Holland, speaking in The Hague on the Threefold Social Order and on education; he emphasised in public the need for a World School Union for the promotion of freedom in the sphere of education. It pained him greatly that a professor at the Technical School, who would have been capable of taking up this idea, did not do so. It could have become a splendid demonstration of free spiritual life over the whole free world, something that could have remained neutral, independent of political happenings.

At Whitsun 1922, at The Hague, Rudolf Steiner gave a series of very impressive academic lectures on anthroposophy and science. I had many opportunities of speaking with him, mostly about medical questions. At that time he wanted the doctors to bring out a medical *vademecum*, a handbook entering right into practical measures; with him, deepest esotericism and concrete action were always in balance. So it was, too, when on one occasion he said to me that if the marketing of Biodoron – the Weleda medicament for migraine – were cleverly done, the Goetheanum could be financed from that source alone. In connection with the *vademecum*, one of us asked what was the latest date when it ought to appear. 'The latest date? June 1921!' he rejoined. (It was already May 1922 when we wrote!)

During this spring I had discussed with a friend the possibility of founding a clinic. I now asked Dr Steiner for his views, saying at the same time that I felt I was really too young and lacked sufficient knowledge of anthroposophy. He consoled me: 'That you are young is of no account, for every day you become that much older. Nor does it matter that you still know little of anthroposophy, for every day you will understand more.' Then he became very serious and recommended me to go to Dr Wegman, 'for she has the true courage for healing'.

In November 1922, he again gave lectures in Holland which were rather poorly attended; in Rotterdam, especially, so few people came that we were very discouraged. But he himself thought differently, for in conversation with a friend he remarked that in Rotterdam there had been a very good audience. One had the impression that he perceived the worth of certain souls, and whether a large or small number of people were sitting there was of less importance to him.

I was still on the medical staff of the mental hospital on one of the islands in South Holland, inwardly rejoicing that I had found the path from Goetheanism to anthroposophy, and Rudolf Steiner as my teacher from an age-long past. But now some older anthroposophists got together and decided that the work was not progressing well, that a group feeling itself spiritually responsible should be formed and should place itself at Dr Steiner's disposal. I was invited to the meeting, although I emphasised that I was not conversant with the problems of the Society. Nevertheless I welcomed the opportunity of contacting Rudolf Steiner. On every occasion there was an atmosphere of festive happiness, whether I was talking to him about a particular case of illness or some other matter, whether the conversation lasted for half an hour or two minutes. Others besides myself will certainly have had the same experience.

A suggestion made with the best possible intentions by someone at the meeting appeared not to please Rudolf Steiner at all. He sat there quietly listening, tapping his foot. I waited in great suspense, wondering what would happen now. 'As long as our Society has such a sectarian character, we shall not progress a single step,' he said. A gunshot could not have had a more electrifying effect. He went on to say that in the way it was functioning at present, our Society could not be taken seriously by the outside world. And then he told us that a Roman Catholic priest had recently asked him for a talk; at last he had been able to speak with somebody about really important world affairs; the priest, too, had been delighted and had invited him to visit him. Rudolf Steiner regretted that he had not found time to accept this invitation; he would also have liked to invite this priest to Dornach, but had abandoned the idea because he could not be sure how the members would behave.

Finally he asked if there was nobody in Holland capable of lecturing to the public? At this there was silence, because one or two such attempts had been made without success; there had been extremely poor audiences. I had given some very elementary lectures at the wish of the members who thought that a qualified doctor might make more impression; true, a few more people came, but always fewer than a hundred. When one of the members present expressed the opinion that I had given one or two quite well-attended lectures, it was an astonishment to me as well as to everyone else, when Rudolf Steiner said: 'Well, then, all you need do is to free Dr Zeylmans for anthroposophical work and offer him a handsome salary.' He turned to me: 'Would you agree to this, doctor?' Now I did not consider that my lecturing activities were of any value; I regarded the lectures as having been quite insignificant, even blundering, performances in which with pain and labour I had strung together the little I knew. But I said: 'Yes, Herr Doktor, if you think I am capable, I will naturally do it gladly.' He repeated that I must of course be free in order to work for anthroposophy. After that there was silence; something different had been expected from him. Only one of the members, Peter de Haan, took the matter up, and to him I said, although inwardly embarrassed, that I would try to move to The Hague in order, possibly, to found a clinic and make a living out of my practice.

When, soon after this, the Goetheanum was destroyed by fire, I was still working in the mental hospital and could not travel to Dornach, because although I was allowed more leave for studies than others, the maximum had already been exceeded. I did not see Dr Steiner again until the Delegates' Meeting in June, 1923. Although I took part in the discussions on the subject of providing funds for building the new Goetheanum, when I actually spoke to him it was, as usual, mainly about patients. Finally, I also asked him about the statues that had been discovered not long before on the coast of Walcheren. Among them was the statue of a goddess by the name of Nehallenia. I had brought photographs with me and showed them to him. 'Yes,' he said, 'that is one of the aspects of the Goddess of Fertility, similar to Herta, of Germanic-Celtic origin. Here you can see the fourfold nature of man indicated: the temple is the physical body, the dog is the etheric body, the astral body is indicated by the fruits, and the child is the unfolding ego. More than that is not yet entirely clear to me. One would have to make further investigations in the neighbourhood itself. The whole of the west coast of Holland is important because from time immemorial there has always been a link with Britain.' The anthroposophical societies in the different countries were to be founded anew, and the founding of the Society in Holland was planned for November, 1923. At The Hague, Rudolf Steiner gave a course of evening lectures with the title *Supersensible Man in the Light of Anthroposophy*. There were also two public lectures and two in the recently founded clinic (I had now come to live in The Hague); also a number of lectures for members. It was a tremendous programme. Both the little clinic –

established to begin with in a private house – and the little school were now inaugurated, and dedicated in the real sense.

I went with a few friends to fetch Dr Steiner from the station. As the train slowly came in and I saw him sitting at the window, I was shocked by his pallor and look of utter fatigue, and at the same time I saw in his face the hallmark of eternity. It was as though the countenance were chiselled out of rock – an impression that went through my very bones. Then came the ordinary conventions: I helped him to get down from the carriage, welcomed those who had come with him – Frau Dr Steiner, Myta Waller, Frau Dr Wegman, Dr Wachsmuth – and when I was accompanying him down the stairway leading from the station, I asked if he had had a good journey. He stopped still in the middle of the stream of passengers, turned to me and said with surprise: 'What do you mean, a good journey?' What he wanted to say was suddenly clear to me. I had seen him arrive, our eyes had met, I had seen who he was, and he had seen that I had seen... and now I was asking whether he had had a good journey. What he wanted to say was: 'Wake up! Don't be conventional!' We were still standing immobile in the stream of travellers. 'I mean only whether there were any outer annoyances,' I said at last. 'Ah, so that is what you mean. Well then, yes, I have had a good journey.'

He visited the little school, which consisted of no more than two or three rooms in a private house, with very few children in three classes, but he conducted the inauguration with as much earnestness and solicitude as if it were already a large school, looked at the children, gave advice about each one individually, in some cases medical advice as well. As the school doctor, I was very often astonished by these medical indications. There was a poor little thin child with an ashen grey skin. 'He is full of fear down into his very organs,' said Dr Steiner. 'He must do the movement for *I* (ee) in curative eurythmy while jumping over a rod... and then, of course, he must take *Prunus spinosa* [Blackthorn] ...' I had never heard of *Prunus spinosa*, for botany was hardly ever included as a subject at the university, and I felt like a stupid child, everything was so new and full of surprises. '*Hypericum perforatum* [St John's wort] ... that you surely know? The leaves are all perforated and one can see the drops of oil,' he said to me as I sat at the back with my notebook. And it continued like this for three whole mornings, with the two class teachers, van Bemmelen and Frau Mulder, and the eurythmy teacher, Fräulein Hoorweg.

The clinic, too, was simply a private house where I worked with one nursing sister; at first we had only a single patient who regarded herself as a permanent boarder. And again Rudolf Steiner behaved as though a big hospital were being opened. I had collected some 35 doctors and senior medical students for two medical lectures which he then gave. The lectures were surprisingly well received, although it was the first time that most of those present had heard anything about anthroposophy. After the second lecture one of the older doctors got up to speak. He said that the lectures had made a great impression upon him, that they represented an integrated system in which, admittedly, there were many gaps, but he realised that these gaps would be closed in further lectures. 'My natural scientific world-view is also an integrated system,' he added, 'equally with gaps to be filled, but these too may disappear. For which system am I to decide?'

The doctor who put this question was sitting at the very back. Dr Steiner walked slowly through both parts of the room to him and said: 'You are perfectly right. More cannot really be said. But it is the heart that makes the decision.'

This doctor telephoned to me the next day and said that although he was not entirely convinced, he wanted to give anthroposophical therapy a 'fair chance', and asked me to treat him for angina pectoris.

After the evening lectures, a group of us always went with Rudolf Steiner to his hotel. After he had had food, we sat round an open fire in the hall and conversation continued, often until very far into the night, about new literary publications, political happenings and other subjects. Dr Steiner was usually full of cheerfulness, told us anecdotes or answered questions. For example, Herr van Leer asked: 'A wonder-working Rabbi such as the Ba'al Shem [the founder of Hasidism, a mystical movement which arose among Polish Jews in the 18th century] must surely have had great powers – is he to be regarded as an Initiate?' 'No, such a man is capable of a very great deal, but was not even a semi-Initiate,' was the reply.

This year, following the burning of the Goetheanum, was marked by the new foundation to be given to the Anthroposophical Society. Dr Steiner, who until then was explicitly not an actual member of the Society but wished his task to be only that of teaching anthroposophy, was hoping that impulses and efforts sufficiently vigorous to give a new form to the work would be forthcoming from the membership itself. A first step was the founding of independent Societies in the different countries. And so in Holland, too, various enterprises had been set on foot in preparation for the actual founding of the Society in the presence of Dr Steiner. In speaking on the subject, he had never given more than indications, and one tried to understand what it was that he really hoped for. But in many preliminary meetings we really did not get much farther than saying that what was wanted was not an 'organisation' but an 'organism'. Many thoughtful ideas with a Goethean trend were expressed in connection with this, but actually we were in a sea of doubt and perplexity.

At this time too – November 1923 – when Dr Steiner was at The Hague, there were meetings in his presence. Reports were given from the different spheres of work; I, too, had to give an address which seemed to me such a poor performance that I felt obliged to apologise to Dr Steiner. He laughed quite cheerfully, and said: 'That kind of thing is by no means bad; not until one has given a hundred lectures can one count upon there having been a good one among them.' I found this a source of real encouragement.

During the discussions about the founding of the Society, Dr Steiner sat for the most part silently waiting. What he wanted, of course, was that the members themselves should find what the situation required. While the talk was proceeding, he studied, for example, the mechanism of the writing-tablet of a lady sitting beside him – the writing could be obliterated by moving a slide; he took out of my hand the tobacco pouch which I had inadvertently drawn from my pocket, scrutinised the zip fastener, then recently invented, and said to me: 'What a pity that one of us did not invent something so ingenious.'

On the evening before the actual founding of the Society he was very downhearted and spoke bitter words about the members, saying that they were full of good intentions, but failed to grasp what was really desired by the spiritual world. We sat there shattered, realising what sorrow filled him and what heavy cares weighed upon him. Conversation began again only slowly, and Dr Steiner explained more clearly his disappointment with the Society everywhere and what he found lacking in it. He said, too, that he had given definite promptings; now, instead of taking them up, people came with quite different, totally inadequate proposals. It was late in the night – the next morning, Sunday, 18th November, was when the actual Foundation Meeting was to take place – when the conversation finally ended. I told Rudolf Steiner that I was willing to accept office as General Secretary of the Society in Holland. Quite unexpectedly, the next morning was the happiest that could possibly be imagined. We made one blunder after another, but Dr Steiner sat there confidently, and finally gave us a draft for the statutes of the Society in Holland. We were to work it out and subsequently bring it into line with the principles of the General Anthroposophical Society to be founded in Dornach at Christmas. After lunch he spoke to me about my functions as General Secretary. 'Remember,' he said, 'from now on you have to bear the whole esoteric and exoteric responsibility for everything that happens in the anthroposophical domain here in Holland.' He took both my hands and gazed at me for some time. That was the last meeting in the year 1923, before the Christmas Foundation.

When at Christmas, 1923, we came to Dornach for the foundation of the General Anthroposophical Society, it was clear to me from the moment when Dr Steiner 'laid the Foundation Stone', that we were witnessing a Mystery-deed that concerned the whole of mankind, the first Mystery-enactment to be performed openly before the world. True, the 800 or so people present were members, but members of such different kinds and stages of development that this deed could certainly be said to have been performed in public. There were friends who felt, as I did, that we had lived through a kind of birth-hour – now I have been born as a spiritual personality. Gradually it dawned upon me how this laying of the Foundation Stone was connected with the original laying of the Foundation Stone of the first Goetheanum on 13th September 1913. At that time the Foundation Stone was laid in the earth in the form of a double dodecahedron, and the forms of the Goetheanum had been able to arise over it. Now, after that Goetheanum had been consumed by fire, all its forces and forms and colours, everything it made visible as a kind of embodied Imagination came back from the spiritual world as Inspiration, in the words of the Foundation Stone Meditation at Christmas, 1923.

The second impression was connected with what Rudolf Steiner planned as the Free High School of Spiritual Science, with three classes. He wanted this High

School to be regarded as an institution standing openly in the world; progress through the different classes would depend entirely upon actual inner development. Here, too the manifest and the secret together: the revealed secret in the Goethean sense.

During these days I also had talks with Dr Steiner which shall be briefly reported here. First of all I asked about a member who had died – she was a painter – and whether it would be possible to form a link with her. Dr Steiner said: 'One can come near her by recalling a definite moment of importance – for example, when one was looking at a picture while she was actually painting it. Such a situation should be visualised in all detail; then, when it becomes a vivid experience, one should damp down the waking consciousness, allow what is now living inwardly in it to flow on and then bear it up to her in the spiritual world, waiting in stillness for a response. That is how contact can be established.'

Another time I asked him about the work now devolving upon me in Holland, saying that I found it very difficult to carry out my duties as a medical practitioner, to help in promoting understanding of anthroposophical medicine, and now also to shoulder the tasks incumbent upon the General Secretary of the Society. I found the last – the work for the Society – especially difficult, for I was less interested in it than in Anthroposophy itself. 'But it is your karma and nothing can be done about it,' he said. As we talked on he repeated this, and yet a third time at the end. In reply to my remark that I found it extremely difficult to combine the functions of doctor and General Secretary, he said: 'It is a very good thing that you, a doctor, should be the General Secretary, for the Society will more and more be in need of healing.' And about the work he said: 'Everything will develop in time, but the first thing to be done is to get the high school established. As for the problems of the Society, you may think of them like this: the Society imposes tasks all the time; it is in the loneliness of the soul that the solutions are found.'

Mention shall also be made of the meeting I had with him in Paris in May 1924. He gave a lecture in the Salle Solferino, in the Boulevard St Germain. Jules Sauerwein, foreign editor of *Le Matin*, translated, and Edouard Schuré, then a very old man, was among the listeners. Between the lectures for the members and all the other demands on Rudolf Steiner I was able, to my joy, to speak with him at some length about the work in Holland. The conversation was always serious and at the same time cheerful. Then one morning I went for a walk, and in the precincts of Notre Dame met Rudolf Steiner and Frau Dr Wegman coming across the great Square; they had evidently just been in the cathedral. I went up to them. 'Have you already been in the Sainte Chapelle?' I asked, meaning the historic 13th-century Chapel that had once been the scene of fiery disputations between the great Dominican scholars of the Sorbonne and those known as the Arabists. 'That is just where we want to go,' answered Dr Wegman, 'but how does one get to it?' As I had just come from there, I showed them the way through the gate, pointed to the little tower that was visible from where we were standing... and that was all. Yet the incident seemed to me to mean more than can be put into words.

During the Christmas Meeting I had already asked Dr Steiner if he would be willing to give a course of lectures on education to us in Holland, and he himself at once suggested the dates. 'What exactly do you want me to do then?' I produced my list of requests – first, a public course on education; secondly, one or two public lectures on medical themes; and thirdly, three lectures for members. He agreed to the whole programme without hesitation. Two other special meetings and an address to young people were subsequently added. We had given a great deal of thought as to where these lectures ought to be held, had visited several likely places and had finally decided on Arnhem, because a fine conference hall on the banks of the Rhine could be rented there. In the neighbourhood there were also memorials of ancient Germanic times, and historic traditions of that kind are rare on the young soil of Holland. In short, we were convinced we had found the right place. But when Rudolf Steiner arrived and was driving to his hotel, he glanced around him and said: 'Surely this is a kind of holiday resort? Apparently it is becoming more and more the custom to combine anthroposophical studies with a summer holiday.' At this we all felt a little embarrassed.

Shortly before I had been obliged to make one of the most difficult decisions in my life. Dr Steiner had telegraphed that as he would be late in arriving, he would not be able to give his first lecture. On 17th July 1924, when Peter de Haan, Michael Tschechow, another Russian actor, and I fetched him from the station at the time indicated, I was appalled to see how deadly tired and ill he looked. We went to the car, and even before it started he said to me: 'So I was not able to give my first lecture this morning. What do you think, Doctor – ought I to make up for it by giving a lecture this afternoon?' I had been obliged to give the opening lecture myself, because several public officials and important guests had come to hear it. Dr Steiner was aware of this. Frau Marie Steiner insisted that a lecture was out of the question because Dr Steiner was exhausted after the many sessions in Stuttgart and simply must rest this afternoon. One could fully sympathise with this, but Dr Steiner, quite unperturbed, looked only at me and repeated that it was for me to decide, since I was responsible for these meetings. 'Do you think I should or should not give this lecture?' Again Frau Marie Steiner interjected that it was out of the question, and again Dr Steiner emphasised that it was up to me to decide; it was my responsibility. Everything in me cried: Rest, rest, cancel the whole programme! But on the other part I thought: other laws hold sway here. At last I said: ' Herr Doktor, I believe you should give the lecture.' He replied quietly – very well then, he would give it.

During these meetings it was impossible not to realise how ill Rudolf Steiner was. When others were lecturing – Dr Schubert, Dr von Baravalle, Mr Van Bemmelen, Mr Stibbe and I – it was heart-breaking to see how exhausted he seemed to be; I noticed, too, with grave anxiety, how emaciated he had become. For all that it was evident on every occasion that in spite of utmost fatigue nothing escaped his attention, and when he was standing at the lecture-desk he was, as always, sparkling with fire, full of life and vitality – one could hardly realise that this was the same man. It was profoundly moving that in the lectures on education, as well as in the address to young people, he should have spoken about Schiller and Schiller's death, about the fire of enthusiasm which consumes a man's being, about Schiller's heart which, at the end, appeared to be almost devoid of physical substance. The inevitable impression was that there, in front of one, was an illustration of what he was speaking about: the fire consuming the body.

At that time in Arnhem I was also able to have talks with him, and asked for advice in the dilemma of having to speak in public about anthroposophical matters of which one knew so little from direct personal experience. 'You may speak about anything in my courses and lectures provided you take care that a year has passed since you studied it,' he answered. We also spoke about another question of principle: that all expressions of modern cultural development to be perceived in painting and literature had always fascinated me, and that I should find it very difficult to put all this aside. He answered: 'Your attitude should be this. You should always have the greatest imaginable tolerance for what comes to manifestation in the world, while at the same time training yourself to let the strictest truth hold sway in presenting anthroposophy.' I realised that this must be the guiding principle in my work.

One evening during those days a few of us were together with him, discussing the point that the 'International Laboratories' in Arlesheim, where the medicaments were prepared, should at last be given an appropriate name. We sat round the table, one after another making suggestions, some humorous, some ingenious and some less ingenious. Dr Steiner sat with his writing-pad in front of him, pencil in hand, listening with a faint, almost mischievous smile. He began to let the pencil play above the pad. Suddenly he made a wavelike movement, coming nearer and nearer to the paper, and finally he said: 'Welle-da... yes, the old Germanic priestess of healing.' And that was how the Weleda Company received its name.

All of us who went to attend the new courses in Dornach in September 1924, felt that we were lifted into other spheres, high above our ordinary consciousness; our very faces changed, we were seeing and hearing beyond the range of our own capacities. As we looked at one another we asked ourselves inwardly: Is that really so-and-so? It was something quite unbelievable and indescribable. We were already living in a spiritual world that was by no means within our grasp. There were moments during the last lectures of the course on Pastoral Medicine when only love and spirit radiated from Rudolf Steiner – with such intensity that it was almost difficult to listen to what he was saying. But the audience was, of course, one to which he could allow his whole being to speak. In the evenings he was giving the great series of lectures on the karmic relationships of individuals. The lecture in which he spoke of Otto Weiniger [See *Karmic Relationships: Esoteric Studies*, lecture 9] was the last I myself was able to hear. That same afternoon, one or two doctors among us, together with Frau Dr Wegman, had been with him. He lay on his couch with a rug over him and gave us a last injunction. I had then to return to my work in Holland.

On 30th March 1925 his death summoned us to Dornach. We shared the vigil by his death-bed, and some account shall now be given of the last night and the direct impressions I received at that time.

Rudolf Steiner lay there in his studio, on his death-bed. What his spirit revealed to me through the picture of death of this I will try to speak. It will be but a feeble stammering, for only the divine-gifted poet can say what is beyond all speech... It was a picture of the joy of gods and the sorrowing of men. 'The friend of God, and the leader of mankind,' as Albert Steffen called him, had passed through the gate of death. Outside in nature the gods were celebrating a festival, because the great leader of mankind came to them. Within, around the death-bed, men were mourning because the friend of God was taken from them. Outside, the spring arrived. The birds suddenly began to sing. The joy of resurrection lived in the plants and animals. The joy of resurrection sought its way to man, entered through his senses, and sank down into his heart. Within, around the death-bed, stood the mourners, and gazed, stricken with grief, upon the beloved countenance. Memories, the most precious and beautiful of their lives, arose. Grief convulsed their souls or was packed away in their hearts. Thus the joy of resurrection and the pain of death met with one another: heavenly joy and human pain.

How wonderful he looked on the first day after his death! As in a light sleep – so peaceful and thoughtful – as if he could awaken at any moment, to tell us what his spirit experienced there above with the gods.

His death had been a prayer, so we were told. He lay for hours in deepest meditation, gazing into far distances. Then his meditation became more and more a prayer. He lay motionless with folded hands. Only a few words had he spoken to his intimate friend and nurse, Dr Wegman. It was only after some hours that he closed his eyes and died – without any agony of death. His prayer on earth was ended.

But to us, it was as if his spirit continued to pray, as if his mighty prayer moved through our sorrowing souls. And in our hearts, where the joy of resurrection and the pain of death were, something blossomed forth and soared aloft, borne upward by his prayer. And that which was for each individual a prayer of thanksgiving became for us all collectively a sure picture of the future.

On the second day, it seemed to me different. There now lay a shadow of grief upon his countenance. It was as if something of the grief of the many hundred of friends who came together from many lands was reflected in this countenance. It was more difficult now to experience the joy of resurrection. But from his shining brow solemn and happy thoughts seemed to float upwards.

Then came the third day. Again a change had taken place. One now saw the face of a saint – griefless and sinless. A face that appeared super-humanly great – but which contained in miniature everything that is good and true and beautiful. Separated from us far beyond our reach – but at the same time near; godlike, but containing all things human. His noble brow was even more radiant than before. In his deep-set eyes, world-secrets lay hidden. His mouth spoke cosmic language. Never were there such hands. They were as strong as the hands of one accustomed to heavy manual labour. But they were spiritualised right into the very muscular fibres. With them he had chiselled the hard wood; with them he had written his clear, flowing writing. To countless numbers he had over and over again given his hand, and everyone had felt it as a blessing...

Six doctors and four others who were near friends of Dr Steiner were allowed, during the last night, to keep the vigil, two by two. The hours we passed there were full of unforgettable beauty and holiness. It was a still and peaceful spring night. The moon shone bright like a sun. Black demonic-looking clouds tried over and over again to darken her radiance – but she threw the sunlight to the earth ever more brightly.

In the studio, now in the coffin, lay the body, unlike any other body of the dead. Lighted candles around threw their golden light upon the black coffin. The scent of flowers filled the air, speaking a delicate language of the soul. The statue of the Christ, with its gestures expressive of world-destiny, rose great and silent at the foot of the coffin.

On the right and on the left, two of us stood watching, guarding the candles that they might burn with an even and quiet flame. How strange and mysterious everything seemed, and yet at the same time how familiar. Pictures from a long, long past rose before us, gleaming like silver in the candlelight – and disappeared. Surely we had been at this scene before...

Then all at once we knew: this is an event that is beyond all time. It points into the long-distant past and into the still more distant future. Past and future are here molten into one and form together an eternal, macrocosmic picture – a picture of the Divine guidance of man and of his cosmic destiny.

Some friends came in and a death-mask was taken. We stood around in silence. When it was evident that the mask had turned out well, we thought with joy: Now, through long years to come, many more will be able to see this expression of deepest wisdom, tenderest love and greatest holiness. The birds were now singing in the early dawn...

We know well that difficult times are before us. But for everyone who in his sorrowing heart has entered into the meaning of the Festival of the Resurrection, the difficult times will be only times of testing – trials of soul that he will have strength to endure. At that time Albert Steffen wrote these moving verses:

Crumbled earth of fallow fields
In a damp wintery grave
Has transformed itself – now yields
The shining figure of a white flower

Whose chalice centre, petalled crown
As visage and wings of light appear –
Christ raises You from the hillside
Up into the holiest sphere.

How all the heavenly folk rejoice,
How the starry choirs resound
At Your earthly beauty which
gently itself from death unbound.

Yes, You come in earthly garment
Yet far removed from all decay –
From this moment angels welcome
Human Beings to Spirit's day.

For the colours of the earth
Now cleansed by You, to them are dear:
Your graceful countenance has joined
Human-kind and God together.

VIGNETTES

Rudolf Steiner at the Rostrum

Friedrich Hiebel

THEN THE EVENING drew near. All available seats of the great hall had already been filled for the morning and afternoon activities, and now there was a throng of people crowding up the steps. There were not enough seats. For the evening lectures, the students, who had got reduced admission and travel stipends, had to exchange their seats every other day for standing room. The advantage of this arrangement was that they might find a place closer to the podium, or even sit on the steps leading up to it, thus coming closer to the lecturer than the people sitting in the front row.

On this first evening, I had a seat in the middle of a completely filled row and waited with intense anticipation for things to start. My eyes focused on the stage, I wondered again and again whether one or other of the people there could possibly be Rudolf Steiner. Seen from a distance, one of the members of the central council of that time resembled Rudolf Steiner, an impression supported by the council member's dark hair and black scarf.

Suddenly the hall fell silent. A few people silently hurried to take their seats. Then we saw Carl Unger ascend to the podium. He welcomed Rudolf Steiner on behalf of the Anthroposophical Society and thanked him for his contribution to the congress. While these brief introductory words were spoken, all eyes turned to the tall figure of the man in black tails who slowly walked from backstage to the center and then let his eyes wander over the audience.

Slowly, Rudolf Steiner walked over to the lectern. The way he walked revealed something of the balance between a soaring freedom from the body and the permeation of earth substance with will. Indeed, Rudolf Steiner's gait was like that of a young man. His face was framed by black hair, which still showed no trace of grey at the age of 60. Lines on the forehead and furrows around the chin and the corners of the mouth bore witness in the spiritual battles of the quest for knowledge, and in their dignity contrasted strangely with the youthful agility of his limbs.

In noblest bodily symmetry, a man stood before us who was the ensouled focus of a world of concentrated spirit-will. Polarities such as that of youth and age seemed to have no validity here. It was as if they were brought into a mysterious balance. Neither his forehead nor his chin were overly pronounced in terms of physiognomy. His nose was itself like a symbol of the symmetry of the whole man.

None of the many carefully taken photographs, none of the probably adequate drawings and busts can fully convey the essence of his stature. For even the best pictures remain silent, and it was only in his word that the essence of his being was revealed, in the word that seemed to take on form in the structure of his sentences and to support itself on the gestures of his arms!

Rudolf Steiner's word now resounded in the great hall, speaking to nearly 2000 listeners. The contrast between the delicate features of his spiritualized physique and the deep resonance of his speech, resulting from breathing deeply with the diaphragm, was surprising. The deep tone of his speech rested in the larynx, vibrated in the chest, and was permeated with the warmth of the heart. There was neither the choppiness of cold intellectuality that is in danger of squeaking in cerebral sounds nor the roar of commands associated with a will-imbued brutish nature.

The word revealed in Rudolf Steiner's speech came as if from organ pipes capable of all modulations, harmonies and configurations, tensions, spirals, cadences, and counterpoints in the cosmos.

He greeted us with the usual formula of polite address, but it sounded as though he had lifted this common expression just now for the first time from the deep treasury of his vocabulary. The words appeared to be chosen very consciously. He began to speak slowly, without the conventional speed prompted by the intellect or routinely unrolled by the will. In uttering the greeting, Rudolf Steiner was actually fully present and truly there in the word with all his heart-filled seer's consciousness.

During the introductory sentences of his lecture, he seemed to keep his eyes almost completely closed, and his glance directed downward. His posture was that of a man listening inwardly. He remained in this inwardly listening stance, gathering himself with all his will forces, for the duration of several long sentences. Seemingly unconcerned about the audience, he appeared to be struggling to find his inner bearings. Indeed, at first it seemed that he was labouring with the wording of the initial sentences. Then came a clearly discernible breakthrough: he opened his eyes, looked directly at the listeners, and began to reinforce his talk with a forceful and diverse language of gestures.

The first third of the lecture was characterized by an intentional breadth of thought, and the speech marked by epic diction. Then the presentation led to an increasingly tender note of heartfelt empathy. The last part of Steiner's talk penetrated noticeably and consciously into the depths of the will. The tempo of the speech grew, the tone became more forceful, the gestures even more drastic.

This introductory lecture, subtitled 'Agnosticism: the Destroyer of Genuine Human Nature,' had a particularly strong impact, like an apocalyptic trumpet call sounding the common chord for all the other lectures on anthroposophy's roots and its fruits in life.

Of the 70 lectures by Steiner that my destiny kindly permitted me to hear, that opening lecture has remained most vividly and indelibly in my memory. That experience combined with a presentiment that developed into a growing certainty: I have encountered this voice already once before! Here, a man stood before me who taught first how to comprehend consciously and in freedom with the head, then knew how to reach people from heart to heart, and finally was able to enter into the depths of the will. . . .

He spoke without any pretension. In the lectures to the members, he spoke much more slowly than in front of the public. He avoided raising his voice and intensifying the diction of his sentences, noticeable at other times and used by him for its effect on the public. He concluded the lecture simply, in quiet culmination. No applause followed. For a time, the listeners remained quietly in their seats. Usually, we got up only after Rudolf Steiner himself had risen again from the seat he had taken after having ended the lecture.

Soon, however, he was surrounded again by people. He gently smiled at one person, warmly shook another's hand. With a slight wave of his hand he greeted those standing at some distance. In leaving, he did not seek out an emergency exit or side door that would have protected him from the onrush of the crowds. Willingly and consciously, he mingled with the crowds of people. On most occasions, he took Marie Steiner protectively by the arm. With the courtesy of an Austrian man? With the elegance of a gentleman? With the demeanor of a man of the world? No. All three were there, elevated to a higher unity.

How much his being, able to penetrate the spirit, and the universality of his genius manifested even in the minutest details of early existence is sufficiently known. He always made a point of considering everyone, even those employed in hotels and restaurants, in their full human dignity and of addressing them accordingly. For example, to the waiter who assisted him in ordering vegetarian dishes, he gave a gratuity, not after the meal but at the beginning, a gift that went far beyond the customary amount of a tip. He was aware that the extra service he wanted required an equally unusual remuneration.

When it seemed justified in spiritual terms, Rudolf Steiner could also sharply admonish people. This is what happened to a desk clerk in a hotel in Vienna when Rudolf Steiner, upon arriving by train in the morning, found the rooms he had reserved not yet ready. The desk clerk of this first-class hotel may have been a snob who imitated the airs of the hotel guests (formerly aristocrats, now the *nouveaux riches*). When Steiner was asked why he had been so indignant – a moment later he was again utterly calm – he said that one had to yell at demons.

An Impression of Dr Rudolf Steiner

W Loftus Hare

THE FAMILIAR PHOTOGRAPHS of Dr Steiner that have appeared in various magazines prepare us for a facial appearance rather narrow and gaunt. They did not help me, however, when I entered the Steinway Hall on last Good Friday evening, but I easily picked out the philosopher from among the group of people moving at the foot of the platform by his modest Continental attire and distinguished appearance. Of middle height with dark, close hair and graceful movements, Dr

Steiner combined the appearance of a German professor and a healthy pastor. When at last he spoke it was clear that he possessed the qualities of expositor and preacher to a matchless degree. Also, being an artist to his finger tips, it was obvious why he spoke in his own tongue, of which he has an absolute mastery, and not in English. Incidentally, he disposed of one of those strange rumours in advance – that he would speak bad German. Though I am no good judge of the German language, I was able to hear every syllable of the six medium-length discourses which Dr Steiner delivered at Easter, and to appreciate the variety of beautiful vowels caught in the grip of jagged consonants so perfectly enunciated. Again, at Oxford in August, I heard Dr Steiner many times. The German construction lends itself to an oratory different from ours, of which Dr Steiner takes full advantage.

Leaving aside for the moment the matter of Dr Steiner's addresses, I would dwell on their form. The speaker has a fine clear voice, capable of great extension of power, deep and manly in tone and flexible to every need of his ideas and his feeling. He never loses control of it or exerts it to its maximum capacity, seeming to have an infinite reserve upon which to draw. In every lecture there is some mood one has not observed before. In view of the fact that a large proportion of an English audience is unable to understand German (upon whom therefore much of the fine eloquence would, in a manner, be wasted), it is a question whether he does not exert himself disproportionately to the need. Thus there is an added formality, somewhat akin to the task of addressing empty chairs, which must increase the burden imposed upon the speaker, who, however, suffers not the slightest embarrassment from it.

It must be evident, to those who hear Dr Steiner's first few sentences, that they are faced by an accomplished, spontaneous and yet disciplined orator, who gives to his voice, his head, his hands and his body a natural freedom of gesture which at the same time is restrained by a certain measure of traditional conventionality. But the gestures are very varied and entirely appropriate to the intellectual content and emotional form of the address.

Ordinarily, it would be something of a strain on an audience to listen to three addresses and three translations covering a period of two and a half hours, but listeners to Dr Steiner soon learn that they may expect a great measure of variety in the appeal he makes to them. He begins with quiet and formal sentences of an expository character and soon holds his listeners under the spell of his power. He speaks of what everyone present has already heard, of anthroposophy as the name given to the *moderne Initiations-Wissenschaft*, a phrase, the constant repetition of which the audience soon gets to understand, marks off the modern from the various sciences of initiation professed in former ages.

The lecture, delivered in three parts, gives Dr Steiner great opportunities for his characteristic rhetoric, which never strays beyond its legitimate limits, which illuminates and beautifies the conception of his dialectic. Two or three times in his address his eyes close and he seems to be depicting for us what he alone can see. And anon he will turn to the audience, addressing it with authority which none seems disposed to resent. Once at Oxford I detected a threatening look; it was contempt at some unworthy activity referred to.

A decided peculiarity in Dr Steiner's mode of address in his more formal utterances is the absence of humour. It is rare to notice this lack in an accomplished orator, but on the other hand it cannot be said that we lose anything by it. Perhaps the non-use of humour is part of Dr Steiner's great reserve; he accomplishes his task easily without it where others would find it helpful. But at Oxford in the lectures on education and social life he showed that he by no means lacks a sense of humour. Occasionally he became almost rollicking. Equally there is no artifice of irony, nor rebuke, no criticism, and what is perhaps more remarkable, no appeal. Dr Steiner does not allow himself the weakness of a direct appeal to the *emotions* over the head of the *intellect*, but strangely enough he does not exalt the intellect itself: rather the reverse. Although decidedly a preacher, he avoids taking us at a disadvantage by the common artifices of wit, antipathy and sentimentality. Moreover Dr Steiner does not shrink from that thoroughgoing formality which gives to his address the only value which a legal document possesses – absolute clarity. Words, phrases and formulae consistently used and often repeated, subordinating aesthetic to intellectual need, give to a lecture by Dr Steiner an additional charm, rather than otherwise. He will not sacrifice ultimate utility to stylistic notions. Where the English use synonyms he will use formulae like a mathematician. But with him formulae are often an integral part of his most poetical and rhythmical cascades of eloquence, which sometimes reach the rapidity and force of a torrent.

From Conversations with Rudolf Steiner

Martina von Limburger

THE FIRST TIME that I heard the name Rudolf Steiner, so incisively important for us, was via England. An uncle of ours lived over there and wrote: 'You are always reading and writing about Annie Besant, and all the time you have a much more significant personality, a Dr Rudolf Steiner, who lectures every week in the Architektenhaus in Berlin.' My parents, who for years had occupied themselves with questions of spiritual science, and had even known Blavatsky personally, travelled to Berlin and came back enthusiastic. I was confined to the house at that time through the grave illness of my husband.

In January 1906, Dr Steiner wished – so it was said – to speak publicly in Leipzig in the *Künstlerhaus*. It was not a very suitable hall as there was a ballroom next door. As he came in and went to the rostrum with elastic, even step, I was struck by his peculiarly harmonious walk and characteristic carriage. It seemed as if his freely held head carried his whole figure. When I was asked later how old he might be, I replied: 'Somewhere between 30 and 60 years old.' His outward appearance and the whole impression of his being had an effect of litheness and youthful freshness, but when he spoke the boundless knowledge that streamed from him made an overpowering impression on one. Already halfway through the lecture I knew: that is what you need, what you have been seeking all the time. By reason of a heavy loss, in which ordinary religion had left me completely empty, I was a well-prepared soil. After a few questions, somewhat primitive as was so often the case, but which Dr Steiner answered readily, he came to our seats with Frau Wolfram, leader of the then small Leipzig Group, in order to make the acquaintance of my father, Oskar von Hoffmann. My father was the translator of Mabel Collins's *Light on the Path*, a book which in early years had been given by Dr Steiner as meditation-exercise almost exclusively, especially the words at the beginning: 'Before the eyes can see, they must be incapable of tears.' He has said that in this language – it was mantric in its metrical form – the working was more powerful than in the English original, and that Hilarion (who lived in the third century AD) had helped in the translation, and from him, as a Greek, had sprung the noble form. Nothing, however, was said of that then. Dr Steiner only asked if he might visit my father, who at that time was 73 years old. The visit took place the following morning when, almost endlessly, he told my parents things of value. He then mentioned that he should return every month and should speak at the house of Frau Bontemps in quite a small circle – there were about 13 people. If my parents would take part they would very welcome, they might also bring their daughter with them who was in deep widow's mourning. Unfortunately he said nothing of my sister who was also present. In my father's former search for spiritual things he had been badly let down and had lost a considerable amount of money. Now he wished purposely to be cautious and therefore said, lightly turning it aside: 'But we are not members.' Dr Steiner smiled: 'That is also not necessary.' However, the others taking part were members, so we were looked on rather askance. From then on Dr Steiner visited my parents every time he came to Leipzig, up to my father's death in 1912.

Statements in Connection with Death.

From our 50th year of life onwards, parts of our being are always passing over into the spiritual world.

Question: When should cremation take place?

Answer: It is good in the case of anthroposophists because it loosens the connection with the physical body more rapidly, but it should never be before three and a half days after death. There still remains till then a connection with the body, like a spiritual umbilical cord. In the case of materialists I should not like to recommend it. They sometimes feel so lost that however dreadful the abandoned corpse is, they still feel that it gives them a sense of union.

Communication with the dead is made easier through spiritual training. But one must strictly avoid bringing about intercourse from selfish motives. On the other hand, should the departed himself strive for it in order to unburden himself of an anxiety, then it is permitted. It can even be that he obtains decided help through it.

There is a danger in seeking for communication because countless beings struggle to communicate with the living, and there is a gruesome 'spirit-rabble' – as Hellenbach strikingly puts it. These are not only deceased human beings but one may have to deal with a whole host of other beings. The most evil of them, it is true, are fettered. That came about with the Death of Christ. As long as we live, elemental spirits are bewitched in us. When a person of a happy nature dies the spirits are set free.

If the one who has died had clung to material things, they continually draw him back. That is a necessary consequence. Not good for him, but he must go through it. One can help him if one tries to think the idea of God into him, to give him belief in the spiritual world.

A person normally meets with the Christ at death. The one who commits suicide has to forgo this meeting. Moreover he is bound to his corporeal nature until the time when he was meant to die, and has to live through again and again what drove him to suicide.

The attraction through dreams is very important for the dead. It has the effect of giving them just what they need. They are helped, moreover, by all that proceeds from love. One should not let one's memory of them deteriorate into egotism, but should strive to increase one's love beyond the grave. Love which does not mourn gives the dead strength to come into the heights. Egotistic love hands a leaden weight upon them.

The living backwards (in Kamaloca) is, as it were, only a private affair and for this reason interest in what is going on still persists. In fact interest in the earth even increases. The fact that Mr X, as you say, did not concern himself with spiritual matters does not prevent him from still being a guide to the child.

Two Incidents

Anna Samweber

WHEN RUDOLF STEINER gave one of his big public lectures at a time when he spoke up for the Threefold Social Order, he always used a special exit which led to the artists' room, from where I accompanied him through a long passage to the main exit. After one of these lectures there were many people standing around who wanted to put their questions and problems to him, and who occupied him for a long time. I was waiting by the side entrance, and I had already got his coat, scarf and hat and was holding them in my arm so that I could pass them to him when he was finally free. After I had stood by the door for some time, he came, took his things from me, went back to the artists' room and put everything back on the hooks.

Then he took one item after the other and put them on. With great surprise I burst out: 'But Herr Doctor, can you imagine how I feel?' He replied: 'And can you imagine how I feel?' We went silently through the dark corridor where I usually led him, as his eyesight was very bad in the dark, when suddenly he said, 'Are you so angry with me that you let me walk into the wall?' Further on, he asked whether I knew why he had acted like that. When I answered in the negative, he replied: 'Think about it.'

When he met me the next day and the day after that, his first question was: 'Have you thought about it?' I became quite upset and when I woke again at night, it came to me. When the people stood around Dr Steiner and besieged him, I had stood self-satisfied with the thought that I had *his* coat, *his* hat, *his* scarf. On the following day Dr Steiner asked me for the fourth time whether I had thought about it. I said: 'Yes, Herr Doctor, I know now why.' He answered: 'You see, Sam, that must not be.' He disliked intensely all personal cult and he gave it no chance to develop around him.

* * * * * * *

Frau Dr Steiner owned a lovely diamond watch with her initials inscribed on the lid. It was broken, and I had to take it to a well-known watchmaker who lived a long way from the Motzstrasse. It was late on a cold and foggy November evening when I made my way in the direction of Nollendorfplatz, where the building site for a subway was situated. I was walking along a long, wooden blank wall when suddenly two human shapes appeared from the dark and attacked me. I remembered that once Rudolf Steiner had told me that if ever I was in need I could call on him. So when these two attackers went for me, the one holding me from behind so that the other could rob me, I called inwardly and spontaneously: 'Doctor, help me!' At the same moment both fellows fell back like lightning and were gone.

When Rudolf Steiner came for breakfast the next morning he greeted me with the words: 'Good morning, Sam. What was the matter that you cried so loud last night?' When I told him about my experience and he had listened quietly, he said simply: 'But I did help you, didn't I?'

Overcoming Formalities

Walter Johannes Stein

WHEN I FIRST CAME into touch with Rudolf Steiner my interest in him knew no bounds, but I had no desire at all to become a member of the Anthroposophical Society. I did, however, want to be present at dramatic presentations which were being given in the summer months at Munich. I therefore went to Munich and found my way to the house where Dr Steiner lived. But I could not get past the staff of those who were looking after him. I was received by a Countess Kalckreuth, a lady whom I afterwards learned to know and to esteem. On that occasion she was rather difficult. She asked me what I wanted. I wanted to see the Mystery Plays. Are you a member? No. Then you cannot witness the plays. Yes, but I have already spoken to Dr Steiner; I have even become his pupil. Maybe, but these presentations are for members only.

I was about to go away in despair, but in that very moment the door opened and Dr Steiner appeared on the scene. He came up to me immediately, held out his hand, and said 'So there you are!' I told him of my unhappy position. I wanted to see the plays, but did not want to become a member; still less so after what had taken place. Dr Steiner looked questioningly at the Countess, but she remained unmoved. At length he said, 'I will have a membership card made out for Herr Stein. It shall not, however, become valid until the moment he goes in through the theatre entrance, and it shall lose its validity in the moment when he leaves the building. That surely will meet the case, Countess?' Of course it would; everything that he said would, but I could not comprehend why he submitted to these formalities.

Armed, then, with such a card, I attended the performances. It would lead me far too far afield if I attempted here to describe what I saw. The plays, of course, have long ago been printed and everyone can buy them. Rudolf Steiner wrote four Mystery Plays and was engaged on a fifth at the time of his death. He wanted to show in these plays how a number of souls pass through repeated lives on earth and undergo destinies which are not to be explained out of one life alone. He wanted to show how karma works.

Deeply impressed by what I saw and heard, I went up to Dr Steiner when the performances were over. 'Well, Herr Stein,' said he, 'did you have a good time?' 'I know now what an ass I was,' was my reply, 'and I have no desire any more to leave the Society.' So I remained therein.

The Man with the Coat

Ilona Schubert

ONE EPISODE WHICH I should not like to forgo took place in Mannheim before a lecture which Dr Steiner was to give. I stood next to him as he was entering the hall. There in front of him stood an elderly gentleman whom the doorkeeper did not wish to admit until he had first handed in his coat to the attendant. Very sadly the man said that in that case he would have to go away again. Dr Steiner then asked him why he did not want to give up his coat and the man replied that he had no jacket underneath. It was just after the war and things of that sort were commonplace. There was really nothing to be ashamed of about it. Dr Steiner said to the doorkeeper that he was the lecturer and that it was his wish that the man should be admitted. The doorkeeper, who would willingly have complied, said however that such a thing was strictly against the rules and he stood to lose his job if he disobeyed them. Then Dr Steiner promised on his part that he would vouch for him if necessary, but that the man had to be admitted otherwise he would not give his lecture.

When he was at home again Dr Steiner explained that it was of great importance for just this man to be present when he spoke. He always scrutinized his audience very carefully and often directed what he had to say to the one or other person. Thus he said to us one day after a lecture in Dornach: 'You must have wondered why I seemingly deviated so much today from the theme we had in hand. There was someone in the hall who made it necessary for me to avoid certain topics. He would have misinterpreted what I said and that would have caused difficulties. I shall return to the theme I had in mind another time.'

A Question of Sleep

Friedrich Rittelmeyer

WHEN I WENT to visit Dr Steiner in Munich in August 1912, another 'theosophical' festival was just over. Two days after the final meeting, at about eight o'clock in the evening, some 10 or 11 people who wanted to speak to him were sitting in the waiting-room, full of deep but at the same time not repellent respect, and who would take up his time until long past midnight. I was told that the whole day long he worked with these people, and by night wrote his Mystery Plays, which were then taken to the printer in the early morning, and immediately rehearsed on the stage. But Dr Steiner was fresh and alert, without a trace of fatigue. People will have to face the astounding fact that he often spent many nights at a stretch with only about an hour's rest. Indeed, without this faculty it is impossible to explain what he accomplished in his life, from the point of view of time. That alone is a phenomenon which the modern mind is incapable of grasping.

Later on, in the year 1919, I felt a great wish for some means of understanding this enigma. I began by asking, in a matter-of-fact way, if it was possible in any way to cut down the hours of sleep, and so extend one's working hours. Dr Steiner at once went into my question, and said in an equally matter-of-fact way, using the impersonal style he nearly always adopted on such occasions, what 'one' would have to do. He was satisfied that I should not make any misuse of what he said, even as applied to myself. But as I do not know if he spoke about it to anyone else, I will only say briefly that there is an exercise in concentration which can be a substitute for sleep and reduce the need for rest to one-eighth of the normal period. 'But it must not be done always,' he said. 'In between there must be real sleep.' So there is a means. The only pity of it is that people are incapable of applying it. I, myself, have never been able to do so, except for a few seconds. When Dr Steiner spoke of matters like this, it was in an absolutely natural way, without the faintest breath of self-aggrandisement or conceit. Nobody on earth could have wrenched his secret from him if he did not wish to divulge it. By the telling of a fact like this, he confirmed his teachings and opened up a mighty vista into the future of mankind.

'Do not worry because there are people waiting,' he said as he received me. 'We will talk over everything we have to say quite quietly, to the end.'

Nearly all of Rudolf Steiner's works in English translation are available through the publishers of this book. Please write to the address below for an Enquirer's Catalogue containing details of basic and introductory titles.

Rudolf Steiner Press
PO Box 955
Bristol BS99 5QN
Great Britain

Distributors in other English-language countries are:

AUSTRALIA Rudolf Steiner Book Centre, 307 Sussex Street, Sydney, NSW 2000

CANADA Tri-Fold Books, 81 Lawton Blvd, Toronto, Ontario M4V 1Z6

NEW ZEALAND Steinerbooks (NZ), 181 Ladies Mile, Box 11-335, Auckland 5

SOUTH AFRICA Rudolf Steiner Publications SA, PO Box 4891, Randburg 2125

USA Anthroposophic Press, RR4, Box 94-A1, Hudson, New York 12534

The Anthroposophical Society

Information on the practical activities in Great Britain based on indications given by Rudolf Steiner are available from the Anthroposophical Society in Great Britain at the address below. There are regional branches of the Society in most areas of Great Britain and contacts for these are also available.

Anthroposophical Society in GB
35 Park Road
London NW1 6XT
Great Britain

Contacts for the Anthroposophical Society in other English-language countries can be obtained from the distributors listed above. For other countries contact

The Goetheanum
CH-4143
Dornach
Switzerland